SKI PIONEERS
OF STOWE, VERMONT

Photo by Marc Sherman
Mt. Mansfield behind the Town of Stowe, Vermont

SKI PIONEERS
OF STOWE, VERMONT

The First Twenty-Five Years

Patricia L. Haslam
Charlie Lord
Sepp Ruschp

STOWE HISTORICAL SOCIETY
2013

iUniverse LLC
Bloomington

SKI PIONEERS OF STOWE, VERMONT
THE FIRST TWENTY-FIVE YEARS

Biographies, Research, Compilation
by Patricia L. Haslam

Photo Selection
by Patricia L. Haslam and Barbara Harris Sorkin

General Editor, Book Design, and Production Manager
by Barbara Harris Sorkin

Cover Design by Robert Roden

Memoir by Sepp Ruschp

The Stowe Reporter articles by Charlie Lord

iUniverse books may be ordered through booksellers or by contacting:

iUniverse LLC
1663 Liberty Drive
Bloomington, IN 47403
1-800-Authors (1-800-288-4677)

ISBN: 978-1-4917-1331-0 (sc)
ISBN: 978-1-4917-1333-4 (hc)
ISBN: 978-1-4917-1332-7 (e)

Library of Congress Control Number: 2013919168

Printed in the United States of America.

iUniverse rev. date: 01/07/2014

Contents

Foreword
by Brian Lindner

Most of the men and women whose stories appear in this book probably never knew me by name. On the other hand, they probably knew of me as one of the "Lindner kids." However, these same folks had a profound influence on my life and my generation, as well as, the succeeding one and yet others well into the future. These folks were pioneers and finally in the pages of this book their stories are told for all to see.

Stowe is a very special town and it isn't just because of Mt. Mansfield or because of the quiet streets or quaint buildings. It's the people and it's the traditions which have created a culture that traces its roots to the people in this book.

Without the 1930's vision and finances of Roland Palmedo, who first identified Stowe and Mt. Mansfield as an ideal location for a ski resort, it might have taken many more decades to bring the young sport to an otherwise agricultural community.

Without the forward-looking views of the early environmentalist Perry Merrill, there is no telling (if or when) state lands could have been developed in partnership with private industry to bring jobs, money and prosperity to the tiny village in the valley.

Without the skiing, surveying, and engineering skills of Charlie Lord when would any ski trails ever have been cut on the mountain? We still ski today on the trails that Lord laid out long before there were any chairlifts and decades before anyone even thought of snowmaking and grooming.

Without Sepp Ruschp, whose business acumen matched his elegance in skiing and matchless skills in communication, there is no telling when our world class ski instructors and others would have been attracted to come to Stowe to build a resort—especially during the Depression and World War Two

Kerr Sparks hired me as a 21-year-old instructor in 1973. To this day I remain proud to have been a member of the Sepp Ruschp Ski

School. Sparks scared me with his outward gruff mannerisms but he ran the best school in the U.S. I recognized it then and I admire him today because of it. He accepted nothing less than full professionalism at all times. He insisted on elegance on skis and his influence affects every turn I make today on every run down the mountain.

Finally, in this book, the stories of the men and women who built Stowe into what we know and admire today are brought together and told in a comprehensive manner. This will serve forever to bring these folks to the forefront of Stowe, American, and world-wide resort history.

If you ski today, dine out in Stowe, hike the mountain or simply live or pass through Stowe, you are experiencing the influence of these pioneer heroes.

Brian Lindner
April 2012

Author's Note

The Stowe Historical Society had been looking for a theme for a new publication. Then, an opportunity presented itself. This opportunity was in the form of Sepp Ruschp's manuscript memoir donated to the Stowe Historical Society in July 2009. To augment the history provided by Sepp, I decided to add essays from early The Stowe Reporter publications by our local historian, Charlie Lord. Charlie wrote from his own knowledge of laying out and cutting trails on Mt. Mansfield, various building projects, and events leading to the founding of the Mt. Mansfield Ski Patrol and the Mt. Mansfield Company. The Mt. Mansfield Ski Patrol has just celebrated its 75th anniversary as the oldest ski patrol in the country. Then, a member of the Society who has had experience working for a New York City publisher offered her services as editor: Barbara Harris Sorkin. After much thought by many members, it was decided to produce a book about a subject that Stowe has been most noted during the past sixty to seventy years: skiing. With such a broad subject to be treated, we decided to produce an initial work which covered the first twenty-five years or so, from the late 1920's to the mid-1950s. A more in-depth publication about skiing after the 1950's, to include further growth of the Mt. Mansfield Company, can be undertaken by others in future years.

If this book were a painting instead, it might be labeled a triptych: a work in three parts, which focuses on the formation of this popular winter sport on Mt. Mansfield. Part I features the physical development of the facilities, the building of the first single chair lift, the World War II years, and the five small companies which comprised the beginnings of the Mt. Mansfield Company. These are presented in the essays by town historian, Charlie Lord, which were first printed in the weekly newspaper, The Stowe Reporter. Charlie was a major figure in this early period. Biddle Duke, current owner and publisher of the, now, Stowe Reporter very kindly gave us permission to reprint these essays, as did John P. Lord, Charlie's son.

Part II is a detailed personal history and reminiscences of Sepp Ruschp, an immigrant from Austria in 1936, who became the president and general manager of the evolving Mt. Mansfield Company. The memoir was an especially exciting "find" because on several occasions this writer and others had urged Maxie Ruschp, wife of Sepp, to take some notes about his early childhood in Austria, his emigration to the United States, as well as his memories about the development of skiing in Stowe. At Mr. Ruschp's retirement celebration in 1978, Maxie said to me, "I will get him to write it at the beach this coming winter at Long Boat Key!" I had no idea this had been accomplished until July 2009 when Tom Amidon brought to the Stowe Historical Society a copy of the Ruschp's memoir which we were very excited to receive. As attorney and executor of the Ruschp estate, Tom gave the Society permission to publish the memoir at some future date. Sepp's daughter, Christi Dickinson was immediately contacted and gave her permission to publish the memoir by her father and said she looked forward to such a publication.

And lastly, Part III consists of vignettes of many, but not all, of the men and women who participated in the formation of the ski industry in Stowe in some fashion. Some of these people were listed at the end of Mr. Ruschp's autobiography as if he had someday intended to further develop brief biographies about them. Other short biographies have been added. All in all, this work could be described as a collective biography.

A key document within the third segment of the book is the letter Roland Palmedo wrote to the Stowe postmaster (Lester Oakes) in 1931 asking about accommodations for skiers in Stowe as he wanted to bring up friends from New York City to check out various ski areas in the northeastern part of the country. The ski industry in town built from that point. The letter is described within the sketch about Roland Palmedo.

While most of these people on the list are now deceased, there are many resources from which to pull together brief biographies: obituaries, references in publications, manuscript sources, and interviews with living friends or relatives to weave the stories.

Many other contributors need to be added to the list of helpers. The scanning by Mike Leach of all of the Mt. Mansfield Ski Club Newsletters, deposited online, has been invaluable. Photographs and other images are included wherever they are available. As a retired Certified Genealogist, having started in 1967, this is what we do: build profiles of people.

Patricia L. Haslam
August 2013

SKI RUNS AND SKI TRAILS
MOUNT MANSFIELD
VERMONT

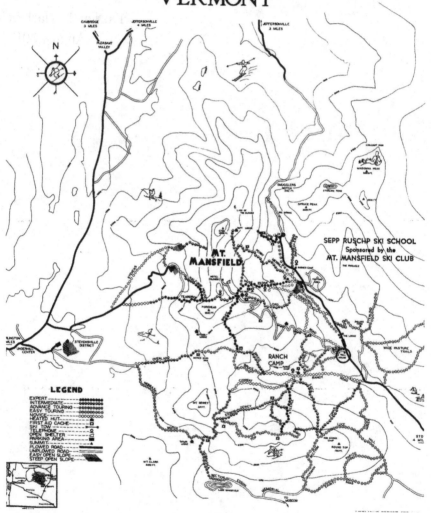

Stowe Historical Society Archives

PART I

The Physical Development of the Mountain

as Described in Essays
by Charlie Lord
from *The Stowe Reporter.*

(These articles have been retyped for this publication. The words and writing style have not been changed. Most of the pictures that appear in each article are the photos which appeared in the original publication.)

Stowe Historical Society Archives
Charlie Lord Cutting the Bruce Trail

CHARLIE LORD
(1902 - 1997)

"Perry Merrill, State Forester, basically gave Charlie a bunch of men and work to do, and that's how the first trails got started... Charlie had a true love of the outdoors." John P. Lord, son of Charlie.

&

"Unbeknownst to me- we were cutting the trail which is now known as the Lord Trail—Perry gave it that name. I said to myself, I'll get even with him. When we cut a new trail, I somehow got that trail named the Perry Merrill." Charlie Lord, 1992, as related to Earline V. Marsh

Everyone loved Charlie and Charlie loved everyone. A self-effacing, likable guy about whom most people in town knew had much to do with early ski development days, but was better known in recent years as the Town Historian. He wrote many articles in periodicals, primarily in The Stowe Reporter and the Newsletter of the Mt. Mansfield Ski Club. The essays that pertain to early ski development are reprinted here with permission of Biddle Duke, publisher of the, now, Stowe Reporter, and by Charlie's son, John P. Lord, now residing in Groton, VT, Charlie's birthplace.

He will be remembered for another large body of work published in The Stowe Reporter whereby he researched and wrote about other local history subjects such as the district schools, place names (Edson Hill, Brownsville, and other settlement areas), but in particular the development of skiing since 1933. Most of his articles appeared in print in the 1970's and 1980's, accompanied by images from his own extensive collection. Much of his collection is scanned and now held in the archives of the Stowe Historical Society. An inventory of his published works can be found at the Society, and copies of The Stowe Reporter are on microfilm, soon to be located at the Historical Society where a reader-printer will be available.

Luckily for Stowe, and for the fledgling ski industry, Charlie was laid off from the Vermont Highway Department in June 1933, during the height of the Depression. A graduate of the University of Vermont, he was a Civil Engineer in Montpelier, and later moved to Stowe. It was in March of that year that the Civilian Conservation Corps was established by President Franklin D Roosevelt. Charlie signed on as a trail engineer with the CCC with best buddy Abner Coleman, and Charlie surveyed and mapped the Bruce Trail from Ranch Valley to what became the Nose Dive, the first racing trail.

20 men from the Civilian Conservation Corps, mostly "local boys" and Charlie Lord,

Stowe Historical Society Archives
Civilian Conservation Corps. at Ranch Camp in November 1933

Charlie remembers a different ski life-style back in the '40's and 50's: "There were no ski bums back then, just bums. We'd drive all over Vermont in search of the best skiing...We were called The Mountain Men. It was a good group: Bish McGill, Huntley Palmer, Art Goodrich, Warren Warner, Art Heitmann, Abner Coleman, George Wesson, Dave Burt, Lindy Lindner, Harry Jerome, Chet

Judge, Lanou Hudson, Bob Cochran, and Luther Booth. We'd climb to the Stone Hut before the lifts were built, spend the night and ski down in the morning."

Stowe Historical Society Archives
C.C.C. Engineer, Charlie Lord at Ranch Camp in November 1933

He worked at the Mountain until 1974 after designing and cutting trails, managing lifts, leading the Mt. Mansfield Ski Club, and performing many jobs for the various entities that eventually became the Mt. Mansfield Company. Charlie's knowledge and trail and lift design were also used at the first chairlift at Mad River, and he designed the first gondola at Sugarbush. Charlie contributed frequent articles to the newsletters of the Mt. Mansfield Ski Club,

At first, Charlie was a single pole skier. In a Mt. Mansfield Ski Club Bulletin of December 12, 1938 Abner Coleman states that, "In 1926 Charlie was an exponent of the Zardsky technique, and the way he could switch down a steep slope with his single staff would have made your eyes jump right out...Now he is an unforgiving purist, and the sight of a stick rider would quake him to the teeth." Later the ski technique became more balanced with two poles. Photographs of him surveying and working outdoors show him smoking a pipe, but it is unknown whether he smoked it while skiing. Probably not.

5

Part of his resume included community memberships and service as well as Mystic Lodge F & AM, Vermont Historical Society, Society of Engineers, Lamoille County Development Association, and Mountain Men of Mansfield, and he was elected a Paul Harris Fellow by Stowe Rotary Club and was awarded for outstanding service to the community.

Charlie was one of the six primary local men who were the core group of promoters of commercial skiing in town in the 1930's and 40's. For this, Stowe is grateful.

The Stowe Reporter
Jan. 18, 1972

Early Days of Ski Development on Mt. Mansfield

by Charles D. Lord

Just when the first ski tracks were made in Stowe and Mansfield is not recorded, but surely by 1910 someone had ventured cross-country on skis. Around 1912 and for several years there were three

Lunch break on Bruce Trail, near junction of Toll Road.

Scandinavian families located in Stowe, one on West Hill, one on Edson Hill and one on Shaw Hill. They traveled back and forth on cross-country or touring skis. They couldn't speak very good English but they sure knew how to ski.

The first recorded ascent of Mt. Mansfield on skis was made in February 1914 by the then Dartmouth College librarian. About this time and perhaps somewhat earlier a local lumberman, Craig Burt, Sr., obtained a pair of skis which he used in getting from one lumbering operation to another. In March 1924, an organized group from Morrisville climbed the Toll Road using skis. Also in February 1926 a group of Stowites did the same. In February 1927, the first recorded overnight party on skis climbed to Taft Lodge where they spent the night and the next day climbed the Profanity Trail, then along the Ridge to the Summit House and then down the Toll Road. These trips required prodigious amounts of energy for the tail was unbroken, the equipment and technique crude when compared to the present day standards.

Nose Dive as it looks today

In February 1921 Stowe held its first winter carnival. A jump and toboggan slide were built on Marshall Hill (where the school Poma Lift now is). In the evening there was a minstrel show by local talent. During the day there were obstacle races, ski joring, exhibition jumping, toboggan rides and snowshoe and ski trips to Mt. Mansfield. Stowe High took over the winter activities and held annual meets at Jefferson High School for years. The meets alternated between Stowe and Jeffersonville and usually various groups would ski through The Notch to participate and spend the night in the town where the meet was held.

Presumably in between the winter of 1927 and 1932, there were other groups who toiled up the Toll Road and slid back down that way. The roads were not plowed and maintained like today and under ideal conditions the foot of Harlow Hill was as far as one could get in a car. Beginning with the winter of 1931-32, more frequent trips were made up the mountain and during the winter of 1932-133, Ranch Camp was opened on an informal basis to local skiers and several old logging roads in that area were brushed out and used.

For a few years previous to 1933, several of us, Abner Coleman, J.F. (Bondy) Bond, Eddie Flanagan, Jimmie Pine, Charlie Slayton, Babe Buxton, Nelson Griggs, to name a few, (all Highway Dept. employees) had gotten interested in skiing. Coleman had been exposed to skiing at McGill in Montreal and Bondy at Dartmouth to early skiing. We had made several trips to the mountains—to those places that were accessible and where there was a road or some kind of a trail to the summit, such as Camel's Hump, Burke Mt., Bolton, Spruce Mt. in Plainfield and Mt. Mansfield. We decided that Mt. Mansfield had the greatest potentialities in that it was the most accessible, had a good summer road to the top, good snow cover and offered excellent vertical drop. At that time, we had no idea that this sport would mushroom into present day size. We were quite content to make these weekly pilgrimages to the mountains and were quite happy with existing conditions.  With the advent of the C.C.C. in June of 1933, word filtered down to us that if we marked and laid out a trail it might be constructed by the C.C.C. During the winter of 1932-33, I recall standing on the Toll Road and looking down towards what was to become the first turn on the Nose Dive and thinking that would be a good place to commence our trail—Abner concurred with me.

So with that impetus we (Ab and I) laid out the Nose Dive during the summer of 1933. We spent many days on this project—there was no old logging road that we could use as a base, except at the very bottom. We originally planned for it to terminate at Barnes Camp and call it the Barnes trail in honor of Willis Barnes who lumbered in this region for many years. However, with the construction of the C.C.C. side camp (now, State Ski Dorm) and activity in the area of the present Mansfield Base House (State Shelter) parking area, the terminus was changed to its present one. The name was also changed to Nose Dive by Perry Merrill, who was the State Forester and directed the activities of the C.C.C.. Construction of the Nose Dive was not started until the summer of 1934 and the trail was given its final smoothing and finishing during the summer of 1935, so that it was actually opened the winter of 1935-1936. To get back to our meandering during this period will say that numerous conferences,

9

meetings, telephone calls and field trips took place. Everything was new—we literally had to feel our way along and were encouraged by the support and interest shown by local and state personalities.

Ranch Camp, an old lumber camp belonging to the Burt Lumber Co., had been used as a focal point the winter of 1932-33, by the Stowe Ski Club. A few old lumber roads had brushed out and some skiing done on these. The trail now known as the Bruce had been laid out during the summer of 1933 by Craig Burt, Sr. and the writer. Seeing as how a work program was already evolved in the Ranch Valley it was decided to commence there.

Consequently on Nov. 1, 1933 about 20 C.C.C. boys and the writer moved into Ranch Camp where we stayed for about 2 months, in which time we cut the Bruce through to the junction with the Toll Road near where the present Nose Dive crosses the Toll Road. We also cut a touring type trail to Luce Hill and Slayton pasture and brushed out several old log roads, including the Conway and Bouyea trails. We moved out of Ranch Camp shortly before Jan. 1, 1934.

So that phase of skiing as we know it today here on Mansfield really began with the construction of the first truly downhill ski trail in 1933. Economic conditions throughout the country were at a low ebb. To move people off the streets and get the situation off dead center numerous government efforts were made to improve the situation. Among these was the formation of the Civilian Conservation Corps, which organized young men in a semi-military force at the disposal of State and local officials to work on recreational, forestry and environmental problems of the day. Several factors were a decisive force in the early development of Stowe. There was already considerable local interest in that there had been winter carnivals, etc., plus the activities of the Stowe Ski Club. Mt. Mansfield and the Toll Road were fairly accessible and the favorable topographic features of the mountain proved to be attractive. Most of the land was owned either by the State Forestry Dept. or the Burt Lumber Company, both of which were highly sympathetic to the growing movement. In addition, there were many individuals whose combined efforts got the ball rolling—so to speak.

The Stowe Reporter

Feb. 1972

Ranch Camp Notes

By Charles D. Lord

Some of the workers during the George Campbell era:

Alton Holbrook	Wilfred Vanasse
Freddie White	Orlo Gibbs
Neil Robinson and team	Kenneth Holbrook
Harold Page and team	Tracy Mansfield
Dick Davis and son, Ralph	David Burt
Art Hamel	Dwight Wiltshire
Leonard Preston	Orvilla Vanasse and
Merton Pike	Team

Inside the cook house there was a wooden barrel into which water continuously ran and from which drinking, cooking and washing water was obtained. One day, a lady skier inquired if she could have a drink of water—Holbrook, as he was called, a kindly soul, but given to rough speech and a loud voice said, "J___ C___, help yourself… there's a whole G___ D___ barrel of it over there in the corner."

Once I was watching George making some pies (apricots were his specialty)…he was talking, as usual, but finishing off the pies at the same time. After he had placed the top crust, he stepped over to the water barrel, and proceeded to pour water over the completed piecrust. I thought he had flipped, but later on, eating the baked product, I realized that this was one of George's cooking secrets. The crust was brown and flaky— just right.

Another time, as related by Art Hamel, it being Xmas time, a bit of hard liquor had been consumed by the help. George had prepared

3 pots of beans for the evening meal and on his first trip from the stove to the table he, being a bit unsteady, tripped and fell, spilling the beans all over the floor. However, as none of the guests were present, they scrapped the beans off the floor, back into the pot and served them to the unsuspecting guests—just as if nothing had happened.

The food at Ranch Camp was simple, but well prepared. All meals were served family style—people sat at long oil cloth covered tables and the food brought to the table in large platters, bowls, pitchers, etc. No one ever went away from the table hungry. It seems that baked beans were ever present—although this may be slightly exaggerated.   The main meal consisted of beans, boiled potatoes, a roast, either of beef or pork, white and brown bread and pie, generally apricot and all you could eat...many a time, I staggered up from the table only to plop into a comfortable chair or nearby bunk. Cooking was done on a wood fired stove or stoves such as were found at that period in lumber camps. The facilities were crude judged by modern standards, but a capable cook, such as George, could turn out wonderfully hearty meals.

The first winter (1933-34), there was only the cook house, which had bunks in one end. Succeeding years saw additional building so that the bunk section of the original cook house was eliminated. It took quite a bit of wood to keep all the fires going. Neil Robinson, Harold Page, and Orvilla Vanasse used their teams to haul wood in from the place of cutting (on Burt land) to the wood shed.

George was a great spieler (slightly exaggerated stories)...he was always telling how he climbed the Bruce at night and visited with George Porter at the Stone Hut and then would ski back down the Bruce. (I doubt if he ever did this). George Porter was an equally good story teller—for instance, he told about driving a dog team in the far north which had so many dogs that the lead dog had ear phones over which signals were received from the driver (George).

The Stowe Reporter
March 22, 1973

The History of Ranch Camp – (Part #1)

by Charlie Lord

This is the first installment in a series of articles on the history of Ranch Camp, the original center of Skiing activities for the Mt. Mansfield Ski Club. The article will be continued over the next couple of weeks and will include pictures and an account of the Mt. Mansfield Merry-Go-Round—one of its first ski races.

****

Just when the first major lumbering operations were commenced in Ranch Valley is not pinpointed. However, Joseph Bashaw established a small farm just west of Ranch Camp in 1843; so it is quite logical to assume that by 1840, lumbering in this area had started. A pent road was surveyed in 1874, as recorded in Book 4, page 139, of the Stowe Town Meeting records. This survey covered that portion of the road from Stowe Forks to the top of Fette hill, which is the only noticeable hill on the road to Ranch Camp. This hill got its name (according to Craig Burt) from a man named Lafayette Houston who hunted and trapped in this area and had a small cabin.

Just easterly of Ranch Camp was located the steam mill of Osman Sanborn. This mill operated around 10 years—it burned around 1910 (according to Jennie Gale who was his daughter). At one time or another there were several lumber camps in Ranch Valley—to name a few, The Conway Camp located on the east slope of Mt. Dewey, the Davis Camp located on the north side of the Bruce Tail at the foot of a steep section near where the State Forest line crosses the Bruce, and the Bouyea Camp located on the Toll Road on the Pole section (according to John McMannis). Also, about ½ mile westerly of Ranch Camp on the Conway trail was located the Butts Camp, which burned. Ranch Camp was also known as the McMannis Camp, according to a Forest Service map of 1916. So for quite a long period (nearly 100 years) the ring of axes and cross-cut saws and the shouts of the teamsters could be heard all over the valley.

How did Ranch Valley get its name? Here's the story as it was passed along—it seems that in the early days, especially around the Bashaw clearing, that area was referred to as the Ranch. So it was logical, as the name became fixed, to call the Valley, the Road, the Brook and the Camp by the pre-fix Ranch. It makes a likely story and maybe there is some truth in it.

With the change in the method of lumbering due to more mobility and movement and improved techniques, it became apparent that the establishment of lumber camps near the site of operations was slowly being phased out and soon became a thing of the past here on the local scene. Thus, it came about that Ranch Camp ceased to be utilized as a lumber camp where the men cut the trees with axes and cross-cut saws and were housed and fed. It was opened by Craig Burt, Sr., as a sort of informal headquarters for the Stowe Ski Club (more in particular for people in the nearby area) during the winter of 1932-33. Before the next winter, the Stowe Ski Club was renamed the Mt. Mansfield Ski Club and its scope of membership enlarged and for a few years Ranch Camp was the center of skiing activities for the club.

In the beginning, there was only one which was known as the "Cook House", in which, besides the cooking and eating space, there were bunks for 10 or 12. George Campbell, an old time lumber camp cook, was in charge. He sure was a good cook as well as a story teller of somewhat questionable (at times) tales. That first year George did most of the work—occasionally helped on weekends by local boys. He cooked on a wood burning stove and his meals were something to rave about, especially his Saturday night supper—baked beans, brown bread, apricot pie and rice pudding. George was an outgoing, friendly and kindly person. He loved to visit and was a genial host.

Neil Robinson and Harold Page sometimes brought in supplies from the "FORKS" using a 4 horse team. These two, plus Alton Holbrook, Dick Davis, Ralph Davis and Dwight Wiltshire, furnished a goodly sample of local color.

Holbrook, as he was generally known, was a kindly man but was given to rough speech at times. However, he was a good backup man for George. Some of the others that worked there in the early years (during busy periods) were Art Hamel, Wilfred Vanasse, Freddie White, Leonard Preston, Merton Pike, Orlo Gibbs, Kenneth Holbrook, Tracy Mansfield, David Burt, Carl Burt, Richard Gale, Orville Vanasse and Burton Morse.

The food at Ranch Camp was simple but well prepared. All meals were served family style. People sat at long oil cloth covered tables and the food was brought to the tables in large platters, bowls, pitchers, etc. No one ever left the table hungry. It seems that beans were ever present thought this may be slightly exaggerated. The main meal (besides beans) consisted of boiled potatoes, a roast of beef or pork, white and brown bread, butter, tea, coffee or milk and desert of either apricot pie or rice pudding.

The facilities were crude, as judged by modern standards, but a capable cook, such as George, could turn out a wonderfully appetizing meal. It took quite a bit of wood to keep fires going, especially as more buildings were added. Neil Robinson, Harold Page and Orville Vanasse and their teams hauled in this wood from nearby cutting sites. In one of the bunk houses was installed a central heater which had its main unit an oil barrel which could be raised and lowered by means of pulleys. Holbrook was patiently showing some guests the mechanics of this rig and upon finishing his demonstration, was asked, "How does it work?" He replied very succinctly, "It don't." He was a native character if there ever was one.

One time Craig Burt, Sr., told one of the employees to cut a certain dead tree, as old sog could aptly describe it. The man said, "Why that is too wet to burn." Craig said, "I know, but it will make smoke and when these city people see the smoke they will be happy."

Ranch Camp was a distinctive institution and its clientele really loved to "get back into the woods." It had an atmosphere all its own and I suspect that even today it would have appeal although it probably wouldn't make much money. Anyway, it had a decisive part in getting the "ball rolling" during the early stages of development.

The trails in Ranch Valley have been silent for 10 to 15 years, but recently, the tourer type skier is developing and once again, the shouts and tracks of skiers are to be heard and seen in the "Valley". Several of the original trails have been reopened and the "Bruce" trail has been skiable most of the time. So it looks like Ranch Valley, Lake Mansfield Valley, Luce Hill, Round Top and the Slayton pasture will be utilized once more on an even large scale.

The Stowe Reporter
March 29, 1973

The History of Ranch Camp – (Part #2)

by Charlie Lord

This is the second installment in a series of articles on the history of Ranch Camp, the original center of Skiing activities for the Mt. Mansfield Ski Club.

* * * *

For the winter of 1934-35, a new bunk house, called the STEM (TEMPO after a turn introduced to this area by Dick Durrance). This structure could house 14 people with separate rooms for men and women. This was the cabin in which the famous stove was installed (Holbrook). Today, it is the only remaining building at Ranch Camp. Rates were quite low, $1 for 3 meals and $1 for lodging. An old barn, just across the road from the Cook House, was fixed up and a few bunks installed. The rates for the next season were slightly higher; $1.25 in the new bunk house and $1.00 in the cook house—for periods of over three days the rate was $2.00 per day for lodging and meals. The winter of 1936-37, another new bunk house, called the Tempo, was available, which could accommodate 18. This was George's last year. For by the next summer, he was failing in health. To all Ranch Camp followers, the memory of George will last a long time. The next year the chief cook was a man known only as "Frenchy"—not much has been recorded about him. The next season, 1938-39, Mr. & Mrs. Conkling were managers—they were there for 3 seasons, or until the season of 1941-42, when Mr. and Mrs. Wm. Henderson were there, beginning the winter of 1942-43 and until the end. The winter of 1949-50 was the last. (Note, the past three winters experienced

17

poor snow conditions). When the Hinmans were there most of the baggage and supplies were transported by dog team. Dave Burt also used an army surplus tracked vehicle known as a "Weasel".

Ranch Camp – March 1936

George Campbell, the hermit of Ranch Camp, after months of secret experimentation, sends word of certain marvelous refinements in his baked bean formula. Bean addicts who may shudder slightly upon hearing the term refinement applied to their particular solace— preferring, rather, a definite hint of biliousness in the concoction— are assured that the refinements were designed to increase one's consumption without destroying in any way the quality.

Ranch Camp – December 1936

George Campbell, raconteur and cook extraordinary, moved into Ranch Camp with his bean pots and pie pans before Thanksgiving Day this year, and has been administering to early season pilgrims ever since. Judging from the amount of food consumed, most skiers do not eat between May and November. One of our better known gourmands, in fact, spoiled a day's skiing for himself by attempting to surmount at one sitting all of the many things that George had prepared. However, there is something about a winter holiday at the Ranch Camp from which even the dangers of over-eating cannot detract, and that is why its list of enthusiasts grows longer each year.

George Campbell at Ranch Camp Cook House(1936-37)

In order to provide room for the increasing number of skiers who visit Ranch Camp, Mr. Craig Burt had constructed another bunk house similar to the one built two years ago. This newest cabin will accommodate 18 people while the other, which is slightly smaller, holds 14. The arrangement of bunk rooms with sliding doors, around a larger room containing the stove, is the same in both buildings; and each bunk has a spring mattress.

The Field Day – April 1939

The Club's informal field day was held on April 2nd 1939 at Ranch Camp under weather conditions so bad that only the more hardy skiers attended. A short but challenging slalom was set by Ab Coleman who thereby expected to win easily, and most certainly would have done so if getting tangled up with all the flags was the object of the race. As it turned out the three Northfield flashes— Goodrich, Wells and Dickinson—divided all the prizes among themselves. The ladies present refused to have anything to do with the races, and a matter of fact, a few of them, after watching the competitors gorge on Mrs. Conkling's dinner, were so unnerved that they did not go near the course. Gad, what a day!

The Stowe Reporter
April 5, 1973

The History of Ranch Camp – (Part #3)

By Bert & Trim Conklin – 1938

Here is the 3rd installment in a series of articles on the history of Ranch Camp – Stowe's 1st "Ski Club".

* * * *

The Ranch Camp now consisted of a complex of several buildings, with the barn-like cookhouse functioning as the center of activities. At one end of this building were a pantry, sink and wood burning cookstove. In the center were a couple of long oilcloth covered tables on which all meals were served family style. The heating system consisted of an iron drum stove supported lengthwise on a stone base.

Bringing in supplies for Ranch Camp (1935-36) are Neil Robinson, driver of the team and Harold Page (in milk can). Photo by Bill Vissering.

One end of the drum contained a door through which two-foot lengths of hardwood could be inserted. A second drum was fitted on top of and parallel to the lower one and the heat and smoke circulated through it before passing up a stovepipe. Beyond a partition at the other end of the cookhouse was a bunkroom containing two lower and two upper king-size bunks.

Outside of the cookhouse was a small double boarded meat storage shed around which snow and ice was heaped during the winter. Nearby was a woodshed where 15-inch split firewood was stored for use in the cookstove. Adjacent to this was a shack in which the camp lighting system reposed. This was a somewhat aged Delco plant consisting of a gasoline engine charger and several storage batteries. As this contraption frequently broke down under heavy usage, a dozen kerosene lanterns were kept available for emergency lighting purposes.

During our first winter a telephone was installed which connected with the outside by means of a wire running through the woods to the Toll House a mile away. As this wire was fastened to trees, high winds often broke it, which necessitated tracing the break on skis or snowshoes.

Skiers were lodged in three bunk houses. The largest, named the Tempo, was partitioned into several small rooms, each of which contained one or two sets of upper and lower bunks. This building was also heated with a double-decker drum-type stove.

A slightly smaller lodging structure, designated as the Stem, also had private rooms but its stove was a vertical positioned drum that flared out at the bottom over a stone fire pit. It could be raised up by means of a rope and pulley with its tail smoke pipe slipping up through an opening in the roof.

The third bunkhouse, the Telemark, was a men's dormitory consisting of a single room containing a number of bunks. The first two winters, Bert and I resided in a sort of second story loft in this building which was reached by stairs that led up from a vestibule. Because our first child, Ann, had arrived in the fall before we went into the Ranch for our third winter there, the Burt Co. had a small two room cabin built for us then which seemed to be deluxe indeed compared with our former quarters.

Ann's first winter was spent in this cabin, her bed being a clothes basket with a pillow for a mattress. Her airings were accomplished by putting her in a box on a toboggan and having her nurse girl pull her around the camp area.

The pride of the Ranch was its Rube Goldberg washhouse which was divided into two sections designated appropriately Christie and Christiana. Both contained flush toilets and hot showers. The showers were supplied by water piped into the building from a small brook above the camp. The water passed through heated coils in a drum stove and was then stored in metal barrels over head.

The camp's consumption of wood in the various heating stoves was, of course, immense. By spring, some forty cords of two foot maple, birch and beech had been converted into BTU's.

The Ranch had a guest capacity of fifty with all bunks filled. We supplied sheets and blankets but the skiers made their own beds (or didn't make them). The rates for lodging and meals were $3.00-$3.50 a day or $18.00-$20.00 a week. This included the backbreaking service of hauling in guests' luggage on a toboggan when necessary, the mile and a half uphill.

Photographed in the Ranch Camp Cook House in 1936 are (l-r) Craig Burt, Sr. (with fork), Leonard Preston, Carl Burt, Wilfred Vanesse (standing), unknown (with clasped hands), Merton Pike and Robert Gale.

Fortunately, the majority of skiers came to the Ranch because they liked its informal atmosphere and its woody isolation. Knowing the score, they would ski in with their duds packed in a rucksack or pack basket on their backs. Some, however, less familiar with our transportation limitations brought suitcases, fur coats and packages.

At the beginning of each winter season, when the bulk of the staple food supplies, equipment, and other numerous and sundry items had to be transported in, horse power was utilized. A local farmer and teamster, Neil Robinson, whose trips in we relished because of his jovial twinkle and dry humor, did this hauling with a wagon, a sleigh or a dray type of winter rig consisting of long poles mounted on runners. Two or four horses were used depending on the size of the loads and the depth of the snow on the woods road. In addition to utilizing his horses at the beginning and end of the season, we also had Neil come in on especially big weekends and occasionally to provide the guests with a sleigh ride.

The rest of the time, our handyman or I had to pull toboggan loads of supplies or luggage in by brute force. It wasn't too much fun to inch along uphill on skis with skis attached to the bottoms pulling a toboggan on which was piled a crate of groceries or meat, a can of milk (yes, we always had fresh milk in camp) and a few suitcases, particularly if the snow on the road was sticky. Sometimes such a trip in took three or four hours.

Our staff consisted of a cook, a handyman, and boys from the village who came in on weekends to wash dishes. Bert and I divided up the management duties with her emphasis being on looking after the planning and preparation of meals. She did the pastry cooking, herself, and would make as many as a dozen and half pies and eight dozen doughnuts on a busy weekend.

As all good things must come to an end, so did our healthy, happy and wonderfully different experience at the Ranch. It was hard work, but it was worth every minute of it.

It has since been enjoyable for Bert and me to pridefully reflect that through the medium of our operation of Ranch Camp, we had a small but active part in the development of skiing at Stowe.

C.C.C. recruits moving into Ranch Camp, November 1933.

The Stowe Reporter

Dec. 1941

Ranch Camp News

by David Burt

"Yea, Neeka! Hike!" That is the cry along the Ranch Road now when Dick Hinman starts his team of nine huskies, down Fette Hill. And as Neeka, the little white leader, heads out straightaway the rest run with a will—and run they must to keep ahead of the heavy sled loaded with three or four hundred pounds of zestful humanity.

People ask whether the dogs are vicious, whether it is safe to pet them; how much wolf blood each has in its veins; and many other questions, all indicating a quickening interest in one of this region's newest attractions. The dogs are not vicious, are very friendly except when in harness, and may even be jealous when one gets more attention than another. However, it may be well to add that the braided whip which Dick always carries on the sled is not purely for atmosphere. There is one quarter strain of timber wolf blood in each of the dogs. This is for the purpose of toughening their mental and physical fiber.

Recently, a private in Uncle Sam's new ski troops tried to race the team from Ranch Camp to Stowe Forks. Arriving about five minutes after Dick had unloaded the sled, all out of breath he exclaimed, "Your dogs sure don't fool along, do they?"

A trip with the team back into the head of Ranch Valley is something to treasure. Up a winding trail over which millions of feet of logs were once hauled, you are carried into the valley. Mount Dewey lies impressively on your left, the Forehead of Mt. Mansfield on your right while the sled creaks over the frosty snow. You stop for lunch beside a small woods fire, and perhaps ramble to the head of Ranch Brook, hunt out an old abandoned log skid-way, discover the huge boulder, split in three chunks, that used to be a landmark for logger and hunter. A bobcat track absorbs the attention of the dogs while Dick spins a yarn about these furtive, predatory animals. Perhaps a snowshoe rabbit scuttles across the trial ahead; a partridge whirrs away in a beautiful flurry of snow.

It is hard to reconcile this world of ancient logging trails and mountain wildness with a world of carefree skiers. Yet both lie within five miles of each other—the one unspoiled, the other unheeding. No wonder you regret the thought of the journey back to the comparative civilization of Ranch Camp, even though a cup of hot tea and plate of cookies await your return.

TUNE IN NEXT WEEK—for more Ranch Camp News—and an account of the Stowe "Merry-Go-Round" Race.

The Stowe Reporter
Dec. 27, 1972

An Early Ski Expedition

as related to Charlie Lord by Art Goodrich

On Saturday PM in March 1938, a group of skiers left Northfield in a Terraplane convertible with a rear end ski rack. Incidentally this was the first model car to appear on the local market with a combined stick and automatic shift; it was amusing to watch the stick flop around when the transmission was automated.

The party consisted of Martin Weinstein (car owner), Mahlon Wells, Merton Dickinson and Art Goodrich. They arrived at the foot of Harlow Hill in mid PM and proceeded to Ranch Camp.

They skied around on the trails at Ranch Camp a couple of hours and then got ready for a real lumber jack meal prepared by that famous lumber camp cook, George Campbell.

The meal consisted of roast beef, gravy browned just right, mashed potato and the driest Hubbard squash, all served family style, with seconds and thirds with apple pie for desert. (WHAT A MEAL). Later in the evening after visiting and resting from the enormous meal, they separated into two pairs.

Marty and Mert skied back down to the foot of Harlow Hill, got in Marty's car, and drove to the foot of the Nose Dive and proceeded to climb up it.

At the same time Mahlon and Art left Ranch Camp and proceeded up the Bruce. It was snowing quite hard by this time but they managed to stay on the trail. The objective of both parties was the newly built Stone Hut where they knew they would find warmth and shelter provided by the hutmaster.

As Art and Mahlon approached the junction of the Bruce and the Toll Road they could hear the voices of the other party approaching on the Nose Dive…so they all arrived at the Stone Hut at the same time and were given a royal welcome by the hutmaster, Reg Springstead. After the usual visiting, etc. and as they were preparing for bed, they realized that perhaps there weren't enough blankets to go around (this was in the days before modern sleeping bags). So they all put on skis, donned their miner-like lites and skied down to the cache at Sta. 13 (just below the Turns) and borrowed the first aid blankets and climbed back to the hut.

After a good nights sleep, they arose fairly early and at about 7:00 the next morning, they phoned down to Frank Griffin's warming shelter (where the Mansfield Base Lodge now is) and ordered breakfast. It took them about 10 minutes to run the Nose Dive and get at their breakfast.

After resting a bit they made two more runs on the Nose Dive that day. A wonderful weekend of skiing and they earned (climbed) every single foot of it.

The Stowe Reporter
Dec. 27, 1973

History of Stone Hut, Mt. Mansfield

by Charlie Lord

Work commenced on the "Stone Hut" around October 1, 1935. Naturally, the first thing was to remove the temporary wooden structure which was built for the winter before. This was done by cutting the building in sections and transporting it to its new location on the bank above the present ski dorm. (Incidentally, this building was demolished or burned up in the Spring of 1967). Foundations were poured and stone masonry proceeded. All concrete was mixed by hand, as well as the mortar, in a large wooden mixing box. Old stone walls in the immediate lowland neighborhood of Stowe were taken apart for materials.

The rafters were peeled poles and the roof and floor, sturdy wooden material. Steel frame windows were used and a large fireplace was incorporated into the southeast wall.

The masonry work was done under the direction of Jimmy Pintello and Clem Chastenay with C.C.C. boys as helpers. The carpenter work was done under the direction of Joe Yong and a small crew consisting of Braman Dalley, Adrian Clark, Duffy as cook and Doyle Hannigan. The crew that did the outside work on the building worked 7 days a week and stayed in the C.C.C. side camp in the Notch (now the State Ski Dorm). After the building was closed in and they were unable to drive on the Toll Road the carpenter crew stayed at the Stone Hut 7 days a week and completed the inside around Feb. 1, 1936. The supervisor or forester in charge of the side camp and directly responsible for the construction was Art Heitmann, who is now Commissioner of Forest & Parks (1970).

Saturday, Nov. 28, 1936, I rode up the Toll Road in a truck that was taking supplies to the crew finishing the latrine building and stayed overnight with them in the Stone Hut. Loren Wright, a carpenter foreman, along with four C.C.C. boys, were doing the work.

While the temporary wooden building was greatly appreciated and well patronized, the new "Stone Hut," so called, has been used extensively over the years, especially during the reign of "King George." Even in this day the Stone Hut fills a need for those wishing to "get back."

The caretakers were Reg Springstead, Freddie Koblenzer, Fritz Kramer and George Porter in that order. They all did a good job, especially George.

Wendy Parrish Post Card Collection
The Stone Hut

The Stowe Reporter
1977

The Shaping of Stowe

By Charlie Lord

Snow comes in many forms and shapes. When it truly shapes up, it is in a distinct crystalline pattern; namely, a six-sided crystal. "Snowflake" Bentley of Jericho, Vermont, was one of the early pioneers in the field of snowflake photography. He took countless pictures of snowflakes and found that while no two flakes were exactly alike, they all, if allowed to form perfectly, were six-sided or hexagonal in shape. Many of these formations were beautiful and intricate and some are used by lace makers.

The next time, while riding up a chair lift and conditions are right, notice the various formations of snow crystals that appear on your clothing.

There is the cold dry snow, wet or sugar snow, hail in various forms and the regular snow which form perfect crystals. All of which is skiable requiring possibly different waxing and of course there is breakable crust and ice which require considerable skill, above the average, to ski successfully.

On Washington's Birthday, February 22, 1932, Roland Palmedo and Jose Machado climbed the Toll Road and spend three days in Stowe and on Mansfield. They reported back favorably to the A.S.C. of New York. At about the same time several other groups also scouted Mansfield and of all the mountains tried, it seemed the most favorable.

One such group consisted of Highway Department employees... Abner Coleman, J.F. Bond, the author, and others...all of whom had been exposed to skiing, Coleman at McGill, Bondy at Dartmouth and the rest by word of mouth.

Mansfield not only had the vertical, it also had good snow, the Toll Road and was the most accessible, so we settled on this mountain. At that time, we had no idea that this sport would mushroom into present-day size. We were quite content to make these weekly pilgrimages to the mountain and were quite happy with existing conditions.

Our equipment was very crude as compared to modern equipment. Skis, poles, bindings, waxes, clothing, trails and technique were all very rudimentary. Instruction was non-existent and what little we knew, we got mostly by trial and error and a few pamphlets. Of course, our very flexible bindings which allowed much movement plus our slow speed saved us from serious injury.

With the advent of the C.C.C. in June 1933, word filtered down to us that if we marked and laid out a trail or two, they might be constructed by the C.C.C. Perry Merrill, who was the State Forester and in charge of the C.C.C. work programs for Vermont, gave us his blessings; so Craig Burt and I laid out the Bruce which goes from Ranch Valley to the Toll Road near where the Nose Dive hits the Toll Road, and Ab Coleman and I during the summer of 1933 and 1934 spent many days laying out the Nose Dive. We, tentatively, called it the Barnes Trail in honor of Willis Barnes who lumbered in that region for many years. However, with the construction of the C.C.C. side camp (now State Ski Dorm), the terminus was changed to the present one. Also the name was changed to its more apt title of Nose Dive by Perry Merrill. Construction of this trail was started in the summer of 1934 and was finished during the summer of 1935. It has been widened, graded and smoothed since the early days to accommodate traffic and technique.

With construction of these trails Ranch Camp was opened to the public the winter of 1934-35—the Toll House and slope and the Lodge opening in 1935-36. The Green Mountain Inn and The Fountain had been open for several years prior on a year round basis. Jennie Gale says that Ab Coleman and I were her first winter (1932-33) guests at the Rocky River Farm. Other lodging places soon followed. The one restaurant was operated by Mr. Boardman followed by Earl Crue.

31

Due to several factors, skiing got off to an early start, here in Stowe. There was considerable local interest with the advent of the C.C.C., sympathetic State Forest Perry Merrill, plus people like Craig Burt, Sr., Frank Griffin, George Gale, Gale Shaw, Sr., Roland Palmedo, etc. Also, there was the favorable topographic features with most of the land being owned by the State or the Burt Lumber Company, and the presence and accessibility of the Toll Road.

As mentioned before, the Bruce Trail was cut and Ranch Camp opened up during the winter of 1933-34. The first down mountain race on the Bruce was Feb. 25, 1934, with Dick Durrance winning easily. Also this was the first winter that Harlow Hill and beyond was plowed. During the summer of 1934, the original Chin Clip was cut—now all grown up. A temporary wooden shelter was constructed by the C.C.C., where the Stone Hut now is.

A winter carnival was held by the M.M.S.C. Feb. 1935, the downhill being on the old Chin Clip with the cross country jumping and slalom held in the village. The slalom hill was the slope (now heavily wooded) directly East and across the road from the present Grand Union Store.

When the Nosedive was a racing trail...

During the summer of 1935, the Nose Dive was smoothed with stumps and rocks being removed so that it was skiable with the beginning of winter. Work was commenced at The Stone Hut Oct. 1 and it was finished in January 1936. The Lodge opened for the first time that winter 1935-36. The weekend of Feb. 1, 1936, the first interscholastic meet was held and on Feb. 23, Bob Bourdon was easily the winner of a downhill on the Nose Dive.

In 1936, Sepp Ruschp arrived on the scene sponsored by the M.M.S.C. and was located at the Toll House which was used as a sports shop, warming shelter, snack bar and guest house under the management of Frank E. Griffin. Ranch Camp was also opened with a new bunk house. George Campbell, who cooked there when it was a lumber camp, was in charge.

Also, at the Toll House was a newly installed rope tow, which ran commercially beginning Sunday, Feb. 7, 1937. Rates were $1.00 per day or $5.00 for the season.

During the fall of 1937 the old Perry Merrill trail was constructed, also the Steeple trail in Ranch Valley—the latter all grown up now. The Nose Dive parking area (200 cars) was built as was a temporary wooden shelter at the side of the present Base House. Also, a practice slope in back of the present Base House (lower end of present North Slope) was constructed and a rope tow installed.

Sepp was at the Toll House with Edi Fuller as an assistant. The Stowe-Mansfield Association was formed with Dr. Barrows as president and Mark Poor as vice president. Ranch Camp was improved with the old barn being turned into a bunk room and a shower room was built. George Campbell was not back as he was terminally ill.

National races for men and women were held on Nose Dive March 4-5 and April 9-10. Several races were held on the Nose Dive, including the Vermont Interscholastic on March 11-12.

During the summer and fall of 1938, fifteen caches were installed by the C.C.C. The first caretaker, Reg Springstead, was at the Stone Hut sponsored by the Vt. Forest Service. New managers at Ranch Camp, Trim and Bert Conklin were on hand. Sepp was back at Toll House with Ali Mauracher as assistant. Jacques Charmoz was at the Lodge as ski instructor. First sugar slalom was April 30, 1939, on the Nose Dive.

During the summer and fall of 1939, the Lord Trail was cut. In June 1939, construction of the Base House (State Shelter) was commenced by the C.C.C. The temporary wooden building was still in use. During early summer of 1939, a preliminary on site study of a chair lift by American Steel & Wire engineers and others was made.

During the fall of 1939, the Rim Rock trail to Taft Lodge was cut. Caretaker at the Stone Hut was Freddie Koblenzer. S-53 was constructed in early winter 1939-40. The parking area at the Nose Dive was enlarged in the spring of 1940. On April 26, 1940, the second Sugar Slalom was held with ideal conditions. Sepp Ruschp Ski School with Sepp as director—with Otto Hollaus, Kerr Sparks and Lionel Hayes as assistants—was started. On June 4, 1940, work commenced on the single chair lift, which was ready for the winter of 1940-41. The Lodge changed hands with George Morrell as the new manager and owner.

On December 9, 1940, the Single Chair Lift began its first season of operation and is still operating (1977). With the advent of the chair lift, skiing entered a new phase—for no longer did the skier have to spend most of the time climbing in order to get a downhill run.

Stowe Historical Society Archives
Single Chair Lift December 1940

Fritz Kramer became the first paid patrolman. George (Harry) Porter became "king" of the Stone Hut. Sepp Ruschp was again director of the ski school with Otto Hollaus, Kerr Sparks, Lionel Hayes, Howard Moody, Everett Bailey, Clem Curtis and Norman Richardson as assistants.

The Skimeister and the Slalom Glade was cut in the fall of 1940. The Base House (State Shelter) was used that winter with Mr. and Mrs. Loren Wright in charge. Ranch Camp opened with Trim and Bert Conkling as managers.

During the summer of 1941, the Nose Dive parking area was again enlarged and a parking fee of 25 cents charged by the Forest Service. Weekly races were held on the Skimeister. On April 11-12, the third Sugar Slalom was held.

In January 1942, the C.C.C. was disbanded as World War II commenced on Dec. 8, 1941.

Harlow Hill was relocated and finished during the summer of 1942.

During the war years, gas was rationed and the majority of skiers arrived by train and bus. Gas coupons were issued to run the Single Chair Lift as it was deemed a recreational necessity. During one season, there was not paid patrol, only Harold Eagleton and Knud Andersen being on hand as volunteers. The Stowe-Mansfield Association established an office in Stowe Village. Erwin (Lindy) Lindner, a medically discharged veteran, became a paid ski patrolman and was on duty the winter of 1943-44.

During the summer of 1945, the Vt. Highway Dept. commenced work on improving the road from Stowe Village to the Mountain. The Mansfield-Stowe Derby was held (informally) during the winter of 1945-46. The present Mansfield T-bar was built and ready for use the winter of 1946-47. The road was surfaced during the summer of 1946. The Junior Program was commenced with Langdon Cummings in charge. The former C.C.C. camp was opened as a ski hostelry known as the State Ski Dorm.

In the fall of 1946 the Burt Company sold to what eventually became the Mt. Mansfield Company 3,000 acres which became known as the Spruce Peak area.

Stowe Center was built the summer of 1948. The Toll House was remodeled during the summer. The ski school had Kerr Sparks in charge with 12 assistants. During the summer of 1949, the By-Pass and Cross Trail from the Slalom Glade to the Perry Merrill was cut. East and West slopes, which had been started the previous winter, was finished and rope tow at Little Spruce were constructed. The Toll House was added on, too. The Mt. Mansfield Lift was purchased by the Mt. Mansfield Company in 1949.

At the town meeting in March 1950, the town voted WET and has remained so to date (1977).

During the summer of 1950, a new nine-hole golf course was established with the first and ninth holes on the Stowe Center side and the other seven across the river reached by a foot bridge. Dr. Barrows officially opened the course.

At Little Spruce, a T-bar was installed replacing the two rope tows. In 1950 The Lodge was sold to the Mt. Mansfield Company.

In the fall of 1951, the Nose Dive was extended to the top of the Nose and the race start was just below the Nose at tree line. On March 22-23, 1952, the men's and women's National Championship was held. During the 1952-53 seasons, the 1,000,000th rider on the Single Chair Lift occurred. During the 1953 sugar slalom Neil Robinson and Perley Millard officiated at the sugaring off pan.

During the summer of 1954, the Big Spruce Double Chair and trails were constructed and used the following winter. The facilities and trails on Mansfield continued to expand. The latest lift built was the gondola on Mansfield, which was constructed during the summer of 1968.

Trails Carved Out

Bruce fall of 1933; Nose Dive summer of 1934-35; Chin Clip (old) fall of 1934; Merrill (old) fall of 1937; Slalom Glade fall of 1940; Lord 1939; Midway Jan. 1940; S-53 (old) March 1940; East and West Slope 1949; Main Street, Sterling 1954; Lullaby Lane 1953; Smugglers 1956; Little Spruce Double Chair Lift trails 1963; Gondola including new Chin Clip and new Perry Merrill 1968; Mansfield (D.C.L.) trails including new Skimeister, Maiden Lane, Hayride, Starr and Goat 1960; the National in 1952-53; and the Tyro, Standard, Gulch and North Slope when the Mansfield T-bar was built in 1946.

Lift Construction

Rope Tows (now all replaced) and Toll House 1936-37; Mansfield (slope back of Base House) 1937-38; Little Spruce 1949-50; T-bars Toll House 1956-57; Mansfield 1946-47; Little Spruce 1950-51; Chair Lifts Mansfield S.C.L 1940; Mansfield D.C.L 1954; Little Spruce D.C.L. 1954; and Gondola on Mansfield 1968

Building Dates

RANCH CAMP, 1933 to 1950—Toll House original building used for several seasons beginning the winter of 1935-36. In 1940 the first addition was built with snack bar, ski shop and warming shelter on ground floor and kitchen, dining room, etc. for guests on upper floors. In 1948, a building across the way was built housing the sport shop, rent and repair, administrative space, ski school and staff quarters. Then in 1949, the restaurant wing was added thus allowing the kitchen and dining room in the Toll House Inn to be moved downstairs. The Toll House Motor Inn was built during the summer of 1964 and completely absorbed the old Toll House. The Toll House restaurant building was completely destroyed by fire in Dec. 1968 and temporary quarters were used the following winter. During the summer of 1969, two new buildings were constructed at the Toll House area—one on the site of the burned building which houses the Administrative offices and the other to the westward, directly across the parking area housing the restaurant, ski school, rent and repair and staff quarters. So now, there are two nearly fireproof buildings plus the Motor Inn on the side of the original little Toll collector's building.

THE LODGE—this was originally a farm building known as the George Harris place. Joe Lance in 1919 added onto the house and opened it as a summer place. Roy Patrick, in 1927, bought out Lance, expanded The Lodge and added the Harlow farms. In 1935-36, it was opened for the winter season for the first time and has been operated summer and winter ever since. George Morrell bought it in 1941 and added onto the place. The Mt. Mansfield Co. acquired it in 1950. They added onto the dining room and also in 1969, a new staff quarters building was constructed to replace those that were in the Den, which was damaged by fire in early 1969 and torn down.

STATE SHELTER (Base House)—opened the winter of 1940-41—built by the C.C.C.—there have been 2 additions, one in 1957 and the other in 1962. It is operated on a concession basis by the Mt. Mansfield Co.

STONE HUT—built by the C.C.C., completed in Jan. 1936, a temporary wooden building on this site was used the winter before.

OCTAGON—built in late 1940's in conjunction with the S.C.L. There have been two additions. On or near this site, in 1857, the first hotel was built on the mountain. Octagon was rebuilt in 1960.

Wendy Snow Parrish Collection
The Octagon Built in Late 1940

MAIN STREET RESTAURANT—built in 1954.

SPRUCE HOUSE—built in 1956 with an addition in 1963.

CLIFF HOUSE—built in 1968, also the Gondola Base, in conjunction with the Gondola.

STATE SKI DORM—built in 1933-34, as a side camp from the main camp (C.C.C.) in Waterbury. Later on, it was remodeled and opened up by State Forest Service in the Winter of 1946-47.

The Stowe Reporter
April 5, 1979

Early Ascents of Mt. Mansfield

by Charlie Lord

The first recorded climb on skis of Mt. Mansfield occurred in 1914 by Nathaniel Goodrich, the then librarian at Dartmouth College. His companion used snowshoes and it was about a dead heat both coming and going. In March 1926, Craig Burt, Sr., his son Craig, Jr. and Robert Wells were the next recorded skiers to visit the top of Mansfield via the Toll Road. In March 1927, Doc Steele and companion were the first recorded to spend the night on Mansfield— they, having climbed the Taft foot trail, spent the night at Taft Lodge and the next day climbed the Profanity foot trail to the ridge and then, to the Summit House and down the Toll Road.

"However, on March 2, 1924, a group from Morrisville climbed Mansfield via the Toll Road. Clovis Couture took the party from Stowe to the foot of Harlow Hill (Stowe Forks) in his Ford converted sno-mobile. The road was unplowed beyond here. It took 4 ½ hours to reach the Summit House in soft unbroken snow. The well or pump house was practically buried so icicles of the veranda were their only source of water.

The gang at the Summit House, March 2, 1924.

Several of the party had leg cramps from too much exercise but after resting and eating their lunch, they began the down run. In the shadows, the snow had hardened and was quite fast. Four of the ten in the party had never skied before and as a consequence they failed to get around some of the shaper turns. The more experienced skiers spent considerable time extricating the novices from the snow banks and bushes. Many shortcuts on the Toll Road were made most of which was unintentional. They established a new record for the run down—38 minutes to Toll House. They enjoyed the expedition very much and suffered no casualties other than tired muscles.

Some of the party had been taught by the Finn by the name of Neil Bine who lived near Lake Lamoille in Morrisville. They even had harnesses of a sort which were home made. Porter Greene made several pairs of nine foot skis at the shop of what is now the Greene Corporation. They were made of native ash and the poles were ash with a solid ring at the bottom. For boots, they were ordinary 12"-14" leather foot wear. Those in this party were Porter Greene, Francis Brown, George Goodrich, Allen Hall, Everett Keeler, Ralph Patch, Starcha Viencek, James Billings and Ralph Drown, as told by Porter Greene who was principle of Stowe High School around 1940!

Before skiing came into the picture, there were others who worked on the mountain. Stuart Nutting, who was born in Stowe and along the last of his working career, was a clerk in Frank Stafford's hardware store. He recalled that one winter when he was only 16 or 17 he bobbed logs down from the Octagon area to the Lookout on the Toll Road and from there the logs were chuted down to a point on the road between the Ski Dorm and the entrance to the Mansfield parking area. At this point, there was a steam sawmill that sawed up the logs. This was about 1883, but no vestige of the chute is now visible. The upper portion of the mountain was heavily timbered with spruce.

Also, there was a lumber camp about halfway up "pole bridge hill" on the Toll Road on the Ranch Valley side which operated around 1900. Lumber men from the "Davis Camp" on the Bruce Trail also operated almost up to the junction of the Bruce and Toll Road (where the Nose dive crosses the Roll Road) and in the vicinity of the Nose Dive and Merrill, there are old log roads that extended up to the bottom of the Turns on the Nose Dive and the Taft Lodge near the Chin. Willie Barnes operated here in this area from what is now known as Barnes Camp.

So Mansfield has been explored in the winter by hikers, skiers and lumber men for over 125 years.

The Stowe Reporter
March 8, 1979

The First Sugar Slalom – 40 Years Ago

By Charlie Lord

It had been a good year, snow-wise, and here it was approaching the last of April 1939. The Nose Dive had been newly cut only four years earlier and was already proving to be a dependable source of good snow.

Corridor section of Nose Dive photographed at the
1940 Sugar Slalom

And as the season approached the end, someone suggested that a slalom race would be a fitting end to the season. The idea was mulled over a bit and then all concerned agreed it was a good idea.

What to name it became the next concern—it just couldn't be another slalom race—a special name had to be given it to make it outstanding. Numerous names were proposed but the name "Sugar Slalom" was finally agreed upon. This name was proposed by the late Roland Palmedo who was one of the early boosters of Mansfield. It was also suggested that the awards be in the form of a pin depicting a maple leaf.

The day of the race was sunny and reasonably mild and skiing was excellent on upper half and good on lower Nose Dive. The slalom was set by Sepp Ruschp and extended from Station No. 13 (just below the turns) to Station No. 35 (one schuss below present finish). The race started at 2 PM, D.S.T. with nearly 100 entries. Milt Hutchinson of Barre had the best men's time of 1:34:2, and Sis McKeon had the best women's time of 1:47:0.

Sugar on snow was served at the finish by the then Stowe-Mansfield (later Stowe Area) Association—Mark Poor, President.

This was in the days before the lift, so everything including the flags, telephones, shovels, sugaring-off pan, syrup and donuts all had to be tugged up the Nose Dive on old metal toboggans, so a lot of work went into the successful race of the First Sugar Slalom.

Andy Mansfield and Dwight Wiltshire presided at the "Sugaring Off." All went well and a beautiful affair resulted. It was a fitting official end of the season although that year there was skiing for another two weeks on the upper half of the Nose Dive. Thus ended the first "Sugar Slalom" only 40 years ago.

The Stowe Reporter

Feb. 7, 1985

Carving the Way Over Mt. Mansfield

by Charles Lord

[Editor's note: this is the first in a series of article on the history of Mt. Mansfield, researched by Stowe resident Charles Lord, and written in collaboration with Stowe Reporter writer Rebecca Widschwenter.]

Over a hundred years ago, tourists and residents alike viewed the stunning scenery from the top of Mt. Mansfield. Unlike today, however, they had a bit more of a challenge in researching the pinnacle of Vermont.

By 1847, some sort of path had been made up Mt. Mansfield, for in the October issue of the Vermont Chronicle that year, reference was made

The long ride up Mt. Mansfield in the old days to the Summit House (follow the arrow).

Photo contributed by Walt Sumes

to a trail on the west side of the mountain in Underhill. The author said that for many years he had desired to visit the mountain. With three others, he spent the night in Underhill and started for the top at 6 a.m.—climbing through mostly unmarked woods.

A 14-year-old Stowe girl was among the first to climb Mt. Mansfield. Starting from the Stowe side with the rest of her party, she said years later that "there was no road or trail of any sort—we traveled through unbroken woods, over rocks and fallen trees."

A larger rock on the Nose was so delicately balanced that a man with a bar could jostle it. After several attempts to dislodge it through blasting, 30 people climbed onto the rock for a view over the precipice. A half hour after they had left, the rock tumbled from its perch with a roar that shook the surroundings.

In 1859, Stillman Churchill acquired what is now the Green Mountain Inn. He was instrumental in making a trail up the Stowe side of Mt. Mansfield, enabling people to reach the top on horseback. Mrs. Churchill, it is said, was the first woman to reach the summit in this manner.

The Halfway House along the Toll Road in 1868. The timber was dragged up the mountain to form the log construction and bark roof (courtesy of Charlie Lord).

Halfway House

W.H.H. Bingham acquired Mr. Churchill's holdings— and having accumulated land on the mountain—he pushed for a road and mountain hotel. A road was completed in 1858 and became known as the Halfway House trail. It led to the Halfway House, a small guest house halfway up the mountain, from which point people could continue on horseback to the summit. The cabin was also used by men who worked on the remaining portion of the road leading to the peak. Mr. Bingham apparently got the town of Stowe to help build the road, for it was legally discontinued as a public road in 1921, according to Stowe Town Meeting records.

the Summit House Hotel atop Mt. Mansfield, torn down in 1964 (photo courtesy of Ruth Nimick).

Summit House

Byron Russell, who was thoroughly familiar with the topography of the mountain, laid out a bridle path and carriage road to the side of the Summit House. In 1870, the carriage road was improved and completed, with a final cost of about $40,000. Henry C. Phillips of New York City was the first to drive a carriage up the length of it.

Tolls were collected at the top by the hotel proprietor—25 cents for a saddle horse, 50 cents for a single team, $1 for a double team, and $1.50 for a four-horse team and $2 for a six-horse team. Some visitors, however, tried to dodge this toll. Along the "Pole Bridge Hill" section there were the remains of a lumber camp where people would leave their teams and walk the rest of the way to avoid the toll. Upon learning of this trick, the proprietor had the building destroyed.

Stagecoach Run

A public stagecoach ran between Stowe Village to the (then) Summit House Hotel and was drawn by four or six horses, conveying guests to the hotel.

Around 1918, the new State Highway through the Notch had been completed and autos were beginning to move about. George Milne of Barre made the first recorded automobile ascent up the mountain. W.C. Adams, then owner and proprietor of the hotel, bought an Oldsmobile which was fitted to carry passengers, mail and supplies from the village to the summit. This allowed guests to arrive at the Summit House in only 1 hour from the village. On its first trip up the mountain, the Olds was loaded with six bales of hay and eight people, including Mr. Adams and the driver, H.B. Blossom. It was a hot day and driving in low gear most of the way proved difficult for the engine. However, they only stopped once to put in 1 ½ quarts of water. The trip took one hour, compared with the 2 ½ hours necessary for a light wagon drawn by two horses and carrying four passengers.

Though Ab Jenkins made the same trip—under race conditions—in seven minutes and 34 seconds, a normal car ride nowadays takes about 20 minutes. The price has gone up a few dollars since the days of the horse-drawn stagecoach, but few other changes have occurred. The view from the top of Mt. Mansfield is still as breathtaking as it was a hundred years ago.

The first Toll House at the bottom of the Toll Road, around 1928.

Photo contributed by Charles Lord

From Tent to Cabin to Mt. Top Hotel (Mt. Mansfield lodging had it all)

By Charles Lord

[Ed. Note: This is the second in a five part series of articles on the history of Mt. Mansfield and Stowe, researched by Charlie Lord, and written in collaboration with Stowe reporter writer Rebecca Widschwenter.]

Long before the multitudes of motels, restaurants and condominiums sprouted up around the Ski Capitol of the East, Mt. Mansfield was a prime spot for lodgings which accommodated hikers and summer tourists.

In 1856, the first overnight lodging was set up for hikers near the site of the Summit House. The tent was erected by David N. Shaw and George Downing, both of Underhill, assisted by the man and boy who carried the floor boards up the mountain. The pair made one trip a day-the man carrying four boards at a time and the boy carrying two-charging 25 cents per board.

Also in 1856, W.H.H. Bingham built a small guest house halfway up the mountain, near a never-failing spring. Known as The Stowe Halfway House, it was from this point that people switched from stagecoach to horseback in order to reach the summit, since Mr. Bingham had at that time built a road only to the halfway point.

Mr. Bingham (W.H.H.) built a second lodge in 1857, on the east ridge about a half mile below the Summit House and near the present location of the Octagon. The following year the house was moved to the Summit and became the nucleus of the Summit House Hotel, then

49

known as the Tip Top House. The original hotel building was 24 by 40 feet. There was a separate barn large enough to stable 12 horses.

In the days before fast travel and refrigeration, a cow and chickens were kept at the summit House during the summer. The so called "Chicken Coop" was later outfitted with a stove and bunks for the benefit of the occasional winter visitor. In the earliest days it was the only shelter on the mountain for skiers.

In 1878 the Summit House was bought by W.B. Bailey. Ownership passed to Charles Churchill in 1893 and W.M. Adams in 1899.

In 1919, the hotel was purchased by the Mt. Mansfield Hotel Company, Inc., with Max Powell of Burlington as president. Associated with him during this period were Mark Lovejoy, Craig Burt, Gale Shaw and William Davis. Charles Riley, Mark Lovejoy, then Charles Riley, Clem Curtis and Albert Vanasse were the successive managers until the hotel closed in 1957. Around 1950, the Summit House became a part of the holdings of the Mt. Mansfield Company, Inc.

In the early 1900's, the Underhill Halfway House was constructed on the Underhill side of Mt. Mansfield. A steep foot trail ran alongside it up to the summit. It is still used by hikers.

The Green Mountain
Club's Taft Lodge around 1925
(courtesy of Charlie Lord)

Also built on the mountain was the Taft Lodge, constructed in the 1920 for the Green Mountain Club with funds provided by Judge Elihu B. Taft and erected under the supervision of Judge Clarence P. Cowles. The foot trail from Barnes Camp to Taft Lodge mainly follows an old lumber road. Most materials for the lodge were hauled by horses.

Logs for the building were cut nearby, Clyde Brink, assisted by Dick Gilchrist, did all the teaming and building connected with the cabin. It has been repaired several times and is still in good shape.

The other three buildings on Mt. Mansfield eventually met their end. The Halfway House on the Underhill side disappeared around 1930, and the Stowe Halfway House ceased to function shortly after the Summit House came into being (though a woodshed was maintained at the site for as long as the Summit House was open).

The Summit House was torn down in 1964 and replaced by a parking area. Just to the west rises a television tower, at the base of which is a building jointly occupied by the television company and the Mt. Mansfield Company. It's now used by the Mt. Company as a summer rest area for hikers and people driving up the Toll Road.

The Stowe Reporter

Dec. 19, 1983

Skiers & Skiing...a Stowe Tradition

By Charlie Lord

[*Ed. Note: The onset of new ski season seems an appropriate time for delving into past years of local skiing. Stowe historian Charlie Lord had provided us with some interesting-and little known-tidbits of Stowe's skiing history, dating back to the first known skiers in our area.*]

Stowe's Skiing Pioneers

At what date the first ski tracks were made in Stowe is not recorded, but surely by 1910, someone had ventured cross country on skis. Around 1912, there were three Scandinavian families located in Stowe: One on West Hill, one on Edson Hill and one on Shaw Hill. They traveled back and forth on touring skis. They couldn't speak very good English, but they sure knew how to ski.

The first recorded ascent of Mt. Mansfield on skis was made in February of 1914 by Nathaniel Goodrich, then Dartmouth College's librarian, along

Lord-Coleman
Nose Dive
1934-35

with a companion, Charles W. Blood, who followed on snowshoes. They spent the better part of a day on the climb and descent.

About this time and perhaps somewhat earlier, local lumberman Craig Burt, Sr. obtained a pair of skis, which he used in getting from one lumbering operation to another. He climbed the Toll Road in February of 1926 with his oldest son, Craig, Jr., and another youth, Bob Wells. It took the greater part of a day and was considered quite a feat.

Quoting Craig Burt, Sr., he said, "Around 1902 to 1905, a few of us took hardwood boards and bent up one end, nailed on a toe strap and thought we were ready to ski. The poles were one inch by one inch hardwood and quite long. There were no grooves on our skis, so control was at a minimum. Our skiing consisted of straight running down a slope near the school. On arriving at the bottom of the run, we carried our skis back up the hill for another straight run. However, 'spills-without-thrills' was not really skiing and we soon lost interest. Some years after 1906, I ordered a pair of skis from the Northland Ski Co. of St. Paul, Minn. These were eight feet long with two grooves. The poles were bamboo and quite long."

So it would appear that aside from the Swedish families, Craig Burt Sr. was about the only skier in town for quite awhile.

Beginnings of Winter Carnival

In February of 1921, Stowe held its first Winter Carnival. A jump and a toboggan slide were built on Marshall Hill (where the school Poma lift, later on, was). In the evening, there was a minstrel show by local talent. During the day, there were obstacle races, ski joring, exhibition jumping, toboggan rides and snowshoes and ski trips to Mt. Mansfield.

All in all, they were complete successes. Among the participants were three Scandinavians from Montpelier, who not only competed, but skied cross country from Montpelier and back in the same day-a distance of 44 miles roundtrip.

During the summer of 1923, the ski jump tower was blown over. After a lapse of several years, a jump was established on the hill behind the present "Pine Cabins," formerly known as the Quincy Magoon place. While the jump was never replaced on Marshall Hill, the toboggan slide was used for several years.

Stowe High School took over the winter activities and held annual meets with Jeffersonville High School for several years. The meets alternated between Stowe and Jeffersonville and, usually, various groups would ski through Smugglers Notch to participate, and spend the night in the town where the meet was held. The following is an anonymous account of one such trip:

"In 1924, the first group from Stowe High School went through the Notch to Jeffersonville, some on snowshoes and some on skis. The trip was made on Friday and the group stayed at different homes in Jeffersonville until Sunday. The snowshoers came home by train to Morrisville and by stage to Stowe on Sunday. There was a carnival between Stowe and Jeffersonville High Schools in ski jumping, cross country and obstacle races. Later that year, a group from Jeffersonville came to Stowe for a weekend and attended a carnival, here. Orlo Jenney, a Stowe High graduate, was the principal of Cambridge (Jeffersonville) High School. In each of the following years-1925, 1926, and 1927, a group from Stowe skied through the Notch on Friday and back on Sunday."

In 1926, Carlyle McMahon, Arnold Moulton, Orlo Gibbs and Gordon (Buster) Canning decided to participate in a carnival and started out late Thursday on a log sled, belonging to Barney McManis, to his home (now the residence of John McManis). They planned to spend the night at Barnes Camp and stopped at Jim Houston's little store (Bottom Notch) and purchased a can of beans and some rolls for supper. Arriving at Barnes Camp around 7:30 they found that vandals had broken every window in the camp. They stuffed mattresses in the windows and built a fire in the large round stove. They hurried upstairs to see if everything was okay and found some stove pipe missing and sparks flying around the room-and the floor covered in pine needles. They went downstairs, put snow on the fire and built another in the kitchen range, which was much safer. Being 26 below that night, the rolls froze, so the beans made up the supper. None dared to sleep, and at daylight the group proceeded to Jeffersonville.

The first place they came to through after the Notch was Morse's Mill, a logging camp about six miles from Jeffersonville. That morning the mill workers were having breakfast when the four stopped there, hungry and tired. But no one offered the group any breakfast, so on they went. A few miles further, Carlyle and Arnold stopped at a farmhouse. The farmer's wife had just taken an apple pie from the oven, and they purchased it, along with a loaf of bread. Orlo and Buster stood the hunger until reaching Hawley's Cafe in Jeffersonville. They participated in the Carnival, spent the night in Jeffersonville and the next day got a ride back to Stowe with Roy Barrows in his model-T Ford.

Toll Road Treks

On Washington's Birthday in February of 1932, Roland Palmedo and Jose Machado climbed the Toll Toad, skied down and spent three days in Stowe. They reported back favorably to the Amateur Ski Club of New York.

Presumably, there were other groups who toiled up the Toll Road and skied back down that way. The roads were not plowed and maintained like today, and under ideal conditions the foot of Harlow Hill was as far as one could get in a car. Beginning with the winter of 1931-32, more frequent trips were made up the mountain, and during the winter of 1932-33, Ranch Camp was opened on an informal basis to local skiers, and several old logging roads in that area were brushed out and used.

Skiing Origins at Mt. Mansfield

That phase of skiing as we know it today, here on Mansfield, really began with the construction of the first truly downhill ski trail in 1933. Economic conditions throughout the country were at low ebb. To move people off the street and get the situation off dead center, numerous government efforts were made to improve circumstances. Among these was the formation of the Civilian Conservation Corps, which organized young men in a quasi-military group and placed this labor force at the disposal of State and local officials to work on recreational, forestry and environmental problems of the day.

Several factors were a decisive force in the early skiing development of Stowe: there was already considerable local interest in that there had been winter carnivals and such, plus activities of the Stowe Ski Club, Mt. Mansfield and Toll Road were fairly accessible and the favorable topographic features of the mountain proved to be attractive; and most of the land was owned by either the State Forestry Dept. or the Burt Lumber Company, both of which were highly sympathetic to the growing movement.

In addition to the formal organizations, there were many individuals who combined efforts got the ball rolling, so to speak.

And finally, there was an abundance of labor in the form of the CCC. All these forces tended to converge, and the net result was the commencement of skiing growth here in Stowe.

A group of CCC workers were based at Ranch Camp during the months of November and December of 1933. Through their efforts was the construction of the Bruce trail, which went from Ranch Camp to a point on the Toll Road near the present junction of the Toll Road and the Nose Dive. Cutting was started on November 6, 1933, and the Toll Road was reached on November 23. It generally followed an old log road most out of the way. The trail derived its name from an old time lumber operator named H.M. Bruce, who in 1890 owned much of the land on which Bruce trail is located. Snow came early that year and was nearly waist deep during the last of the cutting on the Bruce. However, it was completed and used during the winter of 1933-34.

Since those not-so-long-ago days, Stowe has become synonymous with skiing. And as we ski down those powdered slopes of Mt.

Mansfield this winter, we can think of those who crossed the paths before us, and those who made this winter recreation possible.

Dickinson Collection
Crowd of Skiers on Mt. Mansfield

The Stowe Reporter
June 1971

Ski Dates & Construction

By Charles D. Lord

1933

Nov. 1, 1933, to Jan. 1, 1934—C.C.C. cut several trails in Ranch Valley, including the Bruce trail—the crew stayed at Ranch Camp—they also cut some touring trails towards Luce Hill.

Jan. 1934—C.C.C. improved the jump located on the hill near what is now "The Pines" cabins and lodge. [Now Hadleigh House]

First down mountain race held on Mansfield, Feb. 25, 1934, with Dick Durrance as the winner.

Ranch Camp opened to the public for the first time—only the old cook house with bunks therein available.

Preliminary location of the Nose Dive during the summer of 1933—no cutting done.

The winter of 1933-34 was the first in which the road was plowed from the foot of Harlow Hill (old location) to what is now the State parking area at Mansfield. This plowing was done mostly by C.C.C. equipment and men. The month of Feb. 1934 was extremely cold with lots of snow.

1934-35

Constructed the original Chin Clip which dead ended at the top about 1/4 mile below Taft Lodge and ended at VT 108 at the State picnic area-usable during the winter of 34-35. Work started on the Nose Dive during the summer—trail cut through but not usable until late in the season due to rocks and stumps that had not been removed.

Temporary wooden shelter constructed in Nov.-Dec. where Stone Hut now is.

New bunk house at Ranch Camp in addition to main camp- George Campbell, Mgr. (he sure could bake beans).

Accommodations limited to Ranch camp, Barnes Camp, The Green Mt. Inn, The Fountain and a few farmhouses.

For the first ski instruction [to] become available—Jim Trachier was the instructor, sponsored by the Mt. M.S.C. [Mt. Mansfield Ski Club].

Winter Carnival held Feb. 22-24—downhill on Chin Clip, cross country, slalom and jumping held in Stowe Village. The slalom hill being the slope (now heavily wooded) directly east across the road from the Grand Union store. The cross country course was located in the field where the Grand Union now is and westward thereof. The jumping was held at "The Pines" (Hadleigh House) cabins and tourist home.

1935-36

During the summer of 1935, the stumps and stones were removed from the Nose Dive so that it was skiable from the beginning of the season.

Oct. 1, 1935—work commenced on present Stone Hut—it was finished in Jan. 1936.

The Lodge opened for its first winter season.

Toboggans were located at the Stone Hut, Toll Road Halfway, Toll House, Ranch Camp, Barnes Camp and The Lodge.

Toll House opened for first time in winter—Frank Griffin, Mgr.

Jim Trachier, sponsored by the Mt. M.S.C., was again on hand to give instruction.

The Mt. Mansfield Ski Patrol was first officially organized in mid-winter.

First Interscholastic Carnival held Feb. 1—combined with Vt. Championships.

Feb. 23, 1938—First sanctioned race on Nose Dive—Bob Bourdon easily the winner.

Dr. Ernest Wagner, ski instructor, located at The Lodge from March on.

Toll House opened for first time in winter with sports shop, shelter, snack bar and guest house—Vivian Campbell was cook—Wilfred Vanasse worked weekends and steady beginning the winter of '37-'38 and has worked at the mountain ever since. The rope tow was installed on what is now the Toll House T-bar area—it began operating in Dec. 1936. It was bought 2nd hand from Wesley Pope of Jeffersonville. Gordon Bull was in charge of installing it.

Addenda: Re: Date of First Rope Tow

Straight from the horse's mouth, none other than Wesley Pope of Jeffersonville, who says: "I sold the rope tow to Mr. Burt in the fall of 1936 and I put it up with plenty of help furnished by Mr. Burt, plus a pair of horses and drivers. We finished it about the time Sepp arrived around the middle of December 1936. It was 1000 ft long and was powered by a 1927 Cadillac motor." So that pinpoints the date of the first rope tow here in Stowe. Price $900.

Sunday, Feb. 7—big crowd at Toll House slope where newly installed rope tow operated commercially for the first time. The month of January had very poor snow conditions—thaws and freeze ups.

1936-37

Sepp Ruschp arrived in the fall of 1936 as ski instructor, sponsored by the Mt. M.S.C., and was located at the Toll House which was used as a warming shelter, sport shop, snack bar and guest house under the management of Frank Griffin. Rates at the tow were @ $1 per day or $5 for the season.

Jacques Charmoz, ski instructor, was located at The Lodge.

Edson Memorial trail in Ranch Valley cut.

New bunk house at Ranch Camp—George Campbell, Mgr.

Interscholastic Meet Jan. 29-30 sponsored by the U.S.E.A.S.A. and Vt. Headmasters Club.

At least 12 toboggans placed on various trails at strategic spots. Telephones located at the C.C.C. camp (now State Dorm), and the Trout Club near Lake Mansfield.

A rope tow installed on the Bennett farm (where the Mountain Road Motel now is) by Gordon Bull—it was only in one season.

Dick and Jack Durrance in race on Nose Dive Feb. 21—Jack won.

Mt. Greylock races transferred to Mansfield—weather poor and huge traffic jam resulted.

1937-38

Perry Merrill trail constructed during the fall of 1937—also Steeple Trail in Ranch Valley cut.

C.C.C. completed a 200 car parking area at foot of Nose Dive—referred to in the early years as the Nose Dive parking area—they also constructed a practice slope—in back [of the] present State Shelter—all this during the summer and fall of 1938. Temporary shelter was built on site of the present State Shelter.

Sepp Ruschp, ski instructor, on hand at the Toll House with Edi Fuller as an assistant —now called the Sepp Ruschp Ski School.

Frank Griffin moved to Nose Dive parking area and established the Mt. Mansfield Ski School—also installed rope tow on new slope.

Stowe-Mansfield Association (now Stowe Area Association) formed. Dr. Barrows, president and Mark Poor, vice president.

Ranch Camp open—George Campbell not on hand-fifth season for camp. Old barn has been fixed up. New wash room with showers has been built.

Jacques Charmoz back at The Lodge ski school.

Vt. Downhill on Nose Dive Feb. 13.

National races—men's, Mar. 4-5 and women's, Apr. 9-10.

Pins sold at $1.50 to raise money to defray expenses.

Notice of an excursion to Wade Pasture Feb. 27.

Vt. Interscholastic Meet, Mar. 11-12.

Sepp Ruschp ran Hors Concours in 2:55:4 in Vt. Downhill.

Excursion to Luce Hill, Mar. 13.

1938-39

Fifteen ski caches now installed by C.C.C.

Feb. 4, 1939—electric timer used on Nose Dive slalom race—a first—supplied by Dartmouth.

First caretaker at the Stone Hut this winter, Reg Springstead, paid by Vt. Forest Service.

Ranch Camp under management of Trim and Bert Conklin.

Trail survey made fall indicates there are 4.6 miles of expert [trails]; 13.4 miles of intermediate; 12.5 miles of novice; 25.8 miles of touring; 5.2 miles of advanced touring and 3.3 miles of miscellaneous trails in the Mansfield region.

Sepp Ruschp Ski School, with Sepp in charge and in association with Jacques Charmoz at The Lodge—Sepp's direct assistant was Ali Mauracher.

Ranch Camp rates—food and lodging $3 per day or $17 per wk. Breakfasts 40 cents; lunch 50 cents; and dinner 60 cents.

First Sugar Slalom—Apr. 30, on Nose Dive from Sta. 13 to 35—snow conditions excellent.

May 31, 1939—chair lift reconnaissance party consisting of Perry Merrill, Palmedo, Cooke, Sepp, Al Gottlieb, Rogers Adams, myself, and two engineers from the A. S. & W. Co.

Summer and fall 1939—Lord Trail constructed.

June 1939—commenced construction of present State Shelter—there had been a temporary shack at this location in which Frank Griffin operated the Mt. Mansfield Ski School and the food concession. Willi Benedict, Herta Ritchter, Henry Simoneau, Andy Ransome, others were among his roster of instructors.

1939-40

Rim Rock cut in the fall of 1939.

Sepp Ruschp Ski School staffed by Sepp as Director, plus Otto Hollaus, Kerr Sparks and Lionel Hayes.

Ranch Camp rate $2.50 to $3.50 per day—the Conklins, mgrs.

Caretaker at the Stone Hut was Freddie Koblenzer.

S-53 was laid out and constructed mid-winter—completed in March 1940 and named after the C.C.C. camp which built it.

Parking area at the Nose Dive enlarged in spring of 1940.

Apr. 28, 1940- 2nd Sugar Slalom held—ideal conditions—Course from old race start just above Toll Road to sta. 25—first sugar on snow—course set by Sepp.

Midway trail completed in early winter of 1940.

Stowe Historical Society Archives
The Single Chair Lift

June 4, 1940—work commenced on single chair lift—it was completed and used the following winter, 1940-1941.

Sept. 30, 1940—work commenced on the "Octagon."

During the late summer "The Lodge" was purchased by George Morrell.

1940-1941

Dec. 9, 1940—Chair Lift begins first season of operation.

Fritz Kramer caretaker at the Stone Hut for a short while—George (Harry) Porter took over. Fritz became the first paid patrolman.

Sepp Ruschp, Director at the Ski School, with Otto Hollaus, Kerr Sparks, Lionel Hayes, Howard Moody, Everett Bailey, Clem Curtis, and Norman Richardson.

Skimiester being cut in Dec. 1940.

The Slalom Glade cut in the fall of 1940.

Nose Dive By-Pass (original) cut in fall 1940.

State Shelter (now Base House) ready for use winter 1940-1941.

Ranch Camp open with the Conklins as mgrs.

1941-42

Nose Dive parking area enlarged again in summer 1941.

George (Harry) Porter, caretaker at Stone Hut.

Skimiester completed in fall of 1941.

Dec. 1941—State Shelter officially dedicated by Gov. Wills.

Ranch Camp opened with the Hendersons as Mgrs.—dog team instituted—David Burt in charge.

Parking fee of 25 cents at Mansfield parking area.

Weekly Skimiester races on new trail.

Merry-Go-Round Race consisting of four down hill races in one weekend- held on old Chin Clip; Nose Dive; Bruce and Steeple trails—March 7-8, 1942. Norwich, 1st; Dartmouth, 2nd; the Stowe

Snowballs consisting of Dave Burt, Emile Couture, Marilyn Shaw, Betty Ware, and Priscilla Raymond won the mixed group.

Arlberg—Parallel techniques chief topic of conversation.

Apr. 11-12—Third Sugar Slalom

C.C.C. disbanded in Jan. 1942—all trails, public buildings, parking areas, etc. on Mansfield with the exception of the Skimiester was constructed by them—also several trails in Ranch Valley including the Bruce. Most of the boys went into the service and lot of the equipment was used in the construction of the Alaska Highway.

1942 THROUGH THE WAR YEARS

Gas became rationed and practically all skiers arrived by train or bus—private car travel was at a minimum. Gas coupons were issued to run the lift motor as it was deemed a recreational necessity. Service men were given gratis rides. The Lift operated not more than 6 hours a day, 6 days a week. Wood was used as fuel wherever possible.

The Ski School and Ski Patrol staffs were at a minimum—in fact one season there was no paid patrolman—Harold Eggleston and Knud Anderson, volunteers, being on hand most every day.

"Mt. Mansfield Skiing" was issued only once a year and there were no races.

Stowe-Mansfield Association established an office in Stowe.

Ski School winter 1944-45 besides Sepp include Bob Bourdon, Bob DeForest, Joan Stent and Mary Mather. Ski school headquarters at Toll House with branch at State Shelter where there is a rope tow and restaurant.

1945-46

Work by the VT Highway Dept. commenced this summer on improving the road from Stowe Village to the mountain (Nose Dive parking area). It will be hard surfaced next summer. The Mt. Mansfield-Stowe Derby was run informally last winter and is to become an annual event.

1946-47

During the summer the present Mt. Mansfield T-bar was constructed— used the winter of 46-47.

Road from Stowe Village to parking area was paved—completed Oct. 1946.

Beginning of Lullaby Lane from Toll Road to Lifts.

Ski School—Sepp Ruschp, Otto Holhaus, Kerr Sparks, Clem Curtis, Henry Simoneau, John Clement, Stan Gosnay, Roger Paige, Gerald Fisher, Kjell Torke-Hagen, Casie Jones and Frances Harrison- will be at the Toll House and the new T-bar.

Wendy Snow Parrish Collection
Ski School

Dickinson Collection
The Ski School Instructors

Snow came Nov. 24.

Junior program started—Landon Cummings of Barre and Roger Burke of Stowe will direct.

State Ski dorm (former C.C.C. side camp) opened in winter of 1946-47.

In the fall of 1946, the Burt Co. holdings in Smuggler's Notch sold to what eventually became the Mt. Mansfield Co. This transaction covered about 3000 acres including the Spruce Peak area, Sterling Pond, and the Sterling Brook area (just east of the Pinnacle), plus some land on Mansfield.

Six paid men on the Ski Patrol with Howard Moody, leader and Al Arey, assistant leader. Erwin (Lindy) Lindner, former patrol leader, began working for Forest and Parks Dept. as in charge of the State Shelter and parking area.

1948-49

Stowe Center (now called the Centre) was built this summer 1948.

New building constructed at the Toll House to take the place of the original

Toll House—new building will house the ski shop, rent and repair, and office space for personnel, a separate building.

Ski Patrol—Al Arey, leader; George Wesson, assistant leader; and Robert Hawley from last year—new men are Fred Garrity, Stanley Day, and John Chandler.

Ski School with 12 instructors and Kerr Sparks in charge.

1949-1950

New by-pass cut.

Perry Merrill cross trail from Slalom Glade cut.

East and West slope at Little Spruce constructed, serviced by two rope tows in tandem. Also warming shelter and parking area built.

At the Toll House, a wing was added to the new building which will house restaurant, etc. The old Toll House was remodeled by moving kitchen and dining room downstairs into what was the public restaurant.

Mt. Mansfield Lift purchased by the Mt. Mansfield Co.

Ski Patrol—George Wesson, leader; Fred Garrity, assistant leader; Bill Garrity, Don Scholle; Bob Cochran and Francis Menard.

March, 1950- STOWE VOTED WET ALL THE WAY.

1950-51

August 1950—new golf course opens—1st and 9th holes near the Centre—the other 7 holes across the river reached by a bridge cross the West Branch. Dr. Barrows drove the first ball.

T-bar installed at Little Spruce- replaces the two rope tows.

The Lodge sold to the Mt. Mansfield Co. in Nov. 1950.

New cutoff on Lord just below the Lookout in fall of 1950.

1952-53

March 22-23—Men's and Women's National Championships awarded to Mt. Mansfield Ski Club

Nose Dive extended to top of Nose.

1952-53

Karl Frahner and Othmar Schneider, Frank Day, and Gordon Lowe added to Ski School.

1,000,000th skier rides to Mt. Mansfield Chair Life (S.C.L.).

George Campbell died Nov. 20, 1953.

1953-54

Lullaby Lane improved. Slopes at Little Spruce have been widened and smoothed.

Vic Constant downhill started on upper Nose Dive and ran by north side of Octagon, down Lord and standard to bottom. (Same as last year.)

Neil Robinson and Perley Millard at sugaring—off-pan at finish of Sugar Slalom.

20th Anniversary of Mt. Mansfield Ski Club.

1954-55

Spruce Peak Double Chair Life, trails and buildings ready for the season.

1955-56

Summer of 1955— first addition to State Shelter.

Neil Robinson died summer 1955.

1956-57

Billy Woods died Apr. 25, 1957.

Testimonial Dinner for Sepp—Dec. 7, 1958, at Spruce House.

1957-58

Sven Johnson wins cross-country Feb. 1958.

Jump built in lower Ranch Valley, opposite Co. dump.

Hot Rod Corner on Smuggler's Trail completed.

1958-59

Sepp Ruschp Ski School—30 full time instructors including: Othmar Schneider, Karl Farhner, Hans Senger, Rugi Alber, Luis Sturm, Adi Yoerg, and Monique Langlais.

June 15, 1959—Bill Riley skied the Toll road—late snowstorm deposited 8" to 10".

1959-60

Paul Biederman, new permanent Ski Club secretary.

Stuberl opened for the 1963-64 season.

5th American International Races on Mansfield on March 11, 12, and 13, 1960.

Parking charge eliminated beginning of 1965-66 season.

Artificial snowmaking installed at Little Spruce during the summer of 1967.

Double chair lift on Mansfiel—1960.

Double chair lift at Little Spruce—1963.

Gondola and trails at Mansfield—1968.

TRAIL CONSTRUCTION DATES

BRUCE—Nov. and Dec. 1933.

HOUSTON—1933

CONWAY (Edson memorial)—1936

NOSE DIVE—1934 and 1935.

CHIN CLIP (old) – 1934

MERRILL—1937.

RIM ROCK—1939.

CROSS OVER from SLALOM GLADE to MERRILL—1948.

SLALOM GLADE—1940.

LORD –1939.

MIDWAY—Jan. 1940.

S-53—March 1940.

NOSE DIVE BY PASS (old location)—Fall 1940.

EAST and WEST SLOPE—1949.

MAIN STREET and STERLING—1954.

LULLABY LANE—1953.

SMUGGLERS—1956.

LITTLE SPRUCE D.C.L. trails—1963.

GONDOLA trails including new Chin Clip and new Perry Merrill—1968.

MANSFIELD D.C.L. trails including: the new Skimiester, Maiden Lane, Hayride, Starr, Goat and new crossover to Merrill—1960.

NATIONAL—1952-1953.

SKIMIESTER—fall 1941.

MANSFIELD T-bar trails—Tyro, Standard, and North Slope were constructed when T-Bar was installed—1946.

LIFT CONSTRUCTION DATES

ROPE TOWS:
   Toll House—1936-37.
   Mansfield (Slope at State Shelter)—1937-38.
   Little Spruce—1949-50.

T-BARS:
   Toll House—1956-57 (Removed 1962).
   Mansfield—1946-47
   Little Spruce—1950-51 (Removed 1962).

CHAIR LIFTS:
   Mansfield Single Chair Lift—1940.
   Mansfield Double Chair Lift—1960.
   Spruce Peak D.C.L.—1954-55.
   Little Spruce D.C.L.—1963-64.
   Toll House—1962.
   Lookout D.C.L.—1981.
   Little Spruce—1982.
   Triple Chair—1987.

GONDOLAS:
   Mansfield—1968
   4 Passenger Gondola—1989
   8 Passenger Gondola—1992

BUILDING DATES

RANCH CAMP—1933-1950

TOLL HOUSE—original building used for several seasons beginning the winter of 1935-36. In 1940, the first addition was built with snack bar, ski shop, and warming shelter on ground floor. Kitchen, dining room, etc., for guests on upper floors. In 1948, a building across the way was built housing the sport shop, rent and repair, administrative space, ski school and staff quarters. Then in 1949, the restaurant wing was added thus allowing the kitchen and dining room in the Toll House Inn to be moved downstairs. The Toll House Motor Inn was built during the summer of 1964 and completely absorbed the old Toll House. The Toll House Restaurant building was completely destroyed by fire in Dec. 1968 and temporary quarters were used the following winter. During the summer of 1969, two new buildings were constructed at the Toll House area—one on the site of the burned building which houses the administrative offices and the other to the westward directly across the parking area—housing the restaurant, ski school, rent and repair and staff quarters. So now there are two nearly fireproof buildings plus the Motor Inn on the site of the original little Toll collectors building.

THE LODGE—this was originally a farm building known as the George Harris place. Joe Lance in 1919 added on to the house and opened it as a summer place. Roy Patrick in 1927 bought out Lance, expanded The Lodge and added the Harlow farms. In 1935-36, it was opened for the winter season for the first time and has been operated summer and winter ever since. George Morrell bought it in 1941 and added on to the place. The Mt. Mansfield Co. acquired The Lodge in Dec. 1950 and added on to the dining room—also in 1969, a new staff quarters building was constructed to replace those that were in the den which was damaged by fire in early 1969 and torn down. This area is now the Condominium complex beginning in 1981.

Wendy Snow Parrish Collection
Mt. Mansfield Co. Acquired The Lodge in December 1950

STATE SHELTER (Base House)—opened the winter of 1940-41—built by the C.C.C. There have been 2 additions, one in 1957 and the other in 1962. It is operated on a concession basis by the Mt. Mansfield Co.

STONE HUT—built by the C.C.C., completed in Jan. 1936—a temporary wooden building on this site was used the winter before.

OCTAGON—built in late 1940 in conjunction with the S.C.L. There have been two additions. On or near this site, in 1857, the first hotel was built on the mountain [the Summit House].

MAIN STREET RESTAURANT—built in 1954.

SPRUCE HOUSE- built in 1956 with an addition in 1963. There was another addition in 1982.

CLIFF HOUSE—built in 1968, also the gondola base, in conjunction with the Gondola.

STATE SKI DORM—built in 1933-34 as a side camp from the main camp (C.C.C.) in Waterbury. Later on remodeled and opened up by State Forest Service in the winter of 1946-47.

Wendy Snow Parrish Collection
The State Ski Dorm from the Late 1930's

Dickinson Collection
Sepp Ruschp

PART II

The Sepp Ruschp Memoir

(As it appeared in his original memoir but retyped for clarity.)

The Bremen, ship of emigration.

SEPP RUSCHP
(1908 - 1990)

At his 40th anniversary celebration at the Mt. Mansfield Company, [Mr. Ruschp] imparted his philosophy: "Work like hell. Use all the imagination you can and just keep on working. If I had the chance, I would do it again. I have no regrets. I have tremendous pride in what has been accomplished in Stowe and the State."

With war in Europe seemingly inevitable by 1935, Sepp wrote over 90 ski clubs in the US hoping to be hired as a ski instructor, and the newly-formed Mt. Mansfield Ski Club was one of only seven that responded to his inquiries. He came from Linz, Austria in 1936 and he stayed, except for returning to Austria to bring back his bride, Hermine Aistleitner whom he had married in 1935. They sailed from Bremen, Germany on the S.S. Deutschland on October 22, 1937. The ship's manifest lists his given name as Josef Sepp and his occupation as "teacher." "Friend's Name" on the manifest is Frank E. Griffin of Stowe. Three New Yorkers who were also members of the newly-organized Mt. Mansfield Ski Club met him at the port of New York and represented his sponsor, They showed him around New York City, and in a few days put him on the train for Burlington, Vermont. His sponsor and friend, Frank E. Griffin met him at the railroad station and took Sepp under his wing.

When he first arrived in Stowe and viewed the mountain the morning after his arrival, he said, "where are the mountains!" And there was pitifully little snow that season. It must have been discouraging for the new ski instructor more familiar with alpine snow and enormous peaks. As he was to learn, fickle New England weather was an on-going problem.

Soon after he had settled into life in his new home town, he knew he had to find jobs to earn money. One of these was to give lessons to beginning skiers and did so in Montpelier, at Norwich University and University of Vermont. One survivor of these first classes given at Hubbard Park in Montpelier, (uphill in back of the State Capitol building), was young Peter Haslam. Peter, then eight or nine years old and being minimally athletic, attended two or three lessons, but quit because Sepp couldn't speak English very well, and the skis being twice as long as Peter was tall! That was in 1937. After the lessons, Peter slogged through the snow downhill to Spring St. and from there to his home at 25 Liberty St. Interestingly, Abner Coleman and his wife lived in the upstairs apartment there, and the families became friends. Coleman probably promoted ski lessons for Peter to Peter's parents. This connection by the Colemans to the Haslam family was a "small world" moment in hindsight. Ab Coleman, with his buddy and fellow highway engineer, Charlie Lord, designed and cut some of the first trails on Mt. Mansfield.

In Austria, Sepp was a competitor in cross-country, alpine, and jumping events. He was a prominent ski competitor and became the Upper Austrian Combined Champion. He then brought to the US expertise in each of these and taught so many others the sport. These are what gained him the recognition for the local Stowe businessmen to contact him to come to Vermont. He had graduated from technical school in Linz, Austria as a qualified engineer and from there he designed trails, buildings, programs, and then started the Sepp Ruschp Ski School in 1936-7 in Stowe.

Mr. Ruschp returned to his home in Austria in 1937 to bring back his bride, Hermine, whom he had married in 1935, after which he began to prepare for the coming winter season's responsibilities.

The first ski school in the United States was established in 1937 by Ruschp. It was that same ski season that the Eastern Downhill Championships had been scheduled to be held at Mt. Greylock's Thunderbolt Trail over Washington's Birthday on February 22nd. Mt. Greylock was virtually snowless at that time—so a last minute change was made to hold the event at Mt. Mansfield's Nose Dive trail. The Skimeister snow trains from Boston and New York City brought more than 800 passengers to Waterbury, Vt., to be further transported to Stowe. Thousands of other skiers and spectators poured into Stowe so that on Sunday, February 21, 1937, a traffic jam of monumental proportions clogged Route 108 and Stowe. It was estimated that 10,000 spectators in 3000 cars created that bottleneck.

In 1938, Sepp was named winter manager of the Mt. Mansfield Hotel Company. He and Hermine became American citizens in 1943 and a year later he was promoted to director of that company. It was in 1951 that the Mt. Mansfield Hotel Company, the Summit House, the Toll House, The Lodge, and the various lift companies merged to become the new Mt. Mansfield Company of which Sepp became vice-president, treasurer, and general manager. By 1946, he was promoted to president and general manager until 1978 when he was elected board chairman after retirement. In the 1950's, Ruschp was instrumental in founding the Eastern Ski Operators' Association which helped to have ski conditions reported by the National Weather Service. He hosted one of the first, if not the first, international ski competitions in 1952 after World War II. He was appointed organizer for the 1960 Olympics at Squaw Valley when he helped to get the first television coverage for those skiing events.

His goal was to establish a great ski resort which he did with the help of Cornelius (Neil) Vander Starr, a wealthy international insurance executive from New York City. Starr contributed much of his wealth to building Ruschp's dream. Of Ruschp, Starr said in a 1955 article in Sports Illustrated magazine, "Sometimes I find a man who has an inner fire—a man who is perfectly in his métier, his orbit. And when I do, I back him." Starr was founder, president and CEO of American International Group. Starr then pointed to Ruschp and said, "I picked you."

Sepp's Mountain Company was a jacket, shirt and tie company until about the late 1970's. Rules were rules and they were strictly applied at the office, business calls, company-owned restaurants, and special events. Ann (Amidon) Van Gilder remembers "Old Hen" (Henry Simoneau), Sepp, Gordon Lowe, and that group in natty jackets, ties, and LL. Bean boots for Old Hen. In February 1970, a small group of us, [friends of this writer,] were planning to dine at Stowehof, then owned by the Mountain Co. As soon as we arrived and went downstairs, Charlie Black was diplomatically invited to change from his turtle-neck shirt and sport jacket combination to a dress shirt and tie, which they cheerfully supplied, but with his own jacket!

Don Fillion writes in 1977, "In 1936, when Sepp Ruschp arrived in Stowe, there was only the mountain and a few rough ski trails. Now the Austrian-born Ruschp heads the $30,000,000 Mt. Mansfield Corp., the bedrock upon which the ski capitol of the east was built." In 1978, he was elected to the United States Ski Hall of Fame.

The list of his accomplishments is long: former president of the US Ski Association, vice-president of the Federation Internationale de Ski (FIS), expert in ski lifts, built the country's first double chair lift at Mt. Mansfield. He insisted on strict safety practices and clean competitions. Standards were high. He also served on the State of Vermont Development Council and the Economic Advisory Council under five Vermont governors. He was a director at Lamoille County Bank, later the Franklin-Lamoille Bank, and president and director of the USSA and vice president of the international ski organization, FIS.

Sadly, Sepp took his own life after having suffered Parkinson's disease during the last few years of his life. Rev. Douglas Brayton, fittingly, was the celebrant at the mountaintop service. Ruschp and Brayton had begun the now popular Easter Sunrise Service tradition on the mountain. Eulogies were eloquent, spoken by many. Excerpted here, Lloyd "Chip" Lacasse, University of Vermont Director of Skiing, "Ruschp hired people who wanted to ski but could not afford to, giving them a chance to experience the sport." David Rowan, editor and publisher of Ski Area Management magazine praised his "high standards of teaching skiing, and zeal for excellence. We all work and build today on the sure foundation that men like Ruschp built yesterday. The ski sport never had a finer leader."

The memoir is the centerpiece of this work. Ruschp handed it to Bill Riley about October 9, 1980, for editing and he then turned it over to Linda Bates Adams (1943-2001) for typing. At that time Sepp was in the hospital, but expected to come home soon.

In the last segment of the memoir Mr. Ruschp captures the essence of C. V. Starr and Starr's firm, yet gentle, approach to business strategy during which they also became fast friends. That story is best told in his own words, the memoir. At the very end of the manuscript, Mr. Ruschp listed several key names in management about whom he may have intended to write more about in the future. This list is the basis for Part III, "People Remembering People."

Many more names have been added that are important to a fuller understanding about other people who had an impact on the development of the sport of skiing in Stowe.

Patricia L. Haslam
August 2013

Dickinson Collection
Sepp Ruschp, family and friends

FOREWORD

For years my family and colleagues have been urging me to commit to print the experiences and stories of my life from Linz, Austria to Stowe, Vermont.

They tell me I am the only one who knows the real story—the whole story—and that there are people who are interested in sharing this story.

So, in the following pages I will tell my story of Sepp Ruschp—from the years of growing up in Austria to the fifty years of collaboration with the people of Vermont and the development of Mt. Mansfield, its highest mountain.

Sepp Ruschp

Dickinson Collection
Sepp Ruschp

SEPP RUSCHP
BIOGRAPHY
(Intro written 1989)

Sepp Ruschp was born on November 17, 1908 in Linz, Austria and grew up in the shadow of the Austrian Alps where skiing is an integral part of life for a great number of the native population. It is little wonder, then, that he became an expert skier, racer and instructor. During the height of his competitive skiing career Sepp toke private lessons in English and studied business administration.

In Austria at that time, there were many winter resorts with ski schools already established. So when Sepp heard that the Austrian Ski Association had received inquires from ski clubs in the United States about ski instructors and consultants, he immediately realized the possibilities offered by the new sport of skiing in the United States.

Sepp accepted the offer of the Mt. Mansfield Ski Club and came to this country in 1936 as a ski instructor and coach of the University of Vermont and Norwich University Ski Teams. He was aware that this move could be the stepping stone of his future.

In 1938, he became winter manager of the Mt. Mansfield Hotel Company. Under his supervision the original Toll House Inn was built and operated as a lodge and ski shop combines.

When he wasn't busy with his duties with the ski programs at Norwich and the University of Vermont, he was busy teaching around the countryside at night giving lessons under lights in many places—at the local Stowe school program—wherever the need arose.

It soon dawned on Sepp that if he established himself at Mt. Mansfield the pupils would come to him. He could shorten his travel time and increase his instructing time. In February of 1938 he formed a ski school and became one of the first seven instructors to be certified in the United States.

During World War II, Sepp spent over a year at the Bell Aircraft Corporation after serving as a pilot and flight instructor in the U. S. Army Air Force. During this period the ski school and hotel maintained existence with the aid of family and friends.

After the war, skiing boomed as never before in this country. From the first years, Sepp have been a constant promoter of lift facilities on Mt. Mansfield and at the end of the war years, his dream began to materialize. Sepp joined forces with the late C. V. Starr, and together with the support of local businessmen, the Mt. Mansfield Company entered a period of great expansion. Sepp Ruschp became a substantial stockholder of the Mt. Mansfield Company in partnership with C. V. Starr, and was eventually elected President and General Manager. Under his management the Mt. Mansfield Company, Inc.

built nine ski lifts on Mt. Mansfield and
Spruce Peak—with a total capacity of over
eight thousand skiers per hour. In addition
to the lift facilities the Company developed
and operated three hotels, six restaurants,
three ski shops and the ski school. In the
summer the hotels and the gondola lift on Mt.
Mansfield as well as the Country Club golf
course became a part of the overall resort
activities at Stowe.

Despite his duties as president and general
manager of the Mt. Mansfield Company, Sepp
found time to serve as a director of the
Franklin Lamoille Bank and the Mt. Mansfield
Ski Club. Sepp is a past president of the
United States Ski Association (USSA) and a
past vice president of the F.I.S. (Federation
Internationale de Ski). He served on the
organizing committee of the 1960 Winter
Olympic Games at Squaw Valley, California.

In 1978, when Sepp retired from active
management, he stayed on as Chairman of
the Board of Directors of Mt. Mansfield
Company for five years. That same year, for
his devoted service to the sport of skiing
in North America, Sepp was elected to the
National Ski Hall of Fame by the United
States Ski Association.

During this period, Sepp received an
Honorary Doctorate of Law degree from the
Department of Engineering and Business at the
University of Vermont. He also served as a
Fellow at Norwich University and received an
Honorary Doctorate of Business and Management
degree from Norwich in 1989.

After more than four decades as a Vermonter, Sepp's dream had long since come true. He was justly proud of the Stowe area and the Mt. Mansfield Company. But he still nurtured a continuing feeling that the sport of skiing held many opportunities for expansion in Stowe and the State of Vermont. Thus Sepp became a member of the Governor's Economic Advisory Council where he continued to serve under five different administrations.

Sepp was also one of the founders of the Vermont Development Corporation. The VDC was backed by a consortium of twenty-one Vermont Banks who joined forces to support small businesses including the expanding ski industry. After four years, Sepp was named president of this prestigious group, remaining in this position for five years.

Sepp and his wife of forty-nine years, Hermine, spent most of each year in a lovely alpine-styled house, built in 1952, at the foot of Mt. Mansfield. Both played tennis and golf. Hermine remained an active tennis competitor, with many trophies to her credit, until her sudden death due to a heart attack in 1984. His loss of Hermine affected Sepp very deeply, thus he was most appreciative of the great help and support from his family and friends.

Their son, Peter, graduated with a B.A. degree from the University of Colorado and makes his home in Stowe where he follows in his father's footsteps as Director of the Mt. Mansfield Ski School in the winter. Peter is also a director and Vice President of the Mt.

Mansfield Ski School where he remains an avid supporter of the junior racing program. Peter and his wife, Carolyn, owned the Stowe Motel, one of the town's original ski lodges, where they reside with their two children, Andrew and Allison.

Daughter Christina graduated with a B.A. degree from Middlebury College. With her husband Larry Startzel (a former golf professional at the Stowe Country Club) the couple has recently moved from Lansing, Michigan (where Larry was head golf pro at the Lansing Country Club) and built a house in Scottsdale, Arizona. He is the professional director of golf at the well known Paradise Valley Country Club. Larry is also a nationwide official of the PGA (Professional Golf Association) and is co-author of the PGA brochure of tournament regulations.

SEPP RUSCHP
THE EARLY YEARS

I was born in Linz on the Danube on November 17, 1908. My father was an engineer of the Austrian State-owned railroad; his was a government position. My mother did not work, she was a hausfrau. I had one brother, Ernest, who was exactly one year eleven days younger.

(Linz, Upper Austria,

We lived in a "combine" of apartments. Because the government combined the workshop with the worker's home, it was a fringe benefit. Linz was the railroad hub of the old Austrian Empire and was the main repair and construction site for the Austrian State railroads. The officials, according to rank, had apartments given or rented to them at very reasonable prices. As many as 500-600 employees of the Austrian state government occupied different housing complexes.

It was a modest setting, but for us it was somewhat of a luxury as we had four rooms, which was very uncommon at that time. There was a bedroom for my parents, another for myself and my brother, a kitchen-dining room combination and a small sitting room—a total of four rooms on the third floor. It was very comfortable and was maintained by the government.

I was very young when the First World War I began. I clearly remember all the whistles blowing when a general mobilization began. Because of my father's position with the railroad, he was not drafted into active duty at the beginning. Eventually he was inducted into the National Guard Reserve and was trained as a soldier in the army of the old Austrian Empire and attained the rank of corporal. In 1916 he was called to active duty as an engineer and was sent to Poland, where he was the commandant of a troop of sixty men trained to repair and replace railroad machinery that had been damaged by Russian attacks. Once my mother was allowed to take my brother and me to visit our father near the Polish front, where we stayed in a railroad cabin with double-decker beds made of boards from crates. I remember we heard many big "booms"—much shooting in the distance.

Because we had country relatives that had farms, we weren't as hungry as many. Whenever his train returned, my father would help them repair their machinery in trade for eggs, or a loaf of bread or milk. My mother was super— she did everything for the kids.

I was ten years old when the Revolution started in 1918. The army barracks were plundered and burned. I remember we were suffering because we didn't have warm clothing or shoes, and it was so very cold. We had enough medical attention; and I was one of the lucky ones who had fairly good medical and dental care—although I did lose some of my first teeth early on account of the malnutrition. Worse was the unemployment that hit Austria hard, and the lack of satisfactory schooling. Most of the teachers had to be called to active military service. The substitutes were very young and willing but without much experience.

Finally, I think in 1921 or 1922, we got "semmel", which was something like bagels. The white bread was back! That was a great event, and we were able to buy some brown sugar. We ate it plain, and drank it with coffee. We saw the wounded coming from the war. I recall my mother sewing underwear and shirts for the Red Cross and for the soldiers.

In Austria, at age six you go to grad school—"Volkschule" for five years; then three years of Buergerschule which is similar to Junior High School in America. Next, I went to Mechanical engineering school. It was unique because we had eight semesters. Six months of the year we worked in the school on subjects like drafting, drawing, engineering, business then we were farmed out to different plants for "real work"—something like on-the-job training.

In my case, my training sent me to a plant where I worked on high pressure fire engine turbine pumps. From there, I went to the shipyard of Linz, where I worked on the design and tooling up of the diesel engines for boats that would navigate the Danube. The ships were being rehabilitated from war damage in order to continue to supply coal ore and iron ore. One ship I worked on had two 4,500 horsepower diesel engines that were powerful enough to pull heavily loaded tugboats.

At the time the shipping industry was really shaky in Austria and I had heard of some opportunities in the Steyer automobile factory, which was forty-two kilometers from Linz. After I presented my credentials, the director of employment explained that because of my engineering and schooling background, the work he had to offer was above my expectations.

"There is an opening in the versuch (research and design) department," he told me. The head of that department was Engineer Porsche. Today that Mr. Porsche would be the great, great grandfather of the present Porsche automobile family. The position in research and design interested me because I could further my education.

I had no political affiliation then. After the war, the Austrian government was elected

by the majority party, the Social Democrats,
those in industry and those who lived in
the cities. Cities remained mainly Social
Democrats, while in the country people leaned
more towards the People's Party, or the
Christian Democrats—the conservatives. That
was the extent of my political background
at the time. The religion of my family was
Catholic.

When I was about ten years old, my uncle,
who was a great sportsman, introduced me to
skiing. He bought me my first pair of skis,
which were wooden, with no steel edges and
long leather straps for bindings.

There were no ski instructors around Linz.
I went many times to Alberg and took lessons
at Hannes Schneider Ski School, and I won my
first ski race in my hometown of Linz when
I was about twelve years old. From then on
the older members of the ski club took me to
other, higher, beautiful mountains with great
skiing. We did a lot of weekend skiing in the
mountains with alpine clubs within a fifty
mile radius of Linz.

Skiing became a big part of my life.
I competed in many ski races and made
a reasonably good name as a national
competitor. Austria had five states: Upper
Austria, Lower Austria, Vorarlberg, Carinthia,
and Styria. I was the Upper Austria champion
for five consecutive years in the combined
(cross country, jumping, downhill and slalom).

Most of the competitive races were
limited to cross country and jumping.
Living in a city like Linz on the Danube,

training conditions were excellent for these disciplines. There were hills between 3000 and 3500 feet in height, with good terrain for cross country practice in the relatively short time between hours of work, or even after work. We also had fairly good jumping hills nearby, which gave us a great opportunity to train for the combined event. One must not forget that the Olympics in 1928 did not have alpine skiing—the classical combined event consisted of cross country and jumping only.

During my first week of employment at Steyer Automobile in 1931, I received an invitation to the first Gross-Glockner Glacier International ski race. "I shouldn't have missed that one," I thought, "I should have started my job a week later."

The plant manager of the department I was working for was a very nice, tanned, sporty man named Mr. Dopplemeyer. (The Dopplemeyer family is now one of the biggest ski lift manufacturers in Austria.) I showed Engineer Dopplemeyer my letter of invitation from the Austrian Ski Association. He said, "I can not give you a vacation, but you can take a week off, unpaid." He was very eager to let me go.

I went to the race on the Gross-Glockner, one of the highest mountains in Austria with a vertical drop of 4500 feet. I did not win, but I finished in the top ten in a field of 164 competitors. I had drawn the last start number 164, so after a four hour climb to the start, I had to wait almost three hours for my run. Luckily, it was the end of June so the weather was mild, and my result made the

long wait worth it. The race was won by my
friend Friedl Pfeiffer by many seconds. The
race has never been held again to this day,
because the glacier receded and the course
disappeared—so his record still exists.

In sports, as you know, you have certain
advantages when you compete at an advanced
level. In this case, it might be comparable
to a professional football player or a tennis
star in America. In Austria, the skiers had a
good name, which helped open doors for many
personal endeavors.

I had started work at Steyer in May and
I worked until early December. During that
time, Mr. Porsche redesigned the Steyer
"Funfzig"(the Steyer Fifty), that later on
became known at the Volkswagen. The Steyer
automobile company was practically bankrupt,
due to import restrictions by the neighboring
German government. From 6,000 employees
working three shifts, they started to lay off
500 men at a time, and every week I thought,
"When is my time to come?"

Eventually, I got a notice that I was laid
off, so I thought, "Okay, I am arbeitslos
(unemployed), now what?"

It was in 1932 when alpine skiing
began to take enormous strides. The F.I.S.
(International Federation of Ski) was formed,
which sponsored international and national
downhill and slalom races. (Giant slalom did
not yet exist). Because the entire training
time had to be split between the classical
combined Nordic events and the alpine skiing
events of downhill and slalom, we had to

travel from our town into the mountains south of Linz. We had excellent mountains there, including the Dachstein (3000 meters or about 10,000 feet in height) Dachstein was a reasonable training distance from Linz—about sixty miles.

My father and I agreed I could spend the winter racing and concentrating on the state examination to become a professional ski instructor, which was sponsored by the government under the jurisdiction of the Ministry of Education. The examination, if passed, gave one the title of "Staatlich Geprufte Schilehrer" which means a state certified ski instructor. To prepare for that, I went to a pre-course at St. Christoph am Arlberg and raced that whole winter successfully, winning several championships.

The examination itself was very thorough and demanding. One not only had to be an excellent skier, able to negotiate all the types of terrain, but also had to be well versed in the structure of teaching skiing, the dynamics of skiing on a technical basis, and have a knowledge of mountain terrain and its dangers (orientation for ski touring, map-reading, avalanche training, etc.) The Commission—the examiners, namely—consisted of a professor from the University of Vienna, an engineer who understood maps, techniques and dynamics, a doctor for the first aid examination, and the famous Hannes Schneider for the style of teaching skiing. In April 1933, about 160 candidates took part in the examination, about 25% of these passed. I was on. Passing this examination was equal in many skiers' minds to winning a very important race—it was a major accomplishment.

In the years between 1928 and 1936, the Olympic organization finally succeeded in holding alpine events. In those years, many alpine races were held with various levels of importance in the different states of Austria. Time and transportation made competing in some of those races very difficult, but I did as much as I could physically and financially afford. In the same period, a number of lifts and resorts were built in the Alps. Time and money continued to be a great problem. But even more important was the worsening political climate in Austria, which naturally reflected in sports. It was complicated to compete and be a great racer because of the different political affiliations, which always caused rivalry and favorites. You were constantly confronted with decisions about which races to attend and whether you could get a starting permit from the various clubs.

The major movement toward alpine skiing in Austria and central Europe had been originated by the necessity to create new businesses and a new outlook on life after World War I.

In the winter of 1932 to 1933, I competed in Langlauf (cross country), jumping, and downhill as well as slalom. At the same time, I began to realize I had an inner dream that someday skiing would play a key part in my entire lifestyle. I was lucky to do well, and after one of these races when I boarded the train near Vienna, I met someone who would influence my future.

After loading skis into the corner of the compartment (at least four pair), the man sitting across from me looked up from his newspaper, pointed, and said, "That's you, isn't it?" It was a newspaper photograph of me, printed because I had won the four-way event—cross country, jumping, downhill and slalom championship for my state—the "State Championship".

"Yes, that's me," I replied, and he wanted to know what I was doing…just skiing? So we started to talk.

I told him of my employment in the now closed Steyer Company, and that for all practical reasons I was out of a job. He told me he was part of an organization which has lots of stores in Austria with sport departments.

He said, "A man with your experience— rowing, tennis, mountain climbing and skiing— well, we have the equipment, but you have the expertise. Would you be interested in becoming a consultant?" He gave me his card and said to give him a ring or come to Vienna, where he was living.

I went home and told this to my family and my father said, "Sepp, why don't you look into this thing? It may be a complete turnaround for you, but because of your mechanical engineering background, you will need further education in a business school. The factories are all closed due to the political situation, so that career may not work out. Why don't you try it? See what they have to offer."

I went to Vienna where I had to start
out at the bottom just like anybody else. I
served a three year apprenticeship and in the
evening I had to go to school—Handelschule.
When you changed a trade in Austria at that
time, more schooling in that particular line
of employment was required—a sort of "trade
school." If you were accepted into the newly
chosen trade, they would employ you, pay
you as a worker, and then train you. New
training was a requirement for each change.
I would say Handelschule would be the same
as a Business Administration College here.
Additional Aubendschule (night classes)
helped make this possible. I got a degree as
Handelsangestelter (a retail salesperson).
Eventually, I took over as manager of the
sport department of the store in Linz.

Having worked myself comfortably into that
line of buying and selling, I went with the
director of the Vienna store to buy sport
equipment—hundreds of boots and shoes—
in Czechoslovakia. I had been given more
responsibility than that of just salesman
after a short time there. For instance, I
bought 175 pairs of skis in a single order
from the Fisher Ski Company—that was the
biggest order Fisher had in 1932.

The desire to better one's education
and position was constantly hampered by
the political party jealousy and rivalry
in Austria. We had very powerful political
organizations; the Social Democrats of
Austria—today's Socialist Party; the
Chrislichsoziale Partei; today's People's

Party, the "Great German Party"—the main group from the business world, leaning towards National Socialism (Nazism). These power groups were political competitors whose rivalry also invaded the sports world. Each had its own sport organization (ski association), and as we entered the second half of the 1930s the splinter groups in one party had become more radical than the others, especially in the Socialist group. Then the Nation parties began to lean strongly toward the German's Nazism.

The Austrian Ski Association's alpine contingent had successfully gotten through the F.I.S. and adopted the "Vierer Combination"— the four way combination of cross country, jumping, downhill and slalom. I remained very active in ski racing. My team claimed the Austrian National Championship in the ten kilometer relay, where I was anchorman four times. I will never forget that last race. There were eighty competitors in all. We won the Austrian National Championship by nearly two minutes. That was to be the last competitive event I entered in Austria.

After the awards ceremony at the national championships, they handed out little silver skis, the diploma and the cup; and I went downstairs with the others. The President of the Austrian Ski Association said to a group of us, "Do you know, you fellows, what you are going to do with the rest of your life? You cannot race all the time and we don't know what the Germans are going to do." We all knew that there was a sprinkling of Nazi in the Association ski groups, thus we were always careful what we said.

"I have received a letter from America," he said. "The U.S. Ski Association has written that they are interested in schilehers (ski instructors) for different universities, colleges and ski clubs."

After the meeting was over and we had received our prizes, I asked this man if I could talk with him. "Is it personal?" he wondered. "Yes, I am interested in seeing you in your Vienna office because I want to get addresses of ski clubs in the United States," I answered.

Because of the chaotic political situation in 1934, everybody was looking out for himself, and the general outlook on life was very dim. Austria ski schools were gaining fame in the world, opening new opportunities. Austrian instructors were going to New Zealand and Australia; some even went to Japan. In Europe, they went to the Pyrenees in southern France, to Finland and Norway. The, finally, America began to get interested in skiing.

I decided that a feasible solution to the problem of my future lifestyle and career could be solved by starting a ski school of my own. I set my goal to go abroad somewhere to make a new start—to be a pioneer and combine my talents and schooling.

During my racing career I met this very lovely girl, Hermine, who was a great all-round athlete. Hermine was a superb gymnast and track and field competitor. She, too, skied and we climbed a lot of mountains together. In 1935, we were married. We spent our honeymoon climbing the Dolomites—Drei Zinnen, Monte Tofano Mont Cristalo.

Hermine's father had been a railroad officer, on the trains and in the yards. When she was just six months old, he was killed when he slipped between two cars he was working on and fell to the tracks under the train. Both legs were severed at the hip. And he died almost instantly. Her mother was a bookkeeper in the tobacco industry. Between her father's pension from both the job and the accident and her savings from her salary, she was able to purchase a nice house and support her two daughters.

Hermine's mother generously offered to finish off the attic of her house into a little apartment for us when we married. I was a bit dubious about this, knowing in my heart that I was unhappy in Austria, and might not stay there. She told me that was alright, the apartment would be a good investment. She hoped we wouldn't leave, but she wanted to do this for us anyway. So the attic was made into a cozy, flat, with a bedroom, bath and living-dining room and kitchen combination.

Hermine had started out her job training as a seamstress, a tailor, but that didn't last long, as she quickly became bored with the work and was drawn to her love of athletics. Fortunately, she found a friend with similar interests whose father owned an optical business, and because she had enough accounting in school, he hired her to work in his store.

Several days after my meeting with the President of the Austrian Ski Association, I again talked with my father, "What do you have in mind?" he asked.

"I want to look into this American ski instructor business," I answered.

"No!" he exclaimed. "You have a wonderful job, you just got married. Your mother-in-law built an apartment in the attic in her little house. . .

"Yes," I said," but the political situation doesn't appeal to me at all. I'll bet the Nazis are going to be in power in Austria. They will run us. Maybe there will be a war."

It seemed the only way to get out of this impossible situation would be to go to a foreign country. I already knew that Japan wanted instructors, and in Finland they were seeking alpine instructors; but America was still the most appealing. So I wrote a lot of letters.

I went to the president of the Austrian Ski Association in Vienna and he gave me a copy of his letter and all of the addresses. "Wonderful," I said. "I'm going to apply. I shall write to America. I want to go to America as a ski instructor."

Of course, this was a big decision for me and my wife to agree to leave my job, the position that I had worked to attain, to take the risk of going to America with no guarantee I could obtain a permanent immigration visa and enough work to give us the possibility of making a living year-round.

With all this in mind, I went to a private teacher in English. I had English in school as well as some French. This English teacher was a railroad official—a friend of my father. He was a genius in languages and worked in tourist offices in Paris, London, and others in Italy and Czechoslovakia. In other words, he was promoting the Austrian railroads. I believe he spoke five languages and he said he would take me as a student only if I really wanted to learn. He was a socialist, very well educated and well-versed in history and politics. "If you truly want to learn something, and I think you do, I'll take you in." He did, and after many hours of lessons I learned a lot of English from him.

I brought the letters from the American Ski Association to him and said I would like to answer all of them. I wanted to compose a letter, including two or three photos, my racing resume, my educational outline in business and mechanics, and ask if a position were open.

"That's right, all of them." So, ninety ski clubs on that list got the same letter and the same photos. It was an expensive project.

I had replies from a ski club in Colorado Springs, and one from Mt. Hood Oregon, and one from Mt. Rainier. I received a reply from Pecketts in Franconia, New Hampshire and then came the letter from the Mt Mansfield Ski Club.

In reading my resume, Frank Griffin, a director of the Mt. Mansfield Ski Club saw that I had experience as a sport equipment manager. He had a very fashionable men's clothing shop in Burlington and felt it could be a good thing if the Club could sponsor this Austrian instructor and he could get the man a contract with the University of Vermont. I think he had a personal interest in me not only as a ski instructor, but also in the line of sport equipment sales. He was an enterprising man. He also made contact with Norwich University and several other ski clubs in Vermont.

Mr. Griffin approached the Club in Stowe and the University of Vermont with this information. The Board of Directors of the Mt. Mansfield Ski Club agreed to hire a ski instructor. The instructor could make extra money at the University as a coach or trainer and in the Ski School, maybe, up on Mt. Mansfield. His letter of reply was very encouraging.

My English teacher helped me sort things out. "I think that fellow need somebody," he said. "It looks like he could use you. But, Sepp, the federal government is involved, don't do it. You are trying to get out of that situation here, am I right?"

So, I replied to the Mt. Mansfield Ski Club. There was no airmail in those days- all mail was by ship. When the response finally came, it indicated they were very interested and wanted to know under what conditions I would come. My request was: a roundtrip

ticket on a steamer, board and lodging at
a ski lodge near the skiing, and a small
salary. I proposed the sum of $500. And I
agreed, if I should earn more than what the
contract called for, I was willing to share
50-50 with the Mt. Mansfield Ski Club.

It clicked. I had to write immediately
to get a visa and a work permit to come to
America as a ski instructor and it had to be
cleared through the U. S. Labor Department,
etc. This seemed to take forever.

My wife, her mother, and my parents agreed,
reluctantly but unanimously, there was no
future for a young family in Austria, we made
the decision together. I reserved a roundtrip
ticket on a German steamship line.

On December 4, 1936 I sailed on the
steamship "Bremen" to America.

Sepp Ruschp   Dickinson Collection

Dickinson Collection
Sepp Ruschp

STOWE
IN THE BEGINNING

After saying goodbye to all my loved ones at the Linz railroad station, I boarded the train with mixed emotions of sadness and excitement.

The conductor on the train had read the tags on my suitcases designating the Hamburg-American Line and asked if I was on my way to America? My answer was an enthusiastic, "Yes!"

"You know," he said, "in the next car back there are two famous figure skaters—Ida Papetz and Karl Zwack—who are European champions." The train was an express through Germany to Hamburg, and they were traveling to an ice show in America. "I'm sure they would like to meet a fellow sportsman, a ski champion who is also going to America," the conductor suggested.

I went to the first class car (I was traveling third class) and was introduced to the two skaters—beautiful girl and young man. We quickly became friends, and spent much of the train ride chatting. Because we were three nationally known sports figures, we were allowed to travel together. I got out and walked when the train stopped at Regensburg and other cities, but I noticed they never left their car. Finally, I went back in and asked, "Don't you want some fresh air?"

"My dear friend," Karl said, "I'm Jewish. Ida is not but I am and I'm scared stiff. I

won't take one step out there until I am on
my way to the boat." He said he would feel
more at ease once the boat departed. So
when I went out, I brought back chocolate or
whatever they needed. We traveled together
until we parted ways in Hamburg.

My berth on the ship was way below deck,
in tourist class. After about the third day,
I received a little card—an invitation to
five o'clock tea in the first class lounge.
The invitation was from Ida and Karl with
the permission from the captain. Soon I was
on the first class deck. There were many
famous people there, including the boxer
Max Schmeling, who had been in America in
1936 and knocked out the great Joe Lewis.
My friendship with the skaters continued
throughout the voyage, with repeated
invitations to the first class deck.

The captain was a German named Ziegenbein,
of the famous Hansa steamship line. He
treated Ida like a star, as indeed she was.
She was an Austrian rival to Norway's world
famous skater, Sonja Henje. I understand now
why Ida always invited me. I was a young man
in nice sports clothes and seemed a likely
escort. Ida was not married to Karl. She was
married to the president of the Viennese Ice
Club, and he had arranged for her to go to
America to smooth the way for Karl's possible
escape. I don't know what happened to Karl
Zwack after he got to America, but Ida and
I corresponded briefly. She became famous in
Hollywood, divorced her first husband and
married a very rich American.

We had a fairly rough voyage on the Bremen. I remember deboarding the ship in New York City on December 10, 1936 with somewhat shaky legs, where I was met by three members of the Mt. Mansfield Ski Club who were New York residents. One was a newspaperman, Hal Burton, who was a sportswriter for the "Daily News" and a professor at Columbia University. The professor spoke German, which was very helpful to me in my first few hours in America. The language barrier was more of a problem than I had imagined, especially in the first few weeks. Everything was so new. I was awed by the skyscrapers in New York, and felt the loneliness of being in such a different country.

The three gentlemen took me to the Columbia Club for dinner, where they informed me the winter so far had been very warm in Vermont. There had been a big thaw, and the snow mentioned to me by telegram had practically disappeared. They said I should not be discouraged. "In Vermont, there's always snow...especially on Mt. Mansfield." I felt this was not unusual, because in the Alps we sometimes had a thaw before Christmas and things looked grim, but by the holidays we almost always received snow in abundance. So my faith continued.

After dinner, around 11:00 PM, the gentlemen took me back to the station, where I boarded the overnight train from New York City to Burlington, Vermont.

I arrived in Burlington at dawn the next morning. I looked out the window of my

sleeping car and saw Lake Champlain. I was
pretty discouraged because a heavy fog lay
on the lake and it was drizzling rain. As
I stepped down from the train, I did not
see any mountains. Luckily, I had studied
a map beforehand, and knew the Adirondacks
were on one side of Lake Champlain and the
Green Mountains were on the other. But the
distances in America seemed greater than I
had anticipated and I just couldn't see much
of a mountain. I would have to be patient. I
would have to hang on to my faith.

The gentleman who had signed all my papers
to come to America, Mr. Frank Griffin, met me
at the train station in Burlington. He took
me to his store where he introduced me to his
staff. They helped me carry my three bundles
of skis and all my luggage. I had jumping
skis, downhill skis, slalom skis and a lot
of bags because I had brought samples of all
kinds of sport equipment with me. We walked
from the railroad station to his store, then
on to the Hotel Vermont carrying the load on
our shoulders.

Later in the day Mrs. Griffin picked me up
in her car and drove me forty-two miles to
Stowe. The Griffins had a very comfortable
house outside the village, where I stayed
for the first few days. Mrs. Griffin was a
charming person and did everything to make me
feel at home.

The first night, there was a very strong
wind—the drizzle and rain disappeared. In the
morning, I saw in the distance, maybe five
of six miles away, the white line of a white

capped mountain ridge. At breakfast I asked
where Mt. Mansfield was. "Well, if you look
out your bedroom window to the north (which
I had), that's Mt. Mansfield. I was not very
impressed with this little mountain ridge. Of
course, I did not expect great big mountains
like the Alps, but from a distance, that 4,300
foot mountain was not a very imposing sight.

After breakfast, Mr. Griffin drove me into
Stowe Village. I was stirred by the lovely
church with its famous Christopher Wren
temple and the neat white clapboard houses
with their New England-style green wooden
shutters. We drove by the Green Mountain
Inn and turned up the road to Mt. Mansfield.
As we drove the five miles from Stowe to
the mountain, Mr. Griffin pointed out the
different "ski lodges," farmhouses mostly, and
very few of them—which took in a few guests.

Soon we were at the base of Mt. Mansfield,
to the "Toll House", so-called because it
is the starting point of the Mt. Mansfield
Toll Road, which leads to the summit of the
mountain. The cottage there was the summer
lodging for the toll keeper and the manager
of the little souvenir shop.

I learned that the Toll House was to be
the headquarters of my ski School, and also
where I would live. I must say that is was a
simple site. I was quite discouraged because
there was no real ski slope of any kind in
sight. The Toll Road, I had been told, was
an automobile road in the summer time and a
good ski run of four and a half miles in the
winter. There was a tiny slope adjacent to

the lower section of the Toll Road where they had started to build a rope tow.

We drove a bit further up the Mountain Road to a small mountain inn called The Lodge. There, I met the manager, Bob Isham, a very friendly man who welcomed me to Mt. Mansfield. He hoped we could work together to provide a good ski school for the guests.

Because it was a weekend, a few people had come up to ski the Toll Road. I watched them put on their skis and climb up the road in a very clumsy way—they didn't have proper wax or sealskins—it was really quite humorous.

There were only three guests at The Lodge for the weekend. I met them, and proceeded to give them lessons right in front of The Lodge.

In the summer, that slope was a vegetable garden and a horse pasture, with a very gentle slope. I was trying to teach these people the fundamentals of skiing in a pasture! It was my first ski lesson—my first three students in America.

That was on Saturday. Again, I stayed overnight with the Griffins in Stowe, where we had a lovely dinner and more time to get acquainted. On Sunday, when we drove up to the base of the mountain, there were a few more people, including a photographer from the Burlington Free Press who took pictures and wrote a complimentary article—my first publicity, Word got out that an Austrian ski instructor had arrived.

The base of Mt. Mansfield was somewhat unique. There was very little snow-what was left was mostly an icy crust—but the sun was out and it was cool. I looked up at Mt. Mansfield and I was very interested, very excited. I promised myself that as soon as I had the time I would climb this mountain on one of the "trails" and see what the other runs were like. I looked at the trail map that was available at the base. The backbone was the Toll Road; then, there were the Nosedive and the Spruce Trails. Those were the only trails on the map. I couldn't wait to see them and ski them.

Monarch of all he surveys is Sepp Ruschp, ski instructor, on the top of Mount Mansfield

Dickinson Collection
Sepp Ruschp

On Monday morning, I drove with Mr. Griffin to his store in Burlington. I met some of his employees, young salesmen who were curious about ski equipment and how to set up a sport shop. I worked there for the whole day to help them with the first steps. We unpacked some of my skis and equipment and made displays in the different showcases. Soon, there was a corner called the "Sport Department." It looked rather neat—very small, but functional. A few people came into the store to see the new display and I was introduced to them. Most of them were very pleasant, although I couldn't understand them when they talked too fast and I had to keep asking them to speak slowly. They did, and I progressed with my English.

During that same day, I had the pleasure of meeting a couple from Waterbury, Mr. and Mrs. William Mason. Mr. Mason was the president of the Mt. Mansfield Ski Club. Later, I learned why he was so interested in hiring a ski instructor with sporting goods experience. He and his partner, Dan Ryder, had a factory in Waterbury which made wooden handles, but they had just started producing wooden skis. They asked me to come to their factory as soon as I had the time, so they could show me their new product. It took a while before I could get to them, because Mr. Griffin was so eager for me to meet with different ski clubs and be introduced to the athletic directors at the University of Vermont and Norwich University.

In the middle of the week, I visited the University of Vermont, where I got a warm reception from the young team I was

to coach. I tried to set a date for them
to come up to Mt. Mansfield, but they all
said, "Well, we will be able to come once
before the holidays, maybe." They considered
the Christmas holidays their vacation
and I asked, "Don't you go skiing during
vacation?" They said they would try. It
never occurred to them that they should ski
every day in their life in order to be on
the winning race team. They had festivities
in mind and, apparently, were anxious to go
home to see their families. At least, I had
met them.

Later that week, I was introduced to the
Norwich Cadets. Because it was a military
academy, I was impressed with their
discipline. The whole corps marched into the
gymnasium. On the stage, I was introduced by
the athletic director, and Craig Burt, Jr.
(the captain of the ski team) as the new ski
instructor. I gave a short speech, saying
I was very glad to be in America and would
do my best to teach skiing. I excused my
English, but added, "I will probably teach
you more on the slopes than I can explain
to you right now. I am looking forward to
working with you." I received a standing
ovation by about three or four hundred
cadets—an uplifting experience, to say the
least.

During another dinner at his house, Mr.
Griffin introduced me to Craig Burt, Jr.. Mr.
Burt was the president of the Mt. Mansfield
Hotel Company, which owned the Toll House. He
was a lumberman and owned a mill and a great

deal of land. His son, whom I met at Norwich, was also a guest that evening.

December 12 to December 19, 1936 was a week of activities I rather enjoyed because I met a lot of people and most were very enthusiastic about the coming winter. They were also praying for snow. There was very little. Even on Mt. Mansfield, there was only icy crust from the last thaw after the early snow in November. Still it was skiable.

Again, Mr. Griffin, the promoter, took me to the Toll House area to meet a larger group of Mr. Mansfield Ski Club directors and members. I gave a demonstration on skis and a short talk about what I could provide in services. Then, we went to the Waterbury Ski lift. Where? Neither Bill *(Riley)* nor I know the location—here, I did much the same thing—an exhibition and a little talk about technique, equipment, etc. Most of the people had very poor equipment. It was old-fashioned, with clumsy skis and poles. I had a feeling it would be hard to teach them with this primitive equipment. I really didn't want to sound like a ski salesman for Mr. Griffin, but we did sell them quite a number of new skis and more modern boots and bindings.

Mr. Griffin had made arrangements for my services with all of these clubs. The money involved was minor, but the time commitment was substantial. My financial agreement included the ticket to come here, a guaranteed $500 for the season and a fifty-fifty split with the Mt. Mansfield Ski Club on

anything I earned over and above. Naturally,
I was eager to earn more than the Club's
guarantee.

We expected a good number of skiers
for Christmas. I was worried about the
scheduling, because originally I did not know
about the time—consuming travel from one
ski club to the other for night teaching.
I had thought all my classes would be in
Stowe. There was something strange in the
arrangements made by Mr. Griffin. I decided
to try and live with this and somehow work it
out.

I was settling into my little home at the
Toll House, which had been refurbished some.
A glass desk had been added. Displays of some
sport equipment had been set up. And I was
assured that there would be a coffee shop for
the skiers who would come to Mt. Mansfield
with the rope tow. I recommended we have some
rental skis, and in fact, we did gather a few
rental skis and boots, which I tuned to be
usable.

I met the workman who was supervising the
installation of the first rope-tow at Mt.
Mansfield. His name was Andy Mansfield. In
the summertime, he was a handyman at the
Mountain Hotel and took care of Toll Road
repairs with another older Vermonter, Alton
Holbrook. I had some trouble understanding
them because of their "twang." Their English
certainly wasn't what I had learned and now
spoke. They could understand me, but I had
a hell of a time, constantly having to ask,
"Please, slow!" But we got along all right.

The installation of a rope-tow (which I had never seen in Europe) was really a very simple undertaking. As a matter of fact, the tow at Mt. Mansfield was not the first in the east. Woodstock, Vermont was the pioneer in rope tows in the eastern United States—they already had nine.

Stowe's rope tow was quite basic. The drive unit was on top of the hill in a wooden shack. There was on old Model T Ford engine, and the pullies were old car wheels. Wooden posts were set in the ground, and the sheaves carrying the rope overhead pulled up the hill while the ones sliding on the ground held the returning rope, which was in turn held by a counterweight. The counterweight, which was at the bottom, was a gasoline drum filled with sand to tighten the old hemp rope.

Soon after the rope tow was finished, we got some new snow—a few inches. Finally we could test the rope tow. I rode up first and made the track. Of course I got very wet, because of the wet snow on the rope both above and below. The tow was still primitive, but I realized that this was the beginning of something promising.

The living quarters at the Toll House were still sparse. There was a shower, a toilet and washbowl, and two rooms upstairs in the attic. I had one room for myself, with just boxes around a bed. Downstairs was similar space for the coffee shop cook. I found out that the intent was to attract some guests who would stay in the little shack outside, across the brook at the base of the slope—that building used to be a cow barn. Mr. Griffin installed three or four cots downstairs, with mattresses and blankets for all. I couldn't believe that people would come to that shack, but somehow Griffin had enough friends in New York and the newspaperman came up with more. We had one cook, a farm girl named Vivian. Another girl was a waitress and chambermaid combined. There was the handyman who took care of the rope tow, had to clean up after everyone was gone and then, build a fire in the stove that provided the only heat we had. We were camping out. It was more or less like living in the mountain huts in Austria—a bit more primitive—but it was a beginning.

Finally, we had five or six inches of new snow. I was desperately waiting for a chance to get up the mountain to see what it was all about. The first time the sun came out, I waxed my cross country skis and ran up the four and a half miles alone. When I reached the top, I found the "Stone Hut," which had been built by the CCC (Civilian Conservation Corps). Charlie Lord, Ab Coleman and Perry Merrill had done test cuts. There was an identification sign outside and a cache of Red Cross first aid supplies with a toboggan and some blankets indicating it was a first aid station.

A few more steps up from the Stone Hut I found the Nosedive. It dropped steeply. Since I had only my cross country skis on,

I decided not to ski down the Nosedive just then.

After searching around some more, I climbed up to the old Summit House, which was another quarter mile from the junction of the Toll Road and the Nosedive. Of course the house was all boarded up and tied down with ropes so the wind wouldn't blow it away. It was only for summer use. The scene was pretty bizarre looking. This was the "Mt. Mansfield Hotel," an overstatement in my mind. It didn't look like a hotel at all. It looked like a storm hut on the top of the mountain, with old, peeling clapboards and a tin roof. Having checked that out—I skied back down the Toll Road to the Toll House.

The next day, I put climbing wax on my downhill skis and again ascended the Toll Road to the top, which took almost an hour and three quarters. It was then that I made my first run down the Nosedive. I was surprised, amazed, how nice and how challenging the trail was, even though it was very narrow. There were seven tight turns at the top with wind packed snow, but I was used to the wind packed snow of the Alps. I could "swing turn" in that snow. So I skied like that all the way to the long stretch that was later to be called the "Corridor". The run-out of the Nosedive took me back to the Notch Road, through a brook bed, and then, through the woods, where I came upon a wooden chalet, called "Barnes Camp". The man there, Chelsea Lyons, had heard about an Austrian ski instructor who had come to Stowe. His wife made me tea. They had a unique arrangement for heating and cooking—two oil barrels connected with pipes on top, attached to a stone chimney. There was a room with a dozen or more bunks. And Chelsea was also eager for more business. He assured me we would prosper over Christmas and New Year's.

I told the innkeeper that I planned to ski back to the Toll House because most of the highway was not plowed. He was amazed that I had climbed on skis from the Toll House to the summit, skied down the Nosedive and then planned to ski back to the Toll house again. Well, to me Mt. Mansfield was not a giant, so I joked about it. "Oh, that's ok. It's a good hour—plus up the Toll Road and I've skied five or ten minutes on the Nosedive. Now I'll cut around to get on the road which should take about fifty minutes, so in a little over two and half hours I should be out of it."

He was in disbelief. An experience like this, climbing Mt. Mansfield on one side and coming down the other, round trip, on skis, in two hours—was very unusual in this country. Word spread slowly that a young Austrian had something to show a growing admiring crowd of new skiers.

I finally persuaded the athletic director of the University of Vermont to allow the ski team (in spite of exams), to come for a day of skiing on Mt. Mansfield because we had received another substantial snowfall. It

was arranged that the whole team, including
alternates, would come for a day.

I expected them to arrive by at least 9:00
a.m. They arrived well after 10:00 a.m. As
I watched out a window of the Toll House,
I saw a dozen or so young men jumping out
of a rickety old car—they called a station
wagon. They just threw their skis out in
the snow and haphazardly tossed poles, boots
and other gear. I was distressed to see
this sight because I expected a little more
expertise from a University team. I was sure
they hadn't waxed their skis to climb the
mountain, so I explained that they shouldn't
have thrown their skis into the wet snow
because they needed to be waxed. Of course,
they didn't understand that if we were to
use downhill skis for touring, we would
also have to wax them so we could climb.
They had never heard of such a thing—using
climbing wax and downhill wax at the same
time.

I took them into the Toll House, where I
let them warm up while I cleaned their skis.
I waxed about a dozen pairs and then showed
them how to do it. They were fascinated.

Dickinson Collection
Sepp at the Entrance of the Old Toll House, 1937

My idea was to climb up the Toll Road to give the team a good warm up exercise for the trip back down. There were a few shortcuts on the Toll Road and most were rather steep through the woods, which I thought would give them good training ground for the first time. I had no idea what caliber skiers they were, but I figured since the Toll Road was an automobile road in the summertime, it would be a big problem to climb. As I climbed

steadily, I found them falling behind. The
line of twelve got thinner and thinner, but
I kept going. I had decided the good ones
would hang on my tail and reach the top. One
by one they dragged into the Stone Hut where
I had built a fire and brewed some tea with
the ranger who was stationed there. Some were
exhausted. It was then I found out I would
have to teach them more than skiing—they
were not in shape for athletics of any kind.
As we skied down, I discovered that one or
two of them were pretty good. They followed
me (although not through the short cuts) and
they took horrible spills, but they managed
to get down without major upsets.

As I lined them all up in the afternoon
to teach fundamental turns, I ascertained
it would take a long time to make a real
race team of this group. As I mentioned,
there were two who possessed natural ability.
Everett Bailey was one, and Peter Patch was
another. Both became lifelong friends. These
two were very agile and very capable young
skiers—they learned fast from the very first
day; and the enthusiasm of the rest of the
team was unbelievable. They thought I was
some sort of wizard on skis, and I made more
friends than I ever thought I could in one
day.

My feeling was, "Well that's what I'm here
for, and I will teach you as much as I can in
one season."

When their Christmas vacation started, they
disappeared. The captain, who happened to
be Everett Bailey, informed me that the next

organized training we could plan would have to be on the practice hill behind the football stadium in Burlington—if there was enough snow. It was a small hill and there was a jump there, also. We set a date for after the holidays, when we would officially start training together. I told them they would have to put in some serious training hours—a lot of running through the woods, calisthenics and gymnastics—they were to return in tiptop shape. They promised to do it.

I still had responsibilities to Norwich University, the University of Vermont and other clubs. The drive to Norwich and the total teaching time totalled four hours. They paid about $35 an afternoon, which was good money. For the season the University of Vermont paid $350. Some evenings I went up to St. Albans, where I taught by floodlights. I had no car so I had to beg a ride with one of our Stowe workers for a dollar or two. He drove me there and back to Stowe. I remember many evenings of driving back and forth with frozen feet. There was plenty to keep me busy even though there was not much business in Stowe during the week.

Because of the snowfall prior to Christmas, the situation in the whole valley brightened. Everyone was grateful as the vacationers slowly began to return. I was teaching several hour-long lessons a day. Then, came the great questions—nobody knew how much I should charge. I discussed it with Frank Griffin and others; and we came up with a dollar an hour. I said that would be fine.

Since I was the only instructor, I could teach only so many people a day. Having no idea how many people would come, I offered to start lessons at 9:00 a.m. The advice was that 9:00 a.m. was too early. So lessons were at hourly intervals from 10:00 a.m. to 3:00 p.m. with an hour break for lunch. I would be available to teach six, possibly seven, hours per day.

My first Christmas in America was celebrated with the Griffin family. They had invited some friends—college girls and boys. I don't remember exactly who they were, but it was nice because I wasn't alone. Christmas day I was out there teaching again. There were rumors of a big snowfall and there was also talk about a thaw. Not a thaw, we all hoped.

My first celebration of New Year's Eve in America included a big party, a dance, which was sponsored by the Stowe Fire Department. They had a band, and the party was open to the public, so of course, the skiers were invited. We were all sitting around on benches on the sides, talking and watching people dance. I wondered where the tables were, as in Austria, where you could sit down, and have something to eat and drink. To my surprise, I found out there was no such thing! Stowe was a "dry" town—there were no alcoholic beverages served in any lodge or bar. I learned that in America, each community can vote its own liquor regulations, unlike in my country.

That evening some of my college team members were there. One friend invited me to "come out and have a drink." I asked where we were going and the answer was "they are taking us all, come on!" So we went out of the Memorial Building and got into a car. Several people pulled out bottles of whiskey and handed them around for each to have a drink. Well, I tasted one swallow and almost choked because I had never had any raw whiskey. While they urged," Come on, come…" I was smart enough to hold my thumb over the opening of the bottle, pretending it was going down while it really didn't. By midnight, when the party came to an end, there were quite a few "tipsy" girls and boys around. I thought that was a rather curious situation, so different from Austria. Yet it was another lesson in my new country—a custom unknown before to me.

The party was fun, however, because I met some nice people, danced quite a bit, and the only worry was how to get from the Memorial Building back to the Toll House—five miles away. One kind young student was in a similar situation. He wanted to get home because it was getting pretty late. He had a car and agreed to give me a ride. As he started to drive me up to the mountain it began to drizzle, but the closer we came to the Toll House the rain turned to snow, and it snowed quite heavily. We were looking forward to a New Year's Day with freshly fallen snow and for me, more business.

I woke early New Year's morning, looked out my window and it was still snowing. I decided to have a quick breakfast and climb the mountain before my ten o'clock classes. Again I climbed the Toll Road with properly waxed skis, and started to ski down from about the halfway mark enjoying the quiet solitude and the welcome fresh snow. With that run in mind I returned to the Toll house and had a second cup of tea on New Year's morning in 1937, before going out to my first assignment of eight people on the ropetow.

There was very little snow in the east, in general. An advertisement in New York newspapers, sponsored by the ski trains, said Stowe had more snow that anywhere in Vermont. This encouraged an enormous influx of skiers. I could not get over the difference. The five days between Christmas and New Year's were tremendously busy. I was teaching six or seven classes a day. The classes were lined up at the Toll house, where the shop-girl helped me sign up eight to ten for each hour. Sometimes I had as many as sixty people a day, a dollar per person per hour. I could earn—-my God!—$60 a day, or 3000 shillings. The exchange rate was one dollar per five shillings, and that was a damn good income for a European.

Word also got out that Christmas alone was no longer the biggest weekend nor the longes; the combination of the Christmas and New Year's week was even better. So I prepared—I slept many hours each night in order to be fresh in the morning.

I was happy at what had taken place so
far, and I was anticipating great events in
the New Year. As I was the only instructor,
I couldn't divide my classes according to the
ability of the skier. I had to jump around
between a snowplow, a stem Christie and some
who were more advanced. I was quite busy in
order to please all my customers. Apparently
they were pleased, because every time I
finished one class, we shook hands and said,
"See you again, hopefully another weekend
this year, etc." Then another class would
arrive. I ended up dog-tired each day. Looking
back over the holidays, back to the few days
between Christmas and New Years, I couldn't
have been more encouraged.

In my letters home to Hermine, I described
the mountain that had become my new friend,
the people I had met and the many experiences
I had shared so far. She was still living
with her mother and working in the optical
store. I tried to describe what I hoped would
soon be our new home and our new community.

What bothered me a little bit was the
shortness of the Christmas/New Year's holiday
compared to the longer "holidays" of a week
to ten days in Europe. People would say, "Oh,
no, we have to go home. This is only a long
holiday weekend and we don't have a vacation."
Most of the customers were talking about
weekend skiing. I would have to be satisfied
with that.

My elation came to an abrupt halt the
next day, when I looked out the window and
saw rain instead of snow. It rained from the

second to the fifth of January—three days and three nights. We were left with less than a foot at the bottom of the mountain and maybe two or three feet at the top. I hoped the snow would not all wash away. However on the bottom it looked slushy and discouraging and all the people had disappeared.

The first week in January was a disaster because there was absolutely no one at the Mountain—the whole week. I went to Burlington with Frank Griffin hoping to get the University students up to train, but they were still on vacation until the 6th. There was nothing I could do but help out in the store, but sales were down there also. Most people had already bought equipment before the holidays.

The next worry was where to train and ski with my University team, because there was no snow at all in Burlington. I sat down with the captain, Ev Bailey and the athletic director to plan a program. I volunteered to do some gymnastic and running work with them once or twice a week while we waited for more snow on the mountain and chance for them to come to Stowe.

That was wishful thinking. The mountain froze up. There was snow on the top, so I climbed up and skied the crust. I realized that I could not travel to the ski clubs in the different towns, because there was no snow there, either. It was most discouraging. Frank Griffin was not in the best mood. He had his own financial worries, as well as being worried about my guarantee with the clubs. By then I understood enough English to know that something was decidedly wrong.

One evening Frank came up to the Toll House and informed me that The Lodge had employed another ski instructor—a young Frenchman named Jacques Charmoz. I asked Mr. Griffin why this instructor was coming because it was my understanding that he had made arrangements with The Lodge that I was to teach their customers.

Apparently, The Lodge manager had complained that my activities were too diversified. He felt I was not properly providing the Stowe area with the necessary services. I sensed Griffin was overselling me. We seemed to be on the wrong track. I had heard most lodge owners and innkeepers were very pleased with positive reports of my teaching over the holidays, but that they, too, were fearful my arrangement with the ski club was unclear. It was a legitimate concern.

When asked by The Lodge manager to meet Jacques Charmoz, I found out that he spoke hardly any English. I understood a little French and he understood some German, so we got along. I said, "I'm studying English day and night. You'll probably have to do the same thing." When I told Jacques there was no business, I added jokingly, "Well, probably I'll have to teach you in the morning and you will teach me in the afternoon and we will charge each other $20 or $25—we'll make lots of money!" I found Jacques a charming friend. We realized we were both in a strange country

and would have to do the best we could to
survive and make a living.

Still, it had not snowed. So I called Mr.
Griffin and asked if he had anything for
me to do in his store in Burlington. "Oh, I
didn't hire you as a shop clerk, but if you
want to come in, okay."

He picked me up in Stowe the next morning,
and he visibly brightened on our drive to
Burlington, as I explained that I was totally
committed to him and this ski area. During
our conversation we agreed he did oversell me
to the different clubs. And, he admitted he
was worried about how we were going to solve
this problem.

"Well, we will work hard day and night,"
I said. "That's all we can do." So I helped
him in the store. I believe that was the
first inventory they ever made in the sport
department. They had sold most of the samples
I had brought over from Austria, so I ordered
more. Of course, these things took time and
I didn't have anyone helping me write the
orders—I just decided I had to get it done.

One day in the store I met a very charming
couple. "He's a very prominent businessman,
and his wife wants to learn how to ski.
He's a skier and they want to learn more
together," Mr. Griffin told me. Then he added
reluctantly, "I have signed you up for a lot
of private lessons with Mr. and Mrs. Cooke."
I asked how he could sign them up for lessons
in advance without first consulting my
schedule, and he agreed we would have to work
that out.

The first weekend Mr. and Mrs. Cooke came to the Toll House, they were with quite a number of friends—very prominent people in New York society (including Roland Palmedo, who later became president of the company that built the first chairlift in Stowe). I started to give them lessons—again, combining all levels of ability: beginner, intermediate, advanced. It seemed I made a big hit. The Cookes invited me to come with them to Burlington, to their home for dinner. They even drove me to Burlington and back to Stowe.

Again, I felt encouraged because they were supportive. This was certainly a group to attract as vacation people for a class resort.

My mind was spinning with ideas. I knew I could no longer run around to other areas. If I were to do the extra coaching, I would bring an assistant back with me—if I came back. If Stowe was to become a first class resort, it would have to have a lift and a first class sport hotel. If, if… But, all of this would depend upon whether I could get a visa. Things were getting tight "over there" and, of course, this time I would want to bring my wife Hermine with me.

There were, indeed, many arrangements to be made.

Dickinson Collection
Sepp Ruschp, the Businessman

THE RETURN
TO STOWE & A NEW LIFE

In May of 1937, I returned to Austria with a lot on my mind. I knew it would be difficult to get a working visa to return to America, but even if I could arrange that, I would need assurance that my agreement with the Mt. Mansfield Ski Club and the Mt. Mansfield Hotel Company would be straightened out. I could not go back solely as a ski instructor. In addition to upgrading the Toll House to a proper inn, there would have to be a sport and repair shop at the base of the mountain plus an assistant to help with the teaching. I had discussed these necessities with club directors and company leaders before I left. And they agreed that these were reasonable requests.

Hermine and I spent the summer packing and making the necessary arrangements to immigrate to America the following December. Meanwhile, Mr. J. Negley Cooke, a director of the Mt. Mansfield Ski Club, was authorized by the club's Board of Directors to engage a lawyer to draft an employment contract including my arrangements with the Mt. Mansfield Hotel Company, the University of Vermont and Norwich University, a military academy.

We know how much luck plays a big role in life, as it did in this case.

There were only three days of each month when the commission from Washington was available to examine an applicant for a working visa. When my wife and I went to the American Consulate in Vienna for our final examination, we were both shaking like leaves. The consul's secretary did the translating, and I found it easy to understand him, there was another unidentified young man watching the process. In my anxious state, I figured he was a Secret Service agent. I placed all our identification papers and my letters from the Ski Club in America on the table and looked up apprehensively, awaiting our fate.

The young man who had been standing behind me asked, "Didn't you teach skiing in Stowe last year?" What a surprise! Apparently, he knew me.

"Yes," I replied, "and I wish to return."

He remembered I wore a green Tyrolean hat, and said he had taken a lesson from me. Relaxed by this connection, the Consul shoved all my papers aside. He filled out the proper forms, stamped them and Hermine and I walked out with a visa—the happiest couple in the world. In December of 1937, we were on our way to America—this time, together.

Dickinson Collection
Sepp and Hermine at the Toll House

"Home" was to be at the Toll House, where we would live upstairs. During the summer, a small wing had been added to the back of the coffee shop, where a sport and repair shop had been set up. The accommodations and the earnings were still meager, but we managed to make enough money to keep going. I had to buy a car which was a major investment. We continued to pinch pennies to make ends meet, but I remained inspired by the mountain I had come to love.

I was one of seven to pass the U.S. Eastern Ski Association Certification Test for professional ski instructors in 1937 at Suicide Six in Woodstock, Vermont.

In the fall of 1938, my mother-in-law suffered a stroke, and Hermine's family asked her to return to Austria. I agreed she should go. At the same time I began to entertain the idea of moving elsewhere in the states, perhaps to a western ski area, since my plans didn't seem to be making much progress in Stowe.

Hermine left Stowe in September, and I was alone in the Toll House—collecting a toll of $3.00 a car. One day as I sat on the front step, Charlie Proctor, the captain of the Dartmouth Ski team came by. Charlie had been one of the examiners when I passed my instructor's test. He had since graduated from Dartmouth and moved west to be the director of the Yosemite Park area. Charlie hinted there was a position about to open as director of the Yosemite Park Ski School. He asked if I would be interested.

"It depends on the financial arrangement," I replied. He added to my current despair by quipping—it didn't seem I could do a whole lot worse than here. I agreed.

Charlie wanted to know if I had a car and if I were married. Of course, the answer to both was yes. He offered a little chalet for Hermine and me, plus a fixed salary of $5,000 a year and ten percent of the profit of the ski school. There were about ten instructors and the gross business was about $10,000 a year. Tempting, I thought.

I approached the Board of Directors of the Mt. Mansfield Hotel Company to explain the details of this offer. The board called a special meeting at the request of I. Munn Boardman and I was informed that they decided to rebuild the Toll House into a small inn with eight rooms, and I would be the manager. They would add a cafeteria, a sport shop and a new rope tow. This was encouraging; it provided a new opportunity and gave me new hope for the development.

For income, I told the Board that I believed in a percentage instead of a salary. I asked for twenty percent of the Hotel Company profits.

One of the directors asked, "Before or after depreciation?" I didn't understand his question. It was difficult for me to translate the word "depreciation" from German to English. I did not understand that depreciation had to do with the amortization of a capital investment rather than cash operating expenses. When I told them I would look up the word "depreciation" in the dictionary, they were amused. I realized it would be unwise to receive a percentage of the profits after depreciation. So, they agreed from whatever funds we took in, we would subtract operating expenses and I would make twenty percent of the gross profit. I also asked for my own Ski School on the rope tow slope, as well as permission to acquire several more instructors and house them in a nearby chalet. Again, I had an agreement with no written contract, but by now, I knew it was okay to take them at their word.

In the search for additions to my Ski School, I found several recently certified instructors, among them Kerr Sparks, Clem Curtis, and Lionel Hayes. Additionally, one of the Mt. Mansfield Ski Club's top racers, Henry Simoneau, was interested in teaching.

Our meetings of the Board of Directors of the Mt. Mansfield Hotel Company became more frequent. We could see what our minimum needs would be for the next two years. We would have to rebuild the Toll House into a small inn with an expanded coffee shop and sport shop, erect a new rope tow and improve the slopes at the Toll House area.

Of course, the proximity to New York City with its ever growing numbers of ski enthusiasts was a big plus. People like Lowell Thomas, the "Voice of America", would come from New York to climb up and ski down the Nosedive. The Amateur Ski Club of New York, which was a leading social ski club in New England and perhaps in the country at that time, found Stowe very attractive. Many of its members like the Rockefellers, Livvy Longfellow, Roland Palmedo, lots of millionaires—lawyers, brokers, etc.—helped make a name for Stowe, which was good because the public always likes to go where the "big names" choose to go.

Many members of the Amateur Ski Club of New York frequented the Green Mt. Inn on their ski trips to Stowe. I was often invited to dine there with Roland Palmedo, Minnie Dole, Jay Cooke and others. In the course of cocktail conversation, one subject kept coming up: it was not a great joy to climb up

the mountain in order to ski down! At last,
my chance to suggest building a lift arrived.

Mr. Palmedo and Mr. Cooke asked me to map
out a site for the location of a chairlift.
I, in turn, solicited the services of Rogers
Adams, a local civil engineer and contractor
who had a proper transit. We organized a
group to drive up the Toll Road to the Stone
Hut, where set up the transit.

I sited a lift line that would go from
the tree located near the Stone Hut to the
center of the small parking lot at the base
of the mountain. We walked down the line
using a compass to where the lift ends now.
I insisted the lift should go all the way
to the parking lot. The state officials
disagreed. They engaged Rogers Adams to
survey the line they wanted.

Next Mr. Palmedo and group began a
search for a lift company. Again, I made a
suggestion, American Steel and Wire Company
in Sun Valley, which was eventually hired.

Many members of the Mt. Mansfield Ski Club
were not enthusiastic about putting in a lift—
they felt it was "unsporty." Mr. Craig Burt,
Mt. Mansfield Hotel Company president at the
time, was emphatically against the idea. He
felt it would scar the mountain. The feeling
in the community was mixed. Most thought
the idea was very favorable, but there were
some environmentalists who did not want to
"gash up the mountain" and were resistant to
change. Mr. Bodman was so against the idea
of a lift that he sold the Green Mt. Inn for
$22,500 to Parker Perry.

At a Ski Club meeting, Roland Palmedo and Jay Cooke introduced my expansion ideas and began to devise a financial plan for their corporation, the Mt. Mansfield Lift Company. They sold investment units consisting of four shares of preferred stock at $100 a share, and four share of common stock at $1 a share. I bought the minimum number of shares and helped to sell some to others. The $90,000 estimated to build a lift and the Octagon at the top of the chairlift was easily raised.

Charlie Lord and I were sort of "silent partners'. He was named to the Board of Directors and became manager of the Lift Company and I remained a small stockholder. Boone Wilson, an attorney in Burlington, was employed and a very favorable contract with the State of Vermont was negotiated. The Lift Company would pay the state 5% of gross revenue in excess of $45,000. The state included a clause to protect the investment of the Lift Company. It stated that no one could build uphill above 2500 feet elevation or within a radius of ten miles of the new chairlift. The state also reserved the right to take over the Lift Company after ten years, if the facilities were not kept up to standards.

At last Stowe could grow to the level of Sun Valley and Mont Tremblant...we could build a chairlift. In order to become a first class resort, we would need a real first class sport hotel.

Following the Ski Club meeting, we held a Directors' meeting of the Mt. Mansfield Hotel

Company. Mr. Burt, the president, informed us that he had been approached by the owners of The Lodge (a group of Burlington businessmen) with an offer to purchase the place including 375 acres of land for $35,000. After long deliberation, the Board decided this investment was too large. My knowledge of the Lodge and its management had convinced me that we could make the business successful, so I was very disappointed when the idea was turned down. Personally, I was sure a rival group (the Mt. Mansfield Hotel Company) would purchase the Lodge and my dream of having one consolidated company would fall apart. I had to be satisfied with my affiliation as it stood and accept that three companies would exist: Mt. Mansfield Lift Co., The Lodge, and the Mt. Mansfield Hotel Co. with its Toll House, slope and rope tow, and my ski school.

The Mt. Mansfield single chairlift was constructed during the summer and fall of 1940. Opening day was November 17, 1940, coincidentally on my 32nd birthday. Mrs. Anne Cooke and Mrs. Gale Shaw were chosen to be the first to ride the lift and cut the ceremonial ribbon.

There was quite a crowd of officials from New York, Hartford, the Railroad Company (that operated the Skimeister trains transporting skiers from Boston and New York areas to Stowe) and the State of Vermont on hand for the opening ceremony. The primitive way the lift had been constructed caused a problem during this ceremony, because it was necessary to stop each chair to load the dignitaries, who were not properly dresses for skiing. The lift had been designed for continual loading and Mr. Johnson, the engineer representing the American Steel and Wire Company was aghast. He was certain the clutch would burn out. In order to get it going after each stop, we had to latch on to the fifth chair returning to the base and manually pull the down-chairs down. It was a disaster that the lift could not operate. Mr. Johnson and I pooled our engineering knowledge and came up with the theory that the lift motor and the clutch were underpowered. It was like trying to ride a bicycle on sand rather than pavement. We agreed that the lift needed to be modified, and we ordered a different clutch and a bigger motor. All this took a month to retrofit, and the lift finally opened on December 20, 1940 with the capacity of 189 skiers per hour (as compared to the present high-speed detachable quad lift at 1500 per hour).

Meanwhile, Frank Griffin, who held the concessions at the State Shelter in 1938 and was in control of the rope tow lift on the North Slope at the mountain, was not living up to his obligations to the State. I appealed to Perry Merrill, State Park and Forest Director, to acquire these concessions. I now had people on my staff that I felt could help improve the service. Mr. Merrill granted me these concessions: the coffee shop, sport shop and an expansion of my Ski School. I finalized the necessary arrangements with the State and made arrangement for a new rope tow and cleaned up slope.

When I reported this undertaking to the Board of Directors of the Hotel Company, Mr. Burt objected violently. He was afraid that the Toll House business would be harmed, and my commitment to the Hotel Company would be jeopardized by this venture at Mt. Mansfield. At a rather heated meeting, the Board fully realized that any future expansion of the Hotel Company would not materialize as long as Mr. Burt was at the helm. Mr. Boardman reminded Mr. Burt that I had just purchased 10% of the Mt. Mansfield Hotel Company, and he saw no problem in my expansion plans. Since Mr. Burt could not agree with the other Board members and my plans, he had no alternative but to resign.

Mr. Boardman was then elected president of the Mt. Mansfield Hotel Company and our plans started to materialize that year, in 1940. The Board unanimously elected me winter manager of the Toll House area in charge of all new construction of the inn. By this time Hermine had returned from Austria and we moved into the sports shop building.

As the word went out that the Mt. Mansfield Hotel Co. was investing in improvements at the Toll House area, there was no difficulty hiring workmen to carry out the project before the coming winter. Salaries at that time started out at 40 cents an hour, with the highest on the pay scale earning 90 cents an hour.

We continued to examine established resorts like Sun Valley and Mont Tremblant—areas that had built chairlifts. Averill Harriman had begun the development of Sun Valley. Otto Lang went to Mt. Rainier at the same time I came to Stowe. In Franconia, New Hampshire, Sig Buchmeyer was working with the Pecketts to attempt to build a first class ski resort there and the aerial tramway on Cannon Mt. was built in 1940 by the State of New Hampshire. Fred Pabst was starting to develop ski areas in the Midwest, Canada, and eventually Big Bromley in Manchester, Vermont. Ski area development was in full swing.

By now I was better acquainted with the Stowe community, as well as with the wealthy people who liked to visit. One of the men I spoke with was Arthur Dana, a prosperous Stowe landowner. I still had hopes that someone would come along with the resources to form a corporation to develop Stowe as a premier ski resort. Mr. Dana was not interested. He did not want to risk his capital.

I continued to compile my ideas for the development of Mt. Mansfield and adjacent Spruce Peak. I made sketches and maps of lifts and slopes I envisioned would make a "proper ski area." Previously, I had scouted the other side of Mt. Mansfield (the Underhill area) and reinforced my opinion that the Stowe side had better potential, if development could include more trails and a better lift. I was thinking of a T-bar I was familiar with in Europe. It was still my opinion that the newly formed Lift Company of Messrs. Palmedo and Cooke and the Mt. Mansfield Hotel Co. should be one Company.

Half in English and half in German I continued to form my own designs. A frequent ski school student became interested in moving to Stowe and working at Mt. Mansfield. This young woman, Helen Murray, had been coming to Stowe from New York State with her friends for lessons for quite some time and she became interested in the development of the area. She expressed a desire to stay in Stowe and work and thus, she became my assistant.

"Maxie", a nickname Miss Murray acquired in Stowe, was the daughter of a prominent businessman in Utica, New York. Her father died during the horrible influenza epidemic in 1918, and her mother was left a widow with two daughters and a son when Maxie was seven. Her mother moved the family from Utica to Yonkers, New York, where Maxie went to public schools before attending Westover Boarding School in Connecticut. Before her senior year, her mother took her to Europe for the summer to broaden her education. After boarding school, Maxie spent two years at Sweet Briar College. Upon assuming her duties in Stowe, Maxie spent endless hours assisting me in writing my development plans, as well as tending to the general books, reservations, and day-to-day correspondence.

Gradually the town of Stowe began to warm up to me—to regard me as a friend. I gave free lessons to the school children and private lessons to racers. One of those young racers was Marilyn Shaw (McMahon),

157

a daughter of Mt. Mansfield Hotel Company
director, Gale Shaw, Sr., who was a well-known
businessman and influential member of the
Stowe community. Marilyn would go on to be an
Olympic competitor.

My reputation was not only building in Stowe,
but also with the influential persons who
wanted to visit Stowe. I renewed my involvement
with Mr. Mason, a partner in the Derby-Ball
Ski Company, in the design and production of
skis in his Waterbury factory which led to more
connections in business circles in Burlington.
There was finally enough going on to make me
confident that my ideas would work—Stowe could
become a leading ski resort.

After my first winter in Stowe in April
1937, I returned to Austria by boat. There
were many Americans on the boat who were
traveling to Europe to attend the coronation
of the King and Queen of England. Among the
passengers was the well-know author, work-
traveler, and radio commentator, Lowell
Thomas. Mr. Thomas was also one of the
stockholders of the Mt. Mansfield Lift
Company. This was the beginning of a life-
long friendship. Mr. Thomas invited me to
Chicago where he was giving a speech at a pep
rally for the war effort. This turned into
a two-week odyssey where we went on to Sun
Valley, Aspen, Alta, and back to Aspen. It was
a great opportunity for me to see the lifts
and the development in these areas.

Then America was catapulted into World War
II, which affected the whole economy. The
ski industry was hard hit. Eligible people

were drafted into the armed services, so our work force was cut at the Mountain. Most of the male employees left to serve in the armed forces—many became troopers in the 10th Mountain Division. The war had major effects on Stowe as a ski area. The chairlift was only a year old when America became involved in the war and it was operating only a few hours a day. The staff of the Ski School and the newly formed Mt. Mansfield Ski Patrol were minimal and the Mt. Mansfield Ski Club cancelled all competition events.

Because I was not an American citizen I was ineligible to be drafted or even to enlist in the American armed services. Still, I wanted to serve in some way. Through a friend in Stowe, I heard about the Civilian Pilot Training Program at the Burlington Airport. I signed up, took lessons, and after 35 hours I earned a private license for flying. After 250 solo hours, I was eligible for a commercial license and was a candidate for flight instructor. Having successfully completed the requirement, I held this position for two years, during which I lived in the dormitories the University of Vermont provided for over 1000 cadets. I was inducted into the Army Reserve because there was no longer a need for instructors as there were more than a million pilots on duty in the U. S.

In August 1943, Hermine and I became American citizens. Our son, Peter, was born an American citizen in September.

The war was still escalating in 1944; so after reading a newspaper advertisement

recruiting skilled engineers, I joined the
Bell Aircraft Company in Burlington. They
were tooling up B-29's for the big bomber
plant in Marietta, Georgia. Since I had the
proper training, I applied for the job at
Bell, where I was accepted as an expediter
in the tool division because I could read
blueprints—both in metric and in inches.
Working for Bell, I traveled a great deal in
the eastern U. S. for a year, speeding up the
delivery of tools for the war drive. Because
I had been a U. S. Army flight instructor,
I gained preferred status and piloted a
chartered plane to and from the various
suppliers and manufacturers.

Dickinson Collection
Maxie and Hennie

During this time the Toll House was in full operation under the management of my wife and Maxie. I assisted them when I could, and the area became a profitable business. As the war drew to a close in 1945, I was out of both the Army Reserve and Bell Aircraft and moved back to Stowe.

One day in 1946, an interesting letter arrived on fine stationary. It was a reservation for a room at the Toll House. Because of the New York address and the letterhead, Maxie immediately suspected this was not just a run-of-the-mill reservation request, and was concerned that this person might not be comfortable in the casual accommodations of the Toll House. But I suggested we give it a try. The reservation was confirmed and the matter was temporarily forgotten.

In early December, in keeping with my usual morning ritual, I entered The Lodge to greet incoming houseguests. Seated in a corner in the living room was a man I had not seen before. He wore glasses and looked somber. I didn't know him. I exchanged the usual greeting with other guests—"Good morning, Sepp, how are you…nice to see you…sign me up with Lionel, etc." Then I phoned the Toll House to make the necessary arrangements for these lessons. After the bustle was over, the somber man with the glasses walked over to me and said, "I am Neil Starr." As simple as that.

This man, Mr. Starr, began to apologize. He had taken the night train from New York, and someone had suggested he might prefer to stay at The Lodge because the Toll House didn't have private bathrooms. His original reservation was for the Toll House, and he felt he had been rude because he hadn't phoned the change, in advance.

He informed me about a close friend in New York who "thinks you are the best"—Jules Andre. Mr. Andre owned a very fashionable sport shop in the city. Previously, Mr. Starr had skied cross country at Lake Placid, and he skied occasionally in New Hampshire and Sun Valley. His New York friend, Jules Andre, had purchased alpine skis for Mr. Starr, his wife, family and friends. Jules Andre said to Mr. Starr, "if you want to ski—if you really want to learn to ski alpine—you must take lessons from Sepp Ruschp, the Ski School director at Stowe."

As we started our day, Mr. Starr announced he had come to me for lessons because he was an "older" man. He said he didn't want "just any young instructor" leading him around. He wanted private lessons with me. I assured him I was flattered, but I told him I had a business—Ski School—to run. Private lessons with me were not part of the package. "Oh yes, I've seen that you have five or six instructors," he said sarcastically. I didn't quite know what he was getting at.

Explaining that I had to organize the classes before 10:00 a.m. according to ability, assign them to instructors, and then serve as supervisor, I told Mr. Starr perhaps I could squeeze in an hour for a private lesson from 11:00 to noon. We could grab a sandwich to eat outside. He thought that was acceptable. He was alone—just scouting—he came to see what Stowe had to offer.

When we met at the Toll House slope for our first "private" lesson, he saw a mere rope tow hanging there, all soggy and wet. "Do you have a real lift?" he asked.

"Yes", I replied, "the single chairlift is about a mile up the mountain from here." I told him we could drive there in my station wagon. I explained I had planned one run with him down the Toll Road, which would take about an hour, if there was no line at the chair lift.

"A waiting line at the lift!" he exclaimed. "People with private instructors in Sun Valley have a preferred line." I explained to him I had to buy my own ticket here—the Lift Company was owned by a New York group, not me. So we stood in line awhile. He felt that was totally unacceptable—as the Director of the ski school, I should have a special line. However, he put up with the inconvenience and enjoyed himself so much that he stayed for five days. Every day he took a lesson or two— whatever time I could allow. I fit in as many private lessons as possible for Mr. Starr, and on the last day he announced he would no longer come to Stowe by train, he would fly.

During the time Mr. Starr had stayed in Stowe, Hermine always fixed him coffee or tea after skiing. She did the same on the day of his departure, and I joined him before he left by taxi to Burlington for a flight on

Colonial Airlines. I was nervous about what
would happen when I presented him with the
bill. I was so used to people complaining
about the price; even the most wealthy would
try to talk it down or dicker. When he called
me into the room, I noticed he was looking
at the ski school rate folder, so I knew he
had some idea of what was expected. I said
to myself, at least he read it and he knows
he owes me between $150 and $250. Mr. Starr
wrote out a check, folded it and handed it to
me, adding that…yes, he knew it was a little
extra, but I had given him a new outlook on
life.

"You know," he said, "I'm married to a
woman who is quite a bit younger, and perhaps
learning to ski together will impress her.
I am here to size up this place. The Lodge
is not the greatest, but the location is
good and I have looked over some of the
rooms. I will make a reservation soon for a
week vacation, when I can bring my wife and
friends. But during that time I want lessons
with you—not your assistants, as good as they
may be."

Smiling, he said he looked forward to our
next meeting, to which I agreed. He did not
make a move to leave—he was obviously looking
for some reaction from me, so I opened
his check. It was for $1000. "Too much," I
exclaimed," I cannot accept that amount."

"Forget that. Give your wife a present," he
replied. Such an experience was so unique, I
didn't know how to react! I had spent a lot
of my preciously scheduled time with this

prosperous, wealthy man each day he was in Stowe, and had formed some early impressions. He was not well coordinated, and became easily embarrassed, so I tried to look away when he fell and not help him too much. I would stand there and lean on my poles and give quiet suggestions. I could also sense that he had a tremendous ego. However, when you looked into Mr. Starr's eyes, he seemed kind. He was soft-spoken and I had the feeling that he was a warm person at heart. He did not seem dynamic or "tough" during our first meeting in Stowe, although I surmised when dressed for "combat" in the city, Mr. Starr could be formidable.

Because of his apparent tremendous wealth, I felt Mr. Starr could become demanding if he were to come to Stowe often. Still, the way he made demands was gracious, and I remained hopeful that, at last, I had found the major investor who would expand Stowe as a complete ski resort.

This began the "Starr Years".

Dickinson Collection
Starr and Ruschp

THE STARR YEARS

As they say, "necessity is the mother of invention." Because of the transition from war to peace in 1946, I felt strongly that this was the prime time to build additional facilities to meet the demands of post-war leisure time. There was real need for more uphill capacity, as the number of skiers coming to Stowe was increasing. C. V. Starr shared my conviction. That combined with his strong belief that an instructor should not have to wait in line for a lift, enticed Mr. Starr to make an attractive offer.

Cornelius Vander Starr was a self-made millionaire. After serving in the Army in World War I, he became uninterested in his routine job with a steamship company. He used his $10,000.00 savings to launch an insurance company in Shanghai, China, at the age of 27. From that small company, he built up a giant international insurance conglomerate and amassed a fortune. His offices for the American International Group were in New York City. After his visit to Stowe during World War II, he found a new love in Mt. Mansfield. The time seemed ripe for the successful international entrepreneur to join forces with the enterprising young Austrian ski instructor, Sepp Ruschp. It appeared I had found my long sought-after investor and was on the way to realizing my dream.

After returning from his latest ski trip to Stowe in 1945, Mr. Starr called me from his office in New York, "What are your plans?" he wanted to know. I envisioned several things and had compiled a file of plans. He invited me to bring this file to his New York office. After talking it over with my friends, Gale Shaw and Munn Boardman, I decided to go.

At that time I had a design for a small hotel at Little Spruce, where "Henry's Run" (named for long-time mountain manager, Henry Simoneau) is now. I had a plan for a lift there and another on the North Slope of Mt. Mansfield. I had begun to negotiate with Konstamm, a big lift company in Europe which was eventually sold to the Riblet Lift Company in New Jersey. "Well, you are an engineer, a planner and a businessman—what would you do first?" he wanted to know.

I told him first I would build a T-bar lift to replace the two rope tow section on the "Mountain". It would enter State land. Our agreement with the State when we built the chairlift was now showing its restrictions. Starr knew the Burt Company owned land above my proposed top terminal and suggested we negotiate a purchase of land from the Burts in order to go above the 3,000 feet. He didn't like the idea of stopping growth by monopoly!

So we arranged for a meeting with Mr. Craig Burt, the co-owner of the Burt Family Company which owned 400 + acres above the Toll House. "I know you want something, because I have heard about the lift that Sepp wants to build" was Mr. Burt's greeting. "We have kept that land in pretty good shape, and we have given some land to the State. I'm not about to sell one, then fifty acres of land. I'll sell everything or nothing!" he said. The Burt Company owned 3,000 acres on Spruce Peak as well as the 400 acres on Mt. Mansfield.

"You have lumbered the land so you pay taxes. We could be partners or we could buy that acreage," was Mr. Starr's reply.

At the time the Burt family was a dynasty in Stowe. Craig Burt was very protective of his land, while his brother Wayne thought it was worthless. Mr. Starr and I offered the Burts $55,000. They countered with $100,000. In 1947, we eventually bought the Mt. Mansfield and Spruce Peak land for $75,000. The Burt Company reserved the timber rights for their lumber business.

I had estimated the cost of constructing a T-bar from $50,000 to $80,000. Mr. Starr was a bit apprehensive and wanted to know if some local people would help finance the venture. He asked me if I had any money to invest. I told him I had saved about $15,000 and I would be willing to invest it all. "You have the guts to put up all your money?" he exclaimed in disbelief. "I will either lend you all the money or no less than 51%," he said explaining that with more than 50 percent he would have controlling interest. "I will draw up a contract in which I will put up $44,000.00, you will put in your $15,000.00 and we will find some other investors for the rest. We will insure your life for the amount you owe me; then if something happened to you, your wife is taken care of and I will own a lift."

I flew home and called a meeting with the Mt. Mansfield Hotel Company, Mr. Shaw, the Burts, and Mr. Mason from the Ski Club to report the offer. There was quite a debate. Mr. Boardman was elated and impressed that I had ventured into a world that was so strange to me and had come up with an investor as well as being willing to invest my own capital. Others said Mr. Starr was a strange man. His massive wealth frightened them. They feared he could become difficult with his ambitions and gobble us up. "Will Stowe lose its identity as a village?" they worried. In the end the majority said, "Go, we are with you." Thus began a new company, the Smugglers Notch Lift Company.

With the sanction of the majority of the members of the Hotel Company and the Ski Club, the Mt. Mansfield T-Bar was built in 1947. Rogers Adams was the surveyor and right-hand man, Henry Simoneau, Kerr Sparks and Clem Curtis were key participants and Charlie Lord always helped.

The lift was a real clinker, the first with all steel construction. It continuously broke down and I spent almost all of my time helping to repair and redesign the lift, many times working all night. When I explained my dedication to the project to Jack Smith, a friend of Mr. Starr's, he was concerned I was working myself to death. Mr. Smith called Neil about my situation. Mr. Starr called me from Sun Valley. "Can you fix it?" he wanted to know. "Yes," I told him, "but it will take time." He said to do what I had to do, adding "if it works, it is yours and if it doesn't, it's mine and you don't owe me a thing." How generous you can get, I thought.

By this time C. V. Starr and I were on first-name basis (Neil and Sepp). He always stayed at the Lodge, but the manager, Mr. Morrell annoyed him. "Are all the people here like that?" he wanted to know. I assured him that this behavior was just a part of business, a part of life. Mr. Starr wanted to buy the Lodge. He asked about my financial arrangement with the Ski School, the Toll House and the Hotel Company. At the time, I took 20% of the profit from the ski school, had a gentleman's agreement to be winter manager of the Toll House and owned 10% of the Hotel Company.

Neil asked how much the Hotel Company stock was worth. I explained the original investment of $100 a share and suggested he offer double the par value, or $200, and most of the stockholders in the Hotel Company would sell. It was a landslide. Everyone went for it. So now, C. V. Starr and I owned the Hotel Company.

When The Lodge owner, Mr. Morrell, heard of this, he was enraged. It was then that Mr. Starr moved to Stowehof, a lodge on Edson Hill. "Morrell wants $650,000 for The Lodge," he said. I told Neil that including the land, it was not worth more than $250,000.00 and suggested he talk with Mrs. Morrell who reportedly had much invested in the Lodge.

In 1949, we consummated the deal to purchase The Lodge with land for $250,000. Mr.

Starr was elated, "You have made me a million dollars right now," he said "and the land will be worth even more in the future."

We now owned the Hotel Company, The Lodge, the T-Bar lift and the Ski School. My dream of one big company—a complete ski resort— was coming true. We formed the Mt. Mansfield Company. I was offered a fixed salary plus 10% of all profits, a car, living expenses, and a pension after 25 years. A contract was drawn up. And in 1949, I was made President and General Manager of the Mt. Mansfield Company.

Some of the shareholders of the Lift Company and the Hotel Company stayed in as investors in the new Mt. Mansfield Company. Lowell Thomas was one of them and we became lifelong friends. I skied with him the day before he died in 1979, at the age of 89.

Stowe Historical Society Archives
Sepp Jumping

Sepp, "Monarch of all he surveys," ski instructor, on top of
Mt. Mansfield from Winter in Vermont, Crane, 1942

TRIBUTES

From AIG/NY/ Mr. Maurice Greenberg

Citation For Sepp Ruschp From University Of Vermont

Mr. President, I have the privilege to present Sepp Ruschp for the degree of Doctor of Laws, honoris causa.

Sepp Ruschp was born in Linz, Austria, and educated at the Linz Technical School. He was employed successively by the Steyer Company, builders of the Porsche automobile, and a sporting goods company. During this time he was an international competitor in both Alpine and Nordic skiing events, capturing among other trophies the Four-Event Championship of his native country. At an early age, he achieved the coveted status of Austrian Certified Ski Instructor.

Sepp arrived in Stowe, Vermont, on December 10, 1936, at the age of twenty-eight. He brought with him certain talents: the ability to teach and coach skiing, knowledge of business administration and engineering, and an unimpeachable character. His immediate purpose was to become established in this new environment and bring his bride Hermine to join him. This he achieved within a year.

Despite the interruption of World War II, when he served his adopted country as a pilot and flight instructor, Sepp set out to introduce Alpine skiing to Vermont and organize the first technically-qualified ski school in the United States. He shared his competitive expertise as coach of the fledgling ski teams at the University of Vermont and Norwich University, and also coached the school children of Stowe. Two of his early protégés became national and Olympic champions.

As chief executive officer of the Mount Mansfield Company, he planned and executed the development of that mountain--establishing Stowe as the ski capitol of the East. He transformed the sport of skiing into a productive recreational business, while preserving the aesthetic quality of the region. Mount Mansfield became the model for those who have developed like enterprises throughout the nation. As President of the United States Ski Association, he further contributed to the development and organization of the ski industry in this country and abroad.

Sepp possesses a rare degree of honest common sense which he has generously applied to the benefit of his employees, his neighbors, and countless others. He has been consultant or economic advisor to at least seven governors of Vermont. Few people, in our time, have responded so magnificently to the opportunity and the responsibility that our freedoms represent.

By Everett C. Bailey
May 15, 1981.

Christi Ruschp Dickinson's Speech at the 2008 Vermont Ski Hall of Fame

Good evening to everyone at the 2008 Vermont Ski Hall of Fame celebration dinner.

Although it appears that I am sitting in sunny Arizona, my husband, Pat and I, are presently flying over the Pacific Ocean returning from the Women's Golf World Amateur Team Championship that was held in Adelaide, Australia.

Hearty congratulations to the fellow inductees: Allen Adler, Al Hobart, Jan Reynolds and Ned Gillette.

I remember Ned and my brother, Peter, in stiff competition throughout their prep school and college careers.

My father, Sepp Ruschp, grew up in Linz, Austria. His education in engineering provided him the opportunity to work for the Styr Auto Works on the design team led by Porsche, the patriarch of future Porsche automobiles. They actually worked on the design of the prototype of the VW rear engine bug.

Throughout Dad's youth he was always active in sports. He was on a crew team on the Danube. He mountain-climbed and played tennis.

But his passion of course was skiing, both downhill and slalom, but also cross country and jumping.

He won various national competitions throughout Austria.

In the mid-1930's, the political and economic climate was changing and Dad decided to prepare for the state examination to become a professional ski instructor.

He attended the famous Hanne's Schneider Ski School but also was examined by a professor at the University of Vienna.

Dad needed to be versed in map reading, engineering dynamics and first aid. Only a few passed the exam. Among them were Friedl Pfeiffer of Aspen, Sig Engl of Sun Valley, and Dad.

My father and mother were married in 1935 and as the political climate worsened Dad decided to make a career and lifestyle change.

He started to learn English in anticipation of coming to the United States.

He received a letter from Frank Griffin, a director of the Mt. Mansfield Ski Club and as they say, the rest is history.

Dad set sail for America without mother, in December 1936.

He spent his first night in Stowe at Frank Griffin's house, which is now owned by Millie and John Merrill.

When Dad looked out their front window and saw the snow capped mountain range he asked Mr. Griffin:

"Where was Mt. Mansfield?"

Mr. Griffin drove Dad through Stowe. He fell in love with the village atmosphere, the New England style homes and the Community Church with its pristine white steeple.

As they approached the mountain, Dad immediately realized the vast potential that Mt. Mansfield offered.

Dad had the vision that the ski industry and recreational sports was going to explode.

He continued the passion for skiing, Stowe, and Mt. Mansfield for 54 years.

My father, Sepp Ruschp, was passionate about skiing.

He was proud to be an American. He was proud to serve the state of Vermont and he loved his home town of Stowe, and especially the mountain.

He instilled this passion in both my brother and myself. My brother continued in skiing and I turned my focus to golf.

Shortly after I had a knee injury and surgery ending my fledgling ski racing career, he told me that the sport or the game was not important... as long as I remained passionate about any sport, I would always be surrounded by men and women of honor and integrity.

On behalf of my family, I thank the Vermont Ski Museum for the induction of my father, Sepp Ruschp into the Vermont Ski Hall of Fame.

Before I ask my nephew Andrew and my niece, Allison to come forward, a personal thank you to you, Billy Kidd, for presenting this award.

I know that Dad is smiling down over Mt. Mansfield and he thanks you for this prestigious honor.

Dickinson Collection
Family Group in Aspen, Colorado, Christi and Peter in Front and Hermine and Sepp in Back

Hank Greenberg Letter

Read at Mr. Ruschp at 50th Testimonial Dinner 12/10/1986

Dear Sepp:

I am personally distressed that I cannot be with you on this important occasion. A 50th anniversary is important in almost every case, but in your case, more so than most. Your outstanding contribution generally to skiing in America, and especially in Stowe, are unmatched by any other individual alive today. I am personally grateful for all the help and counsel you have provided over the years to me in the affairs of the Mt. Mansfield Company, which continue even today.

Many thanks, Sepp, from all of us at AIG and I hope we are all together to celebrate your 75th anniversary.

With warm wishes for continued good health.
Hank Greenberg

Introduction to the WRFB Radio Interview of Sepp Ruschp by Brian Harwood, Oct. 16, 1977

This actual transcript of the interview with Sepp as transcribed by Brian and donated to the Stowe Historical Society in July 2009. Brian has given oral permission to publish this transcript in the new ski book. This has been retyped from the original transcript, as is.

WRFB Panorama

[BH is Brian Harwood; SR is Sepp Ruschp]

BH I've been trying for years to get you down here! I'm not sure that you're aware of it, but I've been trying to get you down here to talk with you because he is, after all, a very important figure in Stowe and in Lamoille County and in Vermont and in skiing circles around the world. If by now you haven't guessed, I'll tell you that our guest today on Panorama is Sepp Ruschp who recently stepped aside as the Mount Mansfield Company. Welcome. It's good to have you here.

SR It's nice to be here.

BH I'd like to talk first of all about how things were when you came to Stowe. Which was, then, 1937?

SR '36.

BH 36. What did you find here?

SR My first arrival here in 1936 was December 10th. And, we had very similar weather to what we have today. In other words—a drizzling rain. I'd been in Burlington I was leaving Stowe in the dark, so I didn't see much in the morning, it was a clear, sunshine day and the white cap of Mount Mansfield was visible from my window where I looked out. As a matter of fact, I was driven up the first day and the first day I gave lessons to the three gentlemen whom I always think about. One is still alive and he was high ranking in the State Department at one time. He was my first pupil. I was teaching them in front of the lodge there on a very gentle slope. Nothing was running. No ropes or no nothing. We had to climb up and down. And uh, I remember the newspaper man from Burlington and I gave a short interview and they announced that I had arrived to give lessons there. But, after the first few days I climbed Mount Mansfield on the Toll Road with my skis and skied down the Nosedive and there was show there—not a lot, but it was skiable. It was crust and I could see that the Nose Dive has something particularly special. It was down, down, down. It was narrower in those days. But, a great trail. Although I had t run from the bottom of the mountain back to the Toll House base on my skis, which didn't bother me much because I used to run cross country a great deal in Europe. But, I could see that mountain has a great potential right there.

Then, I was introduced to the University of Vermont to the Ski Team and the Norwich Cadets. And another following few days, and I made a little great cheer from the speech therapist my broken English. I had the Cadets and the University students. And, then Christmas came and Christmas we had lots of snow. It 10-11, 11-12 and for lunch they bought me a cup of tea, and a sandwich. I was teaching, teaching, teaching "hour" lessons. And, I worked there all by myself for the whole holiday week until New Year's and New Year's Day. I earned quite a bit of money. It looks very favorable at least to me to have American dollars instead of Austrian shillings.

Then, during the course of the first winter I met many permanent people. Roland Palmedo, Jay Cook[e], his former wife took a lot of lessons from me and also locally I met the Shaw family—they were all youngsters at that time...Lowell Thomas. And, uh, at the end of the first season we had some tough luck with the weather in January, but I made myself busy with coaching the University Teams either dry land or medium snow, mediocre snow. but, the whole thing appealed to me, great potential. Near to the cities, the highest mountain in Vermont. Then we   had the Eastern Championship transferred from Thunderbolt Mountain up to Stowe. Thousands of skiers, here, visitors. That again, gave me reassurance that it's just a matter of time when the skiing could be really developed and something for state, town here, for myself. So, I was encouraged and I had an offer to come back. Then, the following year, I got married and my wife and I came over (the following year). Ever since them I am here.

BH Now, there weren't very many other ski areas, if any, in Vermont.

SR There was Woodstock with rope tows (they had more rope tows). We only had one here. Woodstock was known -- not too any.

BH What, initially, got you to move to Stowe? I mean, you described going up there. But, why Stowe, Vermont? Did somebody know of your talents and say, 'Why don't you come up and try it?'

SR Well, that's a very unique story. I was winning races in Europe, either combined Alpine or cross country jumping, and the last Austrian championship I won the relay and the 18 kilometer and was second and third in downhill. At the prize awarding ceremony, the president of the Ski Association of Austria told us -- a table full of winners -- and said, "What are you going to do in the future when the thing is over?" I asked, "Why do you ask the question?" "Well, he said, "I have a letter here from the National Ski Association in America. They're interested in professional ski instructors and coaches for universities." I took notice of that. I visited the president of Vienna and I got the addresses of several, well, I would think almost 100 ski cubs in America, and I wrote them all. My offer, photo, my racing record, I was an Austrian State Certified Ski Instructor, and sent it out. Amongst one of them was the Mount Mansfield Ski Club. And they wrote me a very nice letter back that they were interested.

And, with the tie-in with the University and Norwich Cadets, the University of Norwich, and the Ski Club here— actually sponsored my first year here. It was luck. I had several other offers. Alberg Ski Club in Colorado, Mount Hood in Oregon. But nothing appealed to me because the proximity of the cities in the East coast. I looked at the map, I studied America, the height of Mount Mansfield, and the snow promises, the record showed there was plenty of snow in Vermont. So, I chose to come to Stowe. And, to Vermont.

BH And, the gradual development began. And, the chair lifts went up, the t-bar.

SR Yes, of course. I always referred to friends, 'Why don't we do this?' Why don't a rope should be lengthened. The trail should be widened. And, we should have inns or a lodge or something like that and, that kind of talking, promoting in general. We were always looking for somebody who would take the lad, who was financially strong enough.

BH There wasn't much of a corporate structure them, was there?

SR No, no. The Mount Mansfield Company owned the summit house and the toll house which is the shelter for the toll keeper. We made a little cafeteria out of it and a sport shop. No, there was nothing here.

BH And then, was it C.V. Starr that actually came in at that point?

SR No, later. The Mount Mansfield Hotel Company owned the slope and the toll house, and I was given the concession for that for a ski school and a rope tow operator, and a small sport shop, and a small coffee shop. One of the older shareholders offered to sell some of the shares to me of the Mount Mansfield Company in '38. I borrowed some money and paid it off, slowly. And then the Mount Mansfield Company (Hotel Company) rebuilt the first Toll House. What I said now, and enlarged the following year with my supervision and so forth. And, then the lodge changed hands, ownership, from outside, from Vermonters to outsiders. And, then '40, Palmedo and Cookie and others skied here, including the amateur ski group from New York. And, every time we talked about the potential, we talked about a lift. What we need is a lift. So, the lift corporation was formed in 1940, and the Mount Mansfield chair lift was built and opened for the winter season of '40-'41. I was a small stockholder then, and helped lay out the thing.

BH Then came the war.

SR Then came the war. Right. Of course, I was not here during the war. I was stationed, fortunately, in Burlington. I joined the Air Force ad became a flight instructor. And, then after the war I worked another year at Bell Aircraft Company as an expediter. I learned a great deal of American business. Company Communications system, etc. Travel. And, then in 1947-48, Mr. Starr came up here -- who was just a skier -- and I got acquainted with him by teaching him to ski. Apparently, he liked me or took a liking of me and, perhaps management abilities which I discussed with him what we could do, should do. And he got encouraged and financed me personally first. He lent me some money to build a T-bar lift. Of course, i had some resentment from others including the senior chair lift people, that I built the competition. That started the ball rolling that the Lodge was purchased, always in some sort of a partnership, corporate set-up. I had the ski school. I had the t-bar lift, 51% control. I had 10% of the Mount Mansfield Hotel Company. And Mr. Starr bought this and Mr. Starr bought that. And, then in '49 we put everything into one basket and we formed the present Mount Mansfield Company. At first, I was Vice President, Mr. Starr President. After a year, he relinquished his position and I became President. And since, I am the President/ General Manager, then, of course, a lot of planning which I did either by dreams or by real, actual designing and laying out Spruce Peak. And that always had to be sold again to either Mr. Starr or jointly to his own shareholders or to banks. And, I have been very successful with Vermont banks. Over years and years and years they've always lend money again. Mortgage money, repaid. With that we developed Mount Mansfield in its present stage.

BH And as that development was going on, there were other ski areas coming along.

SR Yes. Some additions, Mount Tremblant, for instance, in Canada. They built a chair lift a year before this one was built. And Sun Valley started building chair lifts. And, in the east here the aerial tram in Franconia was built by this date. And, Harvey Gibson financed the building of Eastern slope barrier.

BH You'd sort of been the guiding force, though, behind Stowe, and I think in no small way that the community and the Mountain Company is a direct reflection of your own taste and attitudes and management abilities. It's always struck me, as I'm sure it has everyone else, the difference in Stowe, let's say, and other ski areas, other resort areas.

SR Yes.

BH There's a mark her that's decidedly and distinctly different.

SR Well, there are two reasons, I believe, myself. One is that I am, in a way, conservative. I like beauty. I like cleanliness. I like meadows, cut flowers. I was in the Alps. Beautiful hotels, beautiful resort areas. And, somehow, that —I like to transfer into my home state here. And, because of that, and we didn't have millions to tear in and rip something apart —we were better in the long run. We were better off than we did it in piecemeal than in a sophisticated manner, with a little continental atmosphere because I a born and brought up in Europe. So, I think to carry it on, Mr. Starr had a great taste for beauty and cleanliness. He is a connoisseur in gardens and so forth, so I had an easy way to persuade him to do something beautiful.

185

BH Do you think it would be as easy now? I don't mean 'easy' in that sense, but is it as possible now to do what you did and have done in the Mountain Company, if you'd started in 1977 given all the environmental pressures that there are?

SR Uh. It would've been. I would think, quite difficult. Although, we could compare other areas where the state o the officials, whatever, are involved. I would say, if you do it as well as that I think you have a chance. But, it would be more costly, more time consuming. But, in a way, rightly so, because an area or a state could be destroyed by over-expansion, by ruthless exploitation, by 'fast buck' people. Fortunately, the state has made its in-root in environmental controlling. Some are painful, but if you're on the right track, I think you can still do something in this state.

BH Let me ask you a question about what you did in the early years between '36 and, say, 1942 or so, '41.

SR Plans and draw lines, and lift lines and decorate the hotel and the village over here. Not all came true, but a great deal of it.

BH It was, essentially, maintenance.

SR Yeah, Surveying. I did a lot of surveying in the mountain for the Burt Company, who owned most of the forest up here, and also for the state, in a sense.

BH Of course, your training. I don't know, I assume most people know that you're trained as an engineer.

SR Mechanical engineering, yeah. Then I went to business school because I changed from Engineering to Business and sport equipment shops and, so I had two professions, plus the ski instructor certificate.

BH I wonder if you'd talk a little bit about the transition now that's going to occur, or is occurring, between yourself and your successor, Vernon Johnson.

SR Well, Mr. Johnson, who has great experience in resort business. And I believe that he is coming in very low-key, and he's getting acquainted with the community, and slowly with the state. We had many occasions where I've introduced him to different groups. And, again, this week there is another group. a ski club. Uh, and in the meantime, he's studying the management the way I have it managed. I'm sure that he has a different style. I don't know it yet, but every manager will have his own thinking and style. As far as future development is concerned, I have a great deal to say. I'm especially technically. Financially, too. And, I have a personal interest financially. a pretty hefty one in the form of common stock and debentures. So...

BH You'll be on the board.

SR I'll be on the board. Unless I lose my thinking.

BH Let's talk about expansion. You mentioned expansion. Talk about some of the plans that you have in mind for the Mountain.

SR Well, we talked ever since we had the energy crisis and a snow crisis. The number one subject will even out or stabilize our economy here—the company alone, also, the community, is snow making. In the meantime, snow making technique has developed engineering wise. We have one of the best installed in Spruce Peak—only relatively small part because Mount Mansfield has a lot of snow. But, in order to fill the gap of early snow, late snow, and windy day, no question about it. The engineering feat to put snow making on Mount Mansfield encompassed a lot of planning, a lot of engineering, and also financial thinking. We're talking about, perhaps, with a new lift—has to be built in there because snow making alone will not provide enough income to pay for it. It has to be immediately upgraded with another lift. I would say a plan like this would certainly run well over $3 million. Maybe $3 1/2 million. Some other plans are being developed to improve our restaurants and shops and hotels. We talk about, perhaps, $5 million of expansion plans. And, it's being worked on on paper now. And then we have to apply for Act 250 —the Board of Resources. All those things will take months to get approved. And, if and when it's approved and the economy of the country has again further improved. Because we're not out of the weather yet. We don't want to expand and over-expand and then get in trouble financially. Because, the company has to be self-sustaining,. Bottom line is important because we are owned by an insurance company. I mean, part of it, the controlling interest. And, they have to look for earnings. Not just a "welfare institution." And, o a great deal will be what inflation is doing. And one of the biggest items is the energy question —the electricity price and availability. One can go diesel, but then diesel has other headaches…to bring fuel up to the top of the mountain…it's a combination of goals. We're working on it. But, the fuel cost, the energy availability, or the cost of it, has a great deal to do with how far you can go. And what the prices have to be in order to sustain such expenditures.

BH And to make it feasible.

SR Right.

BH Now, you mentioned the word 'insurance.' And that, of course, i in the front or back of everyone's mind depending on how closely associated with the ski industry they are. And, in Vermont, that's a lot of people. $120 million a year. A decision, I don't need to review this for you, I know, but for someone listening, that was made to award $2 1/2 million to a skier who was injured at Stratton Mountain last, two winters ago, I believe it was.

SP Yeah.

BH Now, what is the impact as you see it? Not just on Stowe, but on the ski industry.

SR The impact of this decision is far-reaching. No question. It worries every ski operator, not only in the state of Vermont, because it is nationwide. There are only a few states who have protective law against such a thing. The doctrine of, the assumption of, risk to participate in sport is highly challenged with that verdict. And, this is a very, very far reaching situation. Uh, insurance companies are here to insure us for disasters such a lift break down, a bearing burns out or something like that, and a lift disaster. Which, like an airplane has, right? Like a railroad has. For that we insure it. But, the insurance people for the pleasure of skiing, because there may be a crust o the snow or whatever it maybe that to instigate a loss against, is far reaching. There's no question that if the thing is upheld that the insurance rates will have to go up. Whether we find an insurer to insure us is one thing. And, if we do, how much it will cost? Right now the insurance company ha given us notice that they're going to insure us only from month-to-month, with a provision that upwards and the public has to pay for. Okay, the public is only that much able to pay for. If we hand out millions of dollars to outsiders, where should that money come from? The people have to pay for it.

BH The lift tickets.

SR The lift tickets. And, that is not very easy. IF you take a million and half, you have a million and half rides, if you raise the rate by $1. But, if other losses are coming in, and they are coming in because the risk i challenged now, insurance company must set reserves aside. And, that would run into the millions of dollars. Could run into millions of dollars. And, somebody has to pay for it.

BH Two basic things are happening, as I understand it. One is in the courts where they've appealed the decision of the Supreme Court, and the other is that the ski area operators are attempting to get some legislation.

SR That is a very, very important step, and there are some parallels of other states, only three in the United States, that have a better law than w have. And I'm sure that the legislation has to look into that very seriously. No question about it. And, to protect its industry, too. Otherwise, we are done.

BH Isn't skiing the top, if not one of the top, industries in Vermont in terms of total dollars? We're talking $100 million dollars a year with a budget of $3.4, or 5 million.

SR Uh, it is one of the biggest, not the biggest one, if you go into economy, as farming is here, right, as industry. But, one industry which I always claimed i that outside capital was invested in Vermont, and not from within. Neither from the State or public. So, money was always brought in to construct and build. And then, of course, the value of land has risen. The second home market was a big industry. When you take all this together, I would think that probably the ski industry is a recreation industry. Summer and winter alike, are probably one of the biggest money exchanges. With no cost to us. In a sense.

BH We're out of time.

SR Yeah.

BH The clock runs very quickly when you're talking with someone like Sepp Ruschp. And, we have been for the last half hour or so on Panorama today. Thank you very much. I hear you saying we'll be hearing a lot more from you.

SR Oh, yes.

BH Despite the change in management.

SR Right! I'll have a little vacation now, but I'll be back winter and summer alike.

BH Thanks, Sepp.

1819   1989

NORWICH UNIVERSITY

THE MILITARY COLLEGE OF VERMONT.

The One Hundred Seventieth

COMMENCEMENT

Saturday, May Twentieth

Nineteen Hundred Eighty-Nine

UPPER PARADE   10:30 A.M.

GRADUATION CEREMONY

*Processional   Professor George H. Lane, Jr.
                                                Faculty Marshal

*National Anthem   James Bennett, Director

*Invocation   The Reverend Richard E. May
                                              University Chaplain

Introduction of Honorary Commissioning Officer   W. Russell Todd
   and Commencement Speaker   President, Norwich University

Recognition of Commissionees   General Carl E. Vuono
                                      Chief of Staff, United States Army

Graduation Address   General Carl E. Vuono
                                      Chief of Staff, United States Army

Conferring of Baccalaureate, Master's
   and Honorary Degrees   President Todd

*Norwich Forever.
(All are asked to sing)

Norwich forever, queen of the hills,
When far from thee, still mem'ry thrills recalling
Scenes and old friendships, songs and old cheers
Mem'ries that fade not through the changing years

Closing Remarks   President Todd

*Benediction   The Rev. Richard G. Lavalley
                                         Dir., Newman Apostolate

*Recessional   Professor Lane

Reception for graduates and guests by Webb Hall following the ceremony.

Lunch for graduates and guests served in Harmon Hall following the
ceremony.

Photographs, other than those taken from seats, should be taken only from
the designated area adjacent to the platform group.

*Standing

HONORARY DEGREES

Carl E. Vuono	Doctor of Military Science
K.C. Jones	Doctor of Physical Education
Charles Stuart Adams	Doctor of Business Management
Sepp Ruschp	Doctor of Business Management
John Thomas Evans, Jr.	Doctor of Divinity

CANDIDATES FOR DEGREES
Bachelor of Arts

David Scott Adkins	History
Patricia Ann Albert	Criminal Justice
Jeffrey Lawrence Aubert	Criminal Justice
Thomas Michael Berteletti	Criminal Justice
Brian Robert Bisacre	Criminal Justice
† Maurice Frank Bolduc, Jr.	Peace, War & Diplomacy Studies & History
Steven Andrew Bunting	Peace, War & Diplomacy Studies
Robert Douglas Burke	Criminal Justice
Harding Mudge Bush, Jr.	Peace, War & Diplomacy Studies
Dwight Christopher Cannon	French
Tamara Beth Center	Interdisciplinary Studies
Brian Scott Corcoran	Criminal Justice
Christopher Michael Coveney	Criminal Justice
Thomas Edward Cowern	Political Science
Dwight Almont Cross	History
John Christopher Crowley	History
† Renea Suzanne Curfman	Political Science
† Thomas Matthew Dalton	Political Science
Edmund Danis	Political Science
David John Demers	Peace, War & Diplomacy Studies
Todd Arlyn Dickie	Criminal Justice
Christopher James Dindo	Criminal Justice
G. Richard Donahue	Economics
Brian Patrick Dunn	Political Science
David Erick Elkowitz	Political Science
James Thomas Foye, Jr.	Criminal Justice
Daniel John Gallagher	Psychology
Steven Neville Gibbs	International Studies
Raxaben Gokani	International Studies, Spanish & History

† Army Distinguished Graduate

194

NORWICH UNIVERSITY

MILITARY COLLEGE OF VERMONT   AND   VERMONT COLLEGE

Northfield, Vermont 05663
(802) 485-5011

May 14, 1984

Mr. Sepp Ruschp
Mr. Mansfield Corporation
Mountain Road
Stowe, VT 05672

Dear Mr. Ruschp:

I am very pleased to inform you that you have been nominated by the
Board of Fellows to be a Fellow of Norwich University for an active term
of three years. The Board of Trustees has approved your nomination.

Norwich University would be most honored if you would accept membership.
You will be joining a group of distinguished Americans, alumni and
non-alumni who have indicated a willingness to assist the University
with their expertise and effort.

I will send complete information on the University and the Board of
Fellows shortly after we receive your reply. Please join us. Should
you have questions prior to making a decision, please call me at
802-485-5011, ext. 283 collect.

                                        Sincerely,

                                        James V. Galloway
                                        Major General, USA (Ret.)
                                        Vice President
                                        Liaison Officer

195

Mt. Mansfield COMPANY, INC.

STOWE, VERMONT
05672

SEPP RUSCHP
CHAIRMAN
OF THE BOARD OF DIRECTORS

TELEPHONE
AREA CODE 802
253-7311

May 22/1984

Major General James V. Galloway
Norwich University
Northfield, Vermont 05663

Dear General Galloway:

    Your letter telling me of my nomination to
serve for three years as a Fellow of Norwich
University, reached me in Florida.

    I feel it is a great honor and I accept this
membership with pleasure.

    I am returning to Vermont on June 4th. and
look forward to receiving the information
regarding the Board of Fellows.

            Sincerely,

            Sepp Ruschp.

NORWICH UNIVERSITY

MILITARY COLLEGE OF VERMONT AND VERMONT COLLEGE

NORTHFIELD, VERMONT 05663

(802) 485-5011

W. Russell Todd
President

May 31, 1984

Mr. Sepp Ruschp
Mt. Mansfield Corporation
Mountain Road
Stowe, VT 05672

Dear Mr. Ruschp:

It is my great pleasure to extend to you a warm and cordial welcome to the Norwich University family as a newly elected member of the Board of Fellows.

This action was taken by the Board of Trustees following nomination by Harvey B. Otterman, Jr., Chairman, Board of Fellows. Members of this board, distinguished Americans all, have provided Norwich with a broad spectrum of expertise which has greatly benefit.d the University and its students.

I am delighted that you accepted membership and will look forward to seeing you again.

Sincerely,

W. Russell Todd
President

WRT/s

197

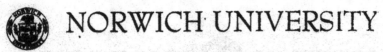

NORWICH UNIVERSITY

MILITARY COLLEGE OF VERMONT   AND   VERMONT COLLEGE

Northfield, Vermont 05663
(802) 485-5011

June 4, 1984

Mr. Sepp Ruschp
Mt. Mansfield Corporation
Mountain Road
Stowe, VT 05672

Dear Mr. Ruschp:

It is my pleasure and privilege to welcome you on behalf of the Fellows as
a new member of the Board of Fellows, Norwich University.

You will find a group of individuals, all distinguished in their respective
fields, who have one common interest: a respect and admiration for our
University and a desire to assist in any way they can.

The University will provide you with the Fellows information package which
will give you up-to-date information regarding the University. Please fill
out the enclosed biographical sheet and return it to the University along
with an 8x10 black and white, glossy photo of yourself (if this is not
convenient, any photo will do) attention of the Vice President who is the
University Liaison.

Should you have any questions, please do not hesitate to contact me or Vice
President James Galloway, who can be reached at 802-485-5011, ext. 282.

Sincerely,

Harvey B. Otterman, Jr.
Chairman, Board of Fellows

HBO/s

198

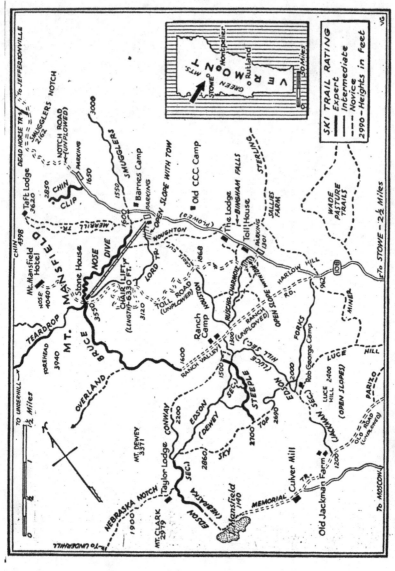

Map showing facilities at Stowe, Vt., where the new 6,330-foot lift has added to the popularity of this Green Mountain resort. Skiing usually is possible here from November until May. NYT 1/17/41

PART III

People Remembering People:

Major Players and Other Participants
during the Developmental Years
of the Ski Industry in Stowe

Meeting the ski train in Waterbury. (Courtesy of the Waterbury Historical Society.) At left: A classic ski poster from the Central Vermont Railroad promoting skiing at Stowe and Mad River Glen. (Reprinted with permission from the New England Ski Museum. For information, call 800-639-4181 or check out their web site at www.skimuseum.org.)

Stowe Historical Society Archives
Skiers Leaving the Waterbury Train Station for Stowe

Wendy Snow Parrish Collection
Skiers Arriving at the Green Mountain Inn

PEOPLE REMEMBERING PEOPLE

This part includes short biographies about major players, some memorable ski instructors, and local racers, as well as other dedicated people who helped build the resort known as "Stowe, Ski Capital of the East." These vignettes include stories from family members and friends who recall their experiences with these ski pioneers, along with obituaries, newspaper clippings, happenings noted in the Mt. Mansfield Ski Club newsletters, and other publications. Readers must remember that memories within these oral histories may differ based on the perspective of the story teller. Interviews were done face-to-face and by letter, telephone, and email. Each has given their permission to use their testimony in these profiles.

Stowe Historical Society Archives
Some Skiers Arriving by Canadian Colonial Airways

[Author note: Many newcomers had lots of questions about Stowe. One frequently asked was the origin of the stylized "S" in the Stowe logo. Sasha Maurer (1897-1961) created several silk-screen posters promoting the Stowe scene in the early 1950's. The earliest poster may have been "There's Always Snow in Stowe," with a stylized "S" in "Stowe." The "S" was soon refined to become the sweeping "S" logo we now see reproduced on almost anything printed, as "Stowe, Vermont, Ski Capital of the East." The Vermont Ski museum has a collection of these posters.]

CRAIG BURT, SR.
1882-1965

Called The Father of Stowe Skiing...The Maharajah
of Stowe. Lowell Thomas, promoter of skiing.

Although Thomas' quote greatly embarrassed Burt, this local boy
nevertheless was a major influence in bringing the sport of skiing to
Stowe. Although he was born in Waterbury VT, Stowe claims him as
a native son. By 1900, when Craig was 16, he was living on Main St.,
Stowe, with his aunt and uncle, Vera and Charles E. Burt and going
to school. But in 1902, his father, Frank O. Burt, died and Craig and
his brother Wayne T. Burt stepped in to carry on the family lumber
business and other enterprises, thereby curtailing Craig's education
at Norwich University, Class of 1904.

The Burts owned and operated one of the largest lumber
companies in the state. In 1883 C.E. and F.O. Burt had purchased
1000 acres of timberland in Stowe Hollow and built a steam mill to

manufacture boards and shingles. Their business built from there. When the big Mt. Mansfield Hotel in the village burned in 1889, the Burts purchased the former hotel property and erected a large steam mill approximately where the present Stowe Post Office and the Green Mountain Inn town houses now stand. They also harvested and processed timber in other mills built on their lands in various forested areas in town.

In those days, skis were an everyday necessity in taking care of outdoor domestic chores as well as the operation of the lumber works in the winter. These skis were fashioned from wooden slats or barrel staves or shaped boards. In 1906, Craig and others made themselves homemade skis for sport. By 1912, he was making skis to travel across his timberlands and is said to have been Stowe's first competent skier. When Craig was about 29 years old, he bought his first commercial skis, made by Northland.

In an October 2011 interview, Denise Burt Cushwa of Stowe, Craig's granddaughter, commented that her grandfather and others had recognized about the turn of the 20th century that the logging business had been in decline for many years and that the development of commercial skiing could provide new, much-needed employment opportunities. Thus began the drive to form a group of local men to aid in this goal. This was about 1920, the same time as the organization of the Stowe Ski Club which later became the Mt. Mansfield Ski Club officially incorporated in 1934. Dedicated to recreational skiing, the Ski Club built a ski jump, ice palace, skating rink, and ski and toboggan runs on Marshall Hill from which the Stowe Winter Carnivals of 1921, 1922, and 1923 were developed. Participants came mainly from Morristown and Waterbury. For those townspeople who preferred to stay warm inside instead of in an ice palace, plans were made and executed to create a minstrel show which performed in churches, clubs, and town meetings. This event raised $1000 which paid for expenses.

Craig Burt is considered the local visionary most responsible for promoting the sport of skiing in Stowe. As skiing caught on, he developed lodging and transportation to accommodate out-of-town skiers. Ranch camp, first a logging camp, was renovated to be the first hostel for skiers. There are many stories written about the legendary Ranch camp-turned-guest-house managed by Trim and Bert (Bertha) Conkling from 1938-1941. Housing was also offered to guests by wives of farmers. Trails, formerly logging roads, were turned into downhill ski runs. Financing for these improvements were by individual contributions, the Ski Club, and the Civilian Conservation Corps, who did the cutting of the trails. In addition to these concerns and all of the consequent activity, Roland Palmedo had already been bringing his friends who were members of the Amateur Ski Club of New York to Stowe to ski since 1931. He had become concerned about skiers injuries. He wrote to Craig and his group about organized assistance for ski injuries and encouraged the formation of a ski patrol. "Our Mt. Mansfield Ski Club elected Charles Lord and me to serve with President Frank Griffin and organize a patrol." writes Craig in his memoir. In 1936, the two, Burt and Lord, provided leadership in the Ski Patrol and defined some of the first procedures for rescuing injured skiers.

In June 1934, the Bennington Banner invited Burt to write them about what had been done at Stowe the past winter. As a result, an article was published in the Banner in 1935 claiming, "Winter sports have been made more of a success in Stowe the past winter probably than anywhere else in Vermont. People in Vermont have argued that the State of Vermont should pay more attention to winter business and that the publicity department of the State would be warranted in spending a little money to make public the advantage that Vermont has to offer winter vacationists."

In an excerpt from the article, "Stowe's Forty Years of Skiing: 1980 Stowe Winter Carnival," is this mention: "In honor of the arrival of Sepp Ruschp as their first ski instructor accepted by the Mt. Mansfield Ski Club in 1936, Craig Burt purchased a secondhand rope tow from a Jeffersonville [VT] man and installed it on a new slope at the Toll House. It was with a 1927 Cadillac motor...etc. Tow rates for that year, 1936, were $1.00 per day and $5.00 for the season."

Thanks to Craig Burt, Central Vermont Railways agreed to transport skiers from Boston and New York—bringing them on snow trains during the thirties and the World War II years. Burt was a busy man! He also tackled the Toll Road to the Summit House which was rebuilt, transforming the road for carriages to a road for automobiles. He was directly involved in the establishment and construction of the Lake Mansfield Trout Club and the Mt. Mansfield Electric Railroad between Waterbury and Stowe Village. Charlie Lord and he laid out the Bruce Ski Trail and other trails across "Burtland."

Denise Cushwa generously loaned this writer her Burt family papers. In this collection are many letters from family members to each other regarding the internal discussions among them having to do with the land sale of Burt properties to C.V. Starr in the late 1940's to 1950.

Lowell Thomas, the radio announcer who did much to popularize skiing in the 1930's, Charles M. (Minnie) Dole, Perry Merrill, and C.V. Starr corresponded with Burt regarding their individual concerns about various aspects of skiing and the ski patrol development. I. Munn Boardman, president of Hickok & Boardman Insurance and Real Estate in Burlington, who was a Mt. Mansfield Ski Club board member, wrote to Burt about "Sepp's new project and the Lift Co." concerns in November 1944.

In one lengthy letter to family members, about 1946-7, the writer, perhaps Carl or Craig Burt, Jr., wrote about the Burt Co. real estate holdings, aside from their lumber business, naming the Ranch Camp, The Fountain, and the Foster Place. The Fountain was a boarding house from 1927. The proprietress then was Lena (May) Norcross along with her husband Wilfred. Their daughter Zelta later ran the business until she retired in 1978. The Foster Place was a farm owned by Gilman Foster until he sold it to Craig Burt. In 1940 Jane Nichols Page happened along with Mr. Burt to inquire about starting up a guest house, by invitation only, to house skiers. A cousin of Jane, Ann (Morgan) (Simoneau) August, managed the Foster Place at different times…Ann described in a 2012 telephone interview that during "post-Foster Place managership," she ran a

Tea Room in the Eggleston's house across from the stable on the Mountain Rd. She was drawing in skiers by the dozens because of her serving of mouth-watering cinnamon toast, the fragrance of which wafted out to the main road. Her familiar nick-name developed in her family because when she was young she was shaped like a polly-wog, hence her nick-name, "Wogs." Ruthie Porter met her future husband, Alex Nimick at the Foster Place. Ruthie was the innkeeper there for three seasons.

Curiously, Wayne and his brother Craig lived in brick houses almost across the street from each other on Maple Street. Both men were involved in community affairs, were bank directors and church officers and town commissioners. Craig was a prime mover in the development of the Mt. Mansfield Electric Railroad (from 1894), a member-at-large with nine others elected at the annual meeting of the Mt. Mansfield Ski Club in 1938 and was instrumental in the organization of the Boy Scouts in town, a Mason, and a member of the Planning Commission. In 1939, Norwich University conferred upon Craig a Bachelor of Science degree in civil engineering in recognition of his many years of service to his community. One of the founders of the Lake Mansfield Trout Club was Craig O. Burt. The Torrent Fire Co. was organized before 1908. Among the officers named was second assistant to the chief; Craig O. Burt.

The Stowe Festival of Music, featuring the Trapp Family, paid this tribute to Mr. Burt in their bulletin in 1965 upon his death:

In Memoriam

Craig O. Burt

"When the Trapp Family first came to America 25 years ago, Craig Burt was their friend and counselor. The Trapp children took him to their hearts right away, and he became "Uncle Craig" to the whole family. He arranged their first concert in Stowe given at the local army camp.

Serving as an advisor in the early plans for the Stowe Festival of Music, he was to have been named Honorary Chairman and would have presented the Stowe Award to the Trapp Family on Friday evening.

Craig Burt, Sr. -- ski pioneer and icon of Stowe."

ROLAND PALMEDO
1895-1977

"Roland Palmedo, president of the Amateur Ski Club of New York, was one of the first winter guests at Stowe in 1932. He became close friends with my son Craig, Jr. and his skiing companions. He immediately arranged a trip with his club. This was the first group of skiers we entertained here..." Craig O. Burt, Sr.

Prolific writer for ski journals, investment banker, pioneer aviator, versatile sportsman, Roland Palmedo devoted his greatest energies to encouraging people to share his greatest passion, the sport of skiing. Palmedo founded and was the early president of the Amateur Ski Club of New York. He was the person who bestowed the name of "Nose Dive Annie" upon Anne Cooke, wife of J. Negley Cooke; because, before there were lifts at the mountain, she would climb the new Nose Drive trail every day, rain or shine, during the ski season.

Palmedo, a wealthy Wall Street financier, was a founder of the Mt. Mansfield Company at Stowe, as well as helped to found Mad River Glen, at Fayston, Vt. He was also a co-founder of the National Ski Patrol System in which he held member card #2. His heart was in skiing. He helped to organize ski resorts in South America, and held memberships in many other ski organizations in the US and abroad.

Within the archives of the Vermont Ski and Snowboard Museum there is a very important letter from Palmedo to the Stowe Postmaster [during the term of Lester Oakes] dated February 19, 1931 inquiring about what accommodations were available to skiers in Stowe as he was planning a ski trip with friends. "Is there a good, clean, comfortable inn in Stowe, open in the winter? What is its name? Is the road over Smuggler's Notch broken in winter?" he asked, as well as "Is there any shelter on top of the mountain where it is possible to spend the night?...", in a total of six questions. Apparently this letter was passed on to C.C. Stafford, secretary of the Stowe Civic Club for an answer. Another letter from Palmedo on March 4 thanked Stafford for his reply—writing that Palmedo "hoped there would be some good heavy snowfalls and cold weather so that a party of friends can come up and investigate your countryside as a winter sport center." This query must have been an eye-opener incentive as to the possibilities for developing skiing as a sport as extended from persons outside the environs of Stowe and Vermont.

In another letter written in November 1932 from Palmedo to Frank Griffin in Stowe, Palmedo writes that they are beginning to think about the coming ski season and getting up to Stowe again. "I have told innumerable people of what a delightful place it is and how hospitable everyone was, so that I expect you will have many more visitors from this part of the country this winter than before. I have written to Mr. Bodman and Mrs. Norcross to inquire about their rates for a little booklet to the members of the Amateur Ski Club of New York with a brief description of the various skiing centers we have discovered." "Mr. Bodman" is the proprietor of the Green Mountain Inn, and "Mrs. Norcross" is Lena (May) Norcross, the proprietor of The Fountain boarding house. Winfred and Lena Norcross were the parents of Zelta who also kept the Fountain running in later years.

Other correspondence between Palmedo, Cooke, and Charlie Lord is held at the New England Ski Museum pertaining to the chronology of the CCC and skiing from the mid-1940's post-war development, up until 1960.

Palmedo's philosophy was this: "I would like to see Vermont ski areas stay as simple and as rustic as possible. I don't think we need to import a lot of plush and sophisticated gimmicks. I am suspicious of man's efforts to improve nature. I can't see that ski resorts need belly dancers, discotheques and other side-show attractions."

C. Minot (Minnie) Dole in his Adventures in Skiing, 1965, page 61, writes: "To the best of my knowledge, the first ski patrol in the East, or the Unites states for that matter, had been organized by Roland three years previously at Stowe. Roland had been one of the few fortunates who skied in Europe and had witnessed the Swiss Parsenn Patrol in Switzerland. Now, the Parsenn Patrol is run by guides and the victim is required to pay for the services. That sort of thing would be out of the question here. Originally Roland had interested members of the Mt. Mansfield Ski Club in Stowe—Craig Burt, A. B. Coleman, Bill Mason, and others—in forming a patrol to be around on weekends when skiers might be on the mountain, locate toboggans, and be ready to assist any skiers that might need help. The Safety Committee felt that the patrol idea should be made more general. Roland did not stop his effort with the Stowe Patrol. But the reports that came from him urged other clubs to start patrols. The groundwork of a real patrol system, such as we have today, was taking shape within a year after the tragic death of Frank Edson which had led us to face the growing accident problem."

The then-new National Ski Hall of Fame was dedicated at Ishpeming, Michigan in early October 1991. Dr. Gretchen Besser contributed an article to the Stowe Reporter with respect to this event. Among all the artifacts and exhibits that are now housed at that facility is the multi-volume library donated by Roland Palmedo. He was a National Ski Hall of Fame inductee in 1968. He is said to have "discovered" Mt. Mansfield as a ski area, and developed Mad River Glen after he became disenchanted with Stowe. Then, in 2006, Palmedo was inducted into the Vermont Ski Museum Hall of Fame.

The State Warming Cabin

FRANK GRIFFIN
1890-1961

He wore many hats. Mr. Griffin's personality was such that he could interest competent men in developing this sport. Craig Burt

Craig O. Burt, Sr. wrote a delightful piece about the versatile Frank Griffin in the June 18, 1961, Vermont Sunday News which appeared just nine days before Frank's death. Frank had been a dairy farmer in Acton, Massachusetts before he became interested in promoting skiing in Stowe. After Frank retired from farming, Burt says, "Frank appeared in Stowe with three airplanes from Boston, to be joined by two Vermont planes. The five planes used the Rocky River Farm on the Mountain Road for a landing field. On October 26-28, there was an air meet. There were air rides—at times were constantly busy. This was at the time when airplanes were beginning to come into more general use and an air ride was a novelty. People came from all over northern Vermont for their first ride on an airplane."

215

In 1929, the Griffins moved to Stowe. Frank did not continue farming but instead he bought the then long-established men's store, Turk's, in Burlington. This was the retail store where Sepp Ruschp occasionally worked to earn money when new to Stowe and paying ski students were meager. Sepp rode to work in Burlington with Frank. In the Ruschp memoir he describes the value of Frank Griffin's participation in giving him a start in Stowe and in skiing. Frank, a director of the new Mt. Mansfield Ski Club, signed the immigration papers Ruschp needed to enter this country. When Ruschp docked in New York City, three Mt. Mansfield Ski Club members who lived in New York, met him, showed him around the city, and then later put him on the train to Burlington, Vermont. Frank met him at the train station. They had a lot to talk about!

Craig Burt gives major credit to Roland Palmedo and Frank Griffin for their interest in aiding and developing skiing in Stowe before World War II. Frank became the first president of the Mt. Mansfield Ski Club, which grew by leaps and bounds. He gained publicity by speaking at meetings in central and northern Vermont towns at every opportunity. He recruited men to ski and work in the developing ski industry in Stowe, and searched for advice from other ski pioneers, many formerly from Europe, such as Erling Strom at Lake Placid, and Otto Schniebs, the Dartmouth coach of that time, among others.

During the early 1930's, directors of the new ski club would meet to discuss various phases of developing skiing in town. These men came from Burlington, Northfield, Montpelier, and Waterbury, long before interstate highways, driving home after dark. No one expected to be reimbursed for expenses in this effort or financial reward. As Craig Burt, explained: "These men should be listed and the list preserved as an example of how progress may be had without money, with knowledge acquired by experience, and without the money bags of our good Uncle Sam. Uncle did come in though, and, later, substantially so. After World War I, and during the depression of 1930, he had a lot of men with nothing to do...we had the work and he had the men," hence, the Civilian Conservation Corps to Stowe to do this work."

Clearly, the development of skiing in Stowe could not have been accomplished without the efforts of the genial and dynamic Frank E. Griffin. He died on June 27, 1961, at Burlington, Vt., at the age of 71 years. He and his wife are buried in Pittsfield, MA cemetery.

Courtesy of Judith A. Gale, Granddaughter
As a Young Man Trapping

GEORGE W. GALE
1886-1964

*The Mt. Mansfield Ski Club incorporated in January 1934 to
promote interest in nature and provide trails for skiing and other
facilities for this sport in Vermont.* Signed by Frank E. Griffin, Fred
M. Pike, Leon G. Bodman, Craig O. Burt, and George W. Gale.

Another member of the core group of local promoters of commercial
skiing in Stowe, along with Charlie Lord, Frank Griffin, Craig Burt,
Sr., and Albert Gottlieb, was George Warren Gale. The three sons
of George W. and Angie (Grout Harris) Gale also became enamored
with skiing: Richard H. Gale born 1918, Robert G. Gale born 1919,
and John S. Gale born 1922. Dr. John is the sole survivor of the
three brothers. Dr. John's daughter, Judith Gale, has compiled his
stories about growing up in Stowe and because he tells his story best
about his father George W. Gale, we will quote liberally from that
manuscript.

George Warren Gale is the brother of Nina Gale who married Howard E. Shaw in March 1895. This was that same year that Howard established the General Store in his own name. In fact, George W. worked for over 50 years with his brother-in-law at the store buying and selling skis for the store, and was also a representative of the Vermont Mutual Fire Insurance Co. in town. He was one of the Village trustees.

At the age of 8 or 10, as John relates, "we skied on barrel staves strapped onto our boots with rubber bands or inner tube strips. At first we skied on the level, but by the age of 11, I was skiing on the hills around Stowe. Marshall's Hill, [south of School St.], was where we would ski and set up slalom flags and practice slalom." That was before the Elementary School was built. By junior high they would climb with skins up Mt. Mansfield after school to get one run in before dark. No lifts then.

Shaw's store was the first Stowe business to sell ski equipment. Frank Griffin had a ski and clothing shop, Turk's, in Burlington, and Dr. John Gale remembers there was some cooperation between Shaw's and Griffin in those sales. Dr. John adds, "Having three sons who were among the early skiers in Stowe, Dad had to have been involved in equipment questions."

"Our first real skis were wooden, made by Northland Co. and soon followed by a company in Waterbury that earlier made such things as scythe snaths. When steel edges for skis became popular, the men who worked at Shaw's started putting them on the wooden skis in the basement of the store. I [John] worked there some during Christmas and spring vacations from college. The edges came in steel strips about 8-10 inches long, with beveled holes about every 1 ½ to two inches; we used a router to remove a strip of wood from each side of the ski, and then drilled holes for each small flat head screw, and fastened the screws by hand. The system worked amazingly well and made a great difference in one's ability to ski on icy or hard packed snow..."

When asked whether it was mostly local people who went up to the Ranch Camp, skiing in and out, John replied, "At first, but then people like Roland Palmedo and other people from New York got involved in promoting skiing in Stowe because they knew Craig Burt."

George W. Gale is distinguished as being Mansfield's first "official" snow-conditions observer. Dr. Gale said that his father did not ski very much. Sometimes his father would go up to Ranch Camp with us on skis. "He didn't use poles. Well, he had one pole, actually a peavy handle which was a device for moving logs… which he would put between his legs and sort of sit on it as a brake going down hill with the pointed arm digging into the snow."

Stowe Historical Society Archives
Charlie Lord, Left, with Ab Coleman, Right

ABNER COLEMAN
1904-2000

A life-long native of Montpelier, Abner Coleman worked for the Vermont Highway Department for 43 years. That is where Abner first met Charlie Lord who also worked there in the 1920's. Arthur Goodrich, Charlie, and Abner were a core group who "prowled" the Green Mountains on skis from the mid-twenties, writes Tom Davis in Vermont Life, winter 1989 issue. They searched for the best place for their kind of skiing. "Mansfield was chosen because it was the most accessible, not because it was the highest peak in the state," said Charlie. Most of the mountain was state forest property or Burt Lumber Company land. Also, the Summit House was a summer destination built near the Nose with the Toll Road for accessibility. And, more importantly, there was plenty of snow in the wintertime.

Abner Coleman remembered in his interview with Tom Davis in 1989 when he and Charlie climbed the Toll Road one of the first few times, that they stopped high on the mountain near the Nose, elevation, 4,062 feet. Coleman said, "It would be kind of fun if we had a ski trail down through there." Thus began the idea for the precipitous Nose Dove as the earliest racing trail in the East. They began marking trails, one of which became the Nose Dive built 1934-1935. Then State Forester, Perry Merrill, named it the Nose Dive.

An early member of the Mt. Mansfield Ski Club founded in 1933, Abner published its first official newsletter on January 25, 1935, known as the Mt. Mansfield Ski Club Bulletin, later the MMSC Newsletter. His major contribution was his column, "Around the Mountain." By 1948, the newsletter editorship had passed to Luther Booth, long-time leader of the Mt. Mansfield Ski Patrol. Abner continued to write many articles for this journal of a historical nature as well as current developments at the Mountain. At the annual meeting of the Mt. Mansfield Ski Club, May 9, 1947, A.W. Coleman was elected president. In the Newsletter of November 1993, the 60th anniversary edition, is a photo of early ski instructors on skis, pre-1940. It includes Sepp Ruschp, Lionel Hayes, Kerr Sparks, and Abner Coleman.

Blake Harrison described the carving of ski trails in his article in Vermont History, Summer-Fall 2003, and quotes Abner Coleman: "As ski promoter and trail builder, A.W. Coleman once reminded a group of engineers, 'While Vermont's terrain is naturally favorable for winter sports, certain developments must be made before the possibilities may be realized fully.'" In a subsequent article for Vermont Life, he added, "Although Nature provides the basic ingredients, her unaided efforts are not quite enough... The Hills are honey-combed with open fields, lumber roads, foot trails, and pastures over which the snow drifts invitingly. The mountains, however, are mostly heavily wooded and there the trails for skiing must be carefully designed and laboriously cleared." And those were the descriptions of the beginnings of trail clearing and subsequent development of the Mountain.

[Author's note: The Colemans were back yard, over-the-fence neighbors of ours when we lived in Montpelier in the mid-1960s.

Mildred Coleman often commented to me that Ab was out of the house at the crack of dawn weekends, or whenever he could, to ski at Stowe in the wintertime. We had no knowledge then about how extensively he had helped to shape the sport of skiing at Stowe. PLH]

Courtesy of Karin W. Gottlieb, Daughter
In Front of His Tent in the Early 1930's

ALBERT W. GOTTLIEB
1904-1978

*"He has been interested in preserving the natural beauty
of state lands and active in promoting the wise use of all
natural resources..." The Stowe Reporter,* Oct. 29, 1970

Al came to Vermont from Schenectady, N.Y. in 1933 after graduating
with a B.S. degree from New York State College of Forestry in 1926
and a M.S. in forestry from Harvard in 1927. The Depression cut
short his plans to earn a PhD.

At the age of 19, he began competing in long distance races. In
December 1924, during a meet at Syracuse University in New York,
he raced against Paavo Nurmi of Finland, who had won several
medals at the Summer Olympics in Paris. Al surprisingly won the
exhibition race against Nurmi. He gave up his competitive running
after graduation in 1927.

Because it was very difficult to find work during the Depression,
Al was out of work for a while. Like many young men of his time, he

224

went wherever he could find work. He came to Vermont to work in a state government program called the CCC. His daughter relates that his first assignment was to climb up 25 of the state's mountain peaks to inspect the fire towers. Al was a forestry foreman in the CCC, 191st Company, living in a tent located in the Little River section of Waterbury. His job was to supervise the clearing of trails for some of the first ski trails on Mt. Mansfield. He married Ruth Flickinger in 1934 and they moved into a house on Maple Street where his daughter, Karin, and her husband now reside. Karin shared in a document about her father that Al worked with Charlie Lord who was the civil engineer and when Al was offered a job as assistant state forester in 1935, it pretty much ended his direct involvement with mountain history.

Karin states that her father was one of the first directors of the Mt. Mansfield Ski Club in its early days, and was a founder of the Ski Patrol. Under his tenure, caches were set up all over the mountain— little roofed containers with corrugated metal toboggans in them and some basic first aid equipment such as splints. Until the '60's at least, the caches were still visible, crumbling on the sides of trails from the ski area side of Mansfield, down the Bruce trail, and as far down as the Trout Club. Her father said the corrugated roofing toboggans tracked very well, but were nearly impossible to turn. That was the time when the first phone system on the mountain went in so accidents could be called in from trailside. These were military field phones. Brian Lindner had this to say about Al in an article:

"For the 1937 season, Al Gottlieb took over as director of the patrol, and set about creating a toboggan-cache system. With the help of the Vermont Forest Service, it was built around Stowe and not just on Mt. Mansfield. At least three of these caches still exist. On the Mountain, Gottlieb secured permission from the state forestry service officials to use fire phones to report emergencies, and this may very well have been the first ski patrol emergency phone system in North America."

Al was promoted to State Forester in 1955 and eventually became Director of Forests. He was a key figure in the development of policies and programs providing a balanced approach toward the adequate protection, proper management and prudent multiple uses of the forest resource. Al served as secretary to the Forest Conservation and Taxation Commission, and laid the ground work which led to the signing of a cooperative forest fire protection agreement with Quebec and New Brunswick Provinces in Canada.

Residing in Stowe, he was very active in town government, was town moderator, tree warden, chairman of the Planning Commission, and president of the Stowe Community Church, as well as president of the PTA.

"When Dad reminisced about Sepp's coming to Stowe, he always recalled with amusement Sepp's first daylight look at the area, 'But where are the mountains?'" Karin recalls another story about her Dad when he was hiking up the S-53 trail and he spied a totally out-of-control skier coming down. "He stepped off-trail out of the way. The guy crashed, rolled, and came to a stop near Dad— all but unrecognizable for the snow all over his (wool) clothes, face, and hat. A pair of glasses lay in a snow bank. Dad took a stab and called, 'That you, Ab?' 'Yeeeaaaaah', came the answer in a disgusted tone. Dad never forgot how comical that was." That guy was Abner Coleman!

Merrill, State Forester, smiles his approval of

Stowe Historical Society Archives

PERRY H. MERRILL
1894-1993

Often called the Patron Saint of Vermont's State Parks and Alpine Ski Areas and the Man who put Vermont on Skis. Rutland Herald's list of the most influential Vermonters of the 20th century.

Perry Merrill of Montpelier served for nearly 50 years in various positions in the Vermont State Forests and Parks system. He was first the state forester, later director, and then commissioner of Forests and Parks. He is said to have been "probably the twentieth-century's single most important figure in shaping modern Vermont's priorities in forestry use and land preservation, and assuring public spaces for recreation and leisure."

After graduating from Syracuse University in the College of Forestry, he went to France during World War I with the ambulance corps, and in 1918 was appointed inspector general of prisoner of war camps in Germany. In 1919 he returned from the war and accepted an appointment as district forester in the Northwest District of the Vermont Forest Service. Through the 1920's he earned a master's degree in Forestry, served as assistant state forester, and by 1929 became state forester. When the Civilian Conservation Corps was created in 1933 Merrill was appointed supervisor of the Corps responsibilities in Vermont. Charlie Lord recalled when Merrill, as state forester, was looking for projects, and word filtered down to Lord and Abner Coleman at the State Highway Dept., that if they marked out a trail or two the CCC might do the work. "You presented your case to Perry Merrill and if he liked what you had, that was it." During this time, in 1935, he was elected Mayor of Montpelier

Merrill's vision for Vermont was founded on the conservation policies of Theodore Roosevelt. He was an aggressive promoter and leader in efforts to purchase land and preserve it for the wood products industry, wildlife habitat, and public use of these resources by Vermonters within a state park system. Merrill supported the creation of ski areas on state-owned land by leasing the land to the developers. The revenue generated from these leases brought in millions of dollars to the state.

Merrill retired in 1966 as commissioner of forests and parks and ran with Richard Snelling as his running-mate for lieutenant governor, which was unsuccessful. He then served two terms in the House of Representatives. He has several books to his credit, the two chief titles of which are, Vermont under Four Flags: a History of the Green Mountain State 1635-1975 (1975), and A History of the Civilian Conservation Corps 1933-1942 (1981).

Middlebury College conferred upon Perry Merrill an honorary doctorate degree in 1955, and in 1964, the 30th anniversary of skiing; he received an award in recognition of his distinguished service to skiing.

CORNELIUS VANDER STARR
1892-1968

*Neil Starr's first visit to Stowe...comes to me as clearly as if
it were only yesterday, although it was almost 25 years ago.
His inquiry to me was "Can one become a good skier at
somewhat over 50 years of age, if he is not the best coordinated
athlete?" He had the energy and determination to accomplish
the almost unbelievable. He became not only an excellent
skier, but also a skiing mountaineer.* Sepp Ruschp, 1968

*There was a strong streak of compassion in him,
which is a wonderful trait to balance the hard-
nosed businessman.* Maurice R. Greenberg

Cornelius Vander Starr was the key figure in the evolution of the
Mt. Mansfield Company. Without him, Sepp Ruschp, would not
have had the financial backing to develop the facilities into the
successful operation that it became. Although Mr. Starr came from
modest beginnings, he rose to become a global entrepreneur. He

was born at Ft. Bragg, Mendocino County, California in 1892, the son of Cornelius "Con" Vanderstar and Frances Arabelle "Belle" Hart of Tennessee. C.V. "Neil" Starr did not know his father long as his father passed away at nearby Noyo, CA 31 Mar 1895 at age 33 of la grippe and pneumonia. Neil was only two years old. Con's obituary appeared in the Ft. Bragg Advocate stating he was "the hotelkeeper at Noyo, born in Illinois where his parents then resided in Washington Heights, Cook County. He had gone to Illinois for a visit in 1889, from Ft. Bragg, then a frontier town, married in Illinois and had three sons. He subsequently moved back to the west coast." Belle then married John Vander Starr, her brother-in-law, at Ft. Bragg in June 1897. They were married only seven years when John passed away in June 1904 at Ft. Bragg. John/Jack, also of Noyo, was cited in his obituary in the Advocate as having operated a liquor business for many years with his brother, Con, at Ft. Bragg. Belle married a third time, Thomas Shelton, in 1911 at Ft. Bragg.

Cornelius and Con Starr, with brother, John, registered as voters in May 1888 as recorded in the 1890 Great Register of Voters of California. The Starr brothers, along with William J. Hart brother of Belle, were all living in the same household in Ft. Bragg in 1910. William Hart was working in the newly-established railroad shop, trains having been introduced just before 1910 which greatly aided shipping for the logging industry.

When Neil was nineteen, about 1911, he set up a shop in Ft. Bragg which carried "fine candies, ice cream, and light sundries." A photo of the store front is included in images in the 1970 publication memorializing C. V. Starr, by C.V. Starr & Co, showing Neil in his apron with his dog, Bob. He sold this business and moved to San Francisco where he enrolled at the University of California at Berkeley where he studied for a year and then left the university. Starr told his good friend Clyde Ware that he did not have time to spend four years at a university. He had waited on tables to pay his way at school that year, sold automobile insurance, and nights he studied for the California Bar exam, which he passed in 1915.

[Inquiries about Starr's year at Cal-Berkeley were made to Wei Chi Poon and Jianye He, reference librarians at the East Asian Ethnic Library at Cal-Berkeley which brought up the fact that they have no file on C.V. Starr in spite of the fact that the special collection and donation of a library in C.V. Starr's name was dedicated in October 2007.

Starr served with the U.S. Army 24th Machine Gun Battalion during World War I, 1917-1918, but never saw service overseas, which he regretted. Instead, Starr became a clerk with the Pacific Mail Steamship Company in Yokohama, Japan. Later, with only 300 yen in his pocket, Starr traveled to Shanghai where he worked for several insurance businesses. In 1919, he founded American International Group, then known as "American Asiatic Underwriters."

Starr was the first Westerner in Shanghai to sell insurance to the Chinese. After his business became successful in Asia, he expanded to other markets, including Europe, the Middle East and Latin America. In 1926, Starr opened his first office in the United States – American International Underwriters (AIU), which was based in New York. AIU wrote insurance on American risks outside the U.S. and thus expanded globally. Starr is not found in the U.S. 1920 Federal census, perhaps because he had journeyed to Yokohama, Japan after his Army service. By 1930, Starr resides in Oakland, Alameda County, California, living with his brothers, and his mother and step-father, Thomas Shelton. In January 1937, he married Mary H. Malcolm.

About 1939, when business in the Orient became difficult with the onset of World War II, the company headquarters was moved to New York City, and about this time he expanded the business to Latin America. Shortly after the beginning of World War II, he registered for draft in 1942 at age 49. In early 1949, AIG left China as Mao Ze Dong led the advance of the Communist People's Liberation Army on Shanghai.

According to the in-house memorial publication of 1970, Starr amazed his friends by taking up the new sport of downhill skiing in

1938 at the age of 46. Five years later during the winter of 1943, Neil and Mary Starr made their first visit to Stowe to ski Mt. Mansfield after having skied at several major ski areas in the West, and in Switzerland, over the years. They persuaded other friends to come along on a trip to Stowe. One day that season, he was in line waiting for the single-chair lift ride up the mountain and criticized the excessive delay with the crowds jamming the loading dock. Starr asked Sepp Ruschp of the Ski School why something was not done about the congestion. Mr. Ruschp then told CVS about his dream of a ski resort to match those in his native Alps. Starr was told, "There just isn't enough money!" Starr asked, "Can't something be done to straighten out things up there?"–meaning the possible consolidation of the five entities which make up the facilities at Mt. Mansfield. Ruschp answered, "Right now I am trying to raise money to build a new lift." On the spot Starr offered to put up enough money to give Ruschp a controlling interest, if Ruschp could raise the rest. In 1950, they had reincorporated the five separate companies into the Mt. Mansfield Co. with Starr a president. The merged companies were The Lodge, the Smuggler's Notch Lift Co. which included the T-bar, Palmedo's Mt. Mansfield Lift Co., the Mt. Mansfield Hotel Co. which included the Ski School, and the Burt Lumber Co. land. By 1952, Starr's total investment was $1 million. The lifts were greatly improved, and Mr. Starr always waited his turn in the lift lines.

In 1951, Neil was instrumental in the success of the first international ski races at Stowe. Starr personally arranged to have such notable skiers as Stein Ericksen, Chico Igaya and others brought to Stowe to participate.

It was under Starr's leadership that Stowe became known as the "Ski Capital of the East." But Starr stepped down as president in 1953 and personally nominated Sepp Ruschp to succeed him. Starr remained as a director and chairman of the board.

CVS was a no-nonsense businessman. He traveled extensively. Ship passenger lists on <u>Ancestry.com</u> record original entries of his many trips to world financial centers.

The memorial book describes Starr's last years within several personal testimonials. After his first heart attack, although he refused to acknowledge it as such, Starr had to give up skiing and tennis. He spent much of his time at his Brewster, NY estate, "Morefar," but passed away December 20, 1968, at age 76, in his Fifth Avenue, New York City, apartment.

C. MINOT "MINNIE" DOLE
1899-1976

"My first visit to Stowe was in the 1934-5 season. After that the winter calendar was pretty well outlined for me. On Fridays, leave the office in New York at 5 PM on the train for [home at] Greenwich, Ct., start driving at 6 PM, arrive Stowe about 2 a.m. and to the Fountain or Green Mountain Inn. Ski all day Saturday and finally tear ourselves loose on Sunday about 4 PM; a steak in Danbury in the late hours, and then to the office early Monday. That was S.O.P. for several years to come." Dole

Another major player in the overall development of the various aspects of the skiing history of Stowe was Minnie Dole, as he was known. In 1936 Minot Dole, an insurance broker from Greenwich, CT, with his office in New York City, was injured in a ski accident in Stowe, VT, when he broke his leg on the Toll Road. He was evacuated by his friends on a piece of corrugated tin roofing material. There is a great deal of background information about Mr. Dole, but his article

234

in the December 15, 1948 Mt. Mansfield Ski Club's Skiing newsletter authored by him, is almost as good as a face-to-face interview.

In that light-hearted piece he wrote for that issue, Minnie Dole notes that it was in January 1936 on his first visit of that winter that he "earned his broken bone pin" on the Toll Road, skiing with his close friend, Frank Edson. "It's always amused me that the Toll Road is classified as a novice trail. I'd rather run the Nose Dive twenty-five times than that [Toll Road] muscle-screamer once." He then describes his skiing accident coming down with Frank's help with his broken leg on a piece of tin and his fanny dragging in the snow. After hospitalization, he spent 15 weeks on crutches, during which time Frank Edson tragically died in a ski race on the Ghost Trail at Pittsfield, MA. Roger Langley, of the Amateur Ski Club of New York immediately asked Dole to lead a safety committee to study causes and prevention of ski accidents.

In his memoir, We Lived in Stowe, Craig O. Burt, Sr. described how they "snared Minnie Dole for a ski patrol for an upcoming race the next day." A group of New York guests were gathered in the Alpen Rosa, an annex to the old Toll House, discussing this and that. The subject of the ski patrol came up. So they appointed Minot Dole on the spot to take care of the patrol. Because of the short notice, Dole had had no time to give any thought to this work. "In the spirit of fun he accepted," said Burt. Dole became very interested in the job and "here it was that he became inoculated with the germ that later helped him to become the father of the National Ski Patrol."

The Craig O. Burt papers also include correspondence with Dole addressed to him at the Amateur Ski Club, at his insurance brokerage business, New York City. In an April 24, 1937 letter, Burt details his and Frank Griffin's concerns "as to the care or possibly the lack of care of different skiers. There is a quiet inquiry being made in the qualifications and methods of some of those responsible for treatment [following accidents] and we will advise you later what works out." Further concerns included "checking the number of people whose tendency is to point their skis downhill regardless of the consequences, and second, the growing tendency of people to seek advice as to suitable locations for them to ski within their ability." Burt had then served as the leader of the Mt. Mansfield ski patrol for the past year.

After the Edson tragedy and his own suffering, Minnie Dole's newly-formed safety committee began to collect data involving skiing accidents, reported the results in a publication, and made many recommendations. This culminated in the establishment of the first ski patrols who were trained to help skiers, to help conduct ski races, and to perform first aid on the slopes. The new National Ski Patrol established in 1938 named Roger Langley Patrolman #1, Roland Palmedo Patrolman #2, and Minnie Dole, Patrolman #3.

Note the lace boot, wooden ski and pre-safety binding era of this early Mt. Mansfield Ski Patrol picture. The building seen faintly in the right center background was the old summer hotel at the top of the Toll Road.

Near the end of 1940, Minnie Dole and John E. P. Morgan had convinced the U.S. Army to create a special military unit trained for winter fighting in the mountains. The now-legendary 10th Mountain Division was born. C. Minot "Mint" Dole, Jr., son of Minnie, commented: "Dad had a government contract as the only civilian agency to screen applicants for potential 10th Mountain soldiers. Each potential candidate had to have three letters of recommendation attesting to their skiing and mountaineering skills. Candidates went directly to Camp Hale in west-central Colorado. Dad screened 25,000 men within the required time-frame of 60 days which were the core of the First Battalion, 87th Regiment. The unit was activated November 15, 1941. The 87th had the highest IQ of any army unit at that time. Men were all from large schools and northern colleges, members of the National Ski Patrol, and amateur ski clubs such as the Hochgebirge Ski Club from Boston."

Stowe Historical Society Archives
"Minnie" with Lowell Thomas

According to Gretchen Besser in her 1983 volume, *National Ski Patrol*: Samaritans of the Snow, "from the Mt. Mansfield ski area alone there were approximately 30 men who enlisted into the mountain troops, the 10th Mountain Division, during World War II, because they were able to ski and endure the hardships of this outfit."

Mint Dole, son of Minnie, spoke on behalf of his father at the October 2010 dedication of the 10th Mountain soldier memorial located at the plaza crossroads between the main Stowe Mountain Resort and Spruce Camp base lodge, an appropriate location for exposure to many visitors. Minnie Dole took a leadership role in helping local and national ski safety programs as well as the establishment of the specialized 10th Mountain Division, major contributions to skiing safety and military defense during World War II. Dole served from 1941-1945. He was honored across the ski industry with plaques, and other awards. A trail was dedicated in his honor at the Berkshire East Ski Area. Dole was inducted into U.S. National Ski Hall of Fame in 1958 and the Colorado Ski & Snowboard Hall of Fame in 1977.

Stowe Historical Society Archives

In the newsletter of the Vermont Ski and Snowboard Museum issue of Vol. 12, #1, Tenth Anniversary Edition, calendar of upcoming events, is posted their new inductees for the October 21st induction dinner at the Trapp Family Lodge which included Minnie Dole, Trowbridge Elliman, Leslie Thompson Hall, Tiger Shaw, Linda Adams, and Sporty Bell.

J. NEGLEY "COOKIE" COOKE
1908-1978

"He must have been one of the best salesmen who ever lived, and fortunate was the business, association, or civic cause to which he applied his prodigious energies and organizational talent."

J. Negley Cooke, better known as "Cookie," was a major financial player in the early development of the sport of skiing. He was a co-founder and a director of the Mt. Mansfield Co. as well as a vice-president and a director of the Mad River Corp. In 1938, he worked with Roland Palmedo to form the Mt. Mansfield Co. These two men created the first aerial chair lift in the eastern United States. Cookie served as a director of the Mt. Mansfield Co. from 1938 until 1974, before he died in 1978.

Skiing became his passion. He and his wife, Ann, grew to love Stowe and built a house in 1959 on Spruce Peak to be closer to the Mountain. This house was razed, along with the Henry Simoneau house, in spring 2003 to make way for pod-housing projects for the new Stowe Mountain Resort. The Cooke's supported many aspects of the ski scene at the Mountain including the loan of their station wagon to be used as an ambulance which was outfitted with a mattress and blankets.

In addition, to helping found the Mt. Mansfield Company and Mad River Glen in Waitsfield, he was devoted to the U.S. Ski Team serving as trustee and honorary vice chairman of the board of the U.S. Ski Educational Foundation This led to organizing local programs and training for athletes around the country for the U.S. ski teams performing in international competitions, including the Winter Olympics. He knew how to fund-raise. In 1968, he organized the first New York Ski Ball, and in 1971, Cookie became the first recipient of the John J. Clair Memorial Award because of his dedication to the sport of skiing in this country. In January 1978, shortly before his death in August, he became an honored member of the National Ski Hall of Fame for his contribution to the sport.

Ann Bonfoey married J. Negley Cooke in 1928 after which they moved to Vermont in the mid-1930s. They were both avid skiers, and Vermont was where she began her racing career. Some elderly residents to this day well remember her as colorful "Nose Dive Annie." [See accompanying essay.]

Cookie married Nancy Reynolds (1915-2005) in 1941. Nancy began skiing while she attended Bennington College in Bennington, Vt., Class of 1937. She was one of America's expert women skiers in the late 1930's and early 1940's. She earned national titles in slalom events, was Closed Downhill and Combined Champion in 1941, and was on the US Women's Ski Team for the FIS Championships in 1938. However, competitions were curtailed because of World War II. For six years, from 1944-1950, she taught skiing for the Brattleboro, Vermont Outing Club. They both worked with Roland Palmedo in making the first chair lift on Mt. Mansfield become a reality. Nancy Reynolds Cooke was elected an Honored Member of the U.S. National Ski & Snowboard Hall of Fame in 1972. Nancy later married Gordon M. Booth in January 1985.

Stowe Historical Society Archives
Charmoz Was a 1936 Olympian for France

JACQUES CHARMOZ
1911-1981

Charmoz taught English to Sepp Ruschp after Sepp
arrived in the US. Sepp Ruschp Memoir.

In January 2012, the Stowe Historical Society was contacted by Mike Leach, of Stowe, to help identify some snapshots sent to him by Frederique Charmoz, daughter of Jacques Charloz Charmoz who was one of the first ski instructors and arrived shortly after Sepp Ruschp in 1936. This contact opened up an interesting and insightful view into the life of Mr. Charmoz.

When Charmoz first began to ski he would draw and sell cartoons to magazines to pay his expenses. This was at the age of 15 years when he was traveling from Paris to Chamonix. His cartoons later appeared in a book written by Roland Palmedo many years ago, his daughter said.

A.W. Coleman, editor of the Mt. Mansfield Ski Club newsletter of December 12, 1938, reports that "Sepp Ruschp has made many friends during the past two years running his ski school with headquarters at the Toll House. His assistants are Ali Mauracher, late of the Greenwich Outing Club, and Jacques Charmoz, the resident instructor at The Lodge and a familiar figure at the mountain." In a January 1939 newsletter, Coleman again reports that during the week after Christmas 1938, Sepp, Jacques and Ali gave among them over 500 ski lessons..."The school is clicking perfectly, and everyone is enthusiastic over the way it is being run. It is hoped that our members will not miss this opportunity for increasing their skiing enjoyment."

Ms. Charmoz hopes to write a biography of her father and the many facets of his varied interests and abilities. Jacques was born in 1911 in Paris, France. By the age of 20 years he was mountaineering, skiing including racing and competitions, along with other adventurers from France, Germany, Switzerland, Italy and America. Frederique found his pilot's license in Chile in 1936 at the Santiago Aeroclub Museum, and his logbook in Indochina. He flew with the Canadian Ferry Command of the Royal Air Force during World War II. Jacques first met her mother in Malibu, CA in 1946 after the war, where he was then training on Boeing airplanes. He made exploration movies between his travels in South American and North America, she thinks, for a Pan American film company, but is not sure of the exact name of the company.

Stowe Historical Society Archives
Lowell Thomas Broadcast at the Green Mountain Inn

GARY FISHER
1924-2012

"When asked what he enjoyed most about skiing, he said, 'Going fast! " Obituary, *Stowe Reporter*, June 28, 2012.

Gary was first a ski patrolman and then became a ski instructor. He was on Sepp Ruschp's short list of people at the end of his memoir about whom Sepp may have wanted to develop additional information.

At age 14, Gary was a star on the Stowe High School ski team. His winter occupations started at the Mountain in 1945 as a ski instructor and then becoming to the ski school director and the first manager at Toll House.

In an email from Hesterly Buckley in March 2010, she recalls various employees of the Mountain Co. "Gary was the head of the beginner and intermediate ski school for many years. All he had to do was watch someone walk out to the bottom of the hill and he knew just which class to put him or her into!"

Helen Wilhelm Wright describes Gary as always being at the Toll House when she was a ski instructor there, including directing the massive traffic snarls on the busiest days.

In later years, Gary worked for Ed Billings doing carpentry, along with Eric Berringer, Ted Tormey, Billy Adams, and Peter Haslam, Jr. "Gary did mostly finish work as his knees were shot from teaching skiing for so many years," recalls Peter.

Gary married Joy Hermann in 1952 at Stowe when his occupation was "ski instructor." Joy was one of the few documented women who were students at the private school, "West Hill," in the 1940's, better known as "The Bride's School." The women were taught homemaking skills by the owners, Mrs. Johan (Sonja) Bull and her friend Countess Susie Sparre. The carrot which attracted the young women was the newly-popular winter sport of skiing. This is where she met her future husband.

After 37 years at the Mt. Mansfield Co., Gary retired. He was honored in 2011 with a 50-year pin as a member of the Professional Ski Instructors of America. He had also been a ski instructor examiner.

Sadly, Gary Fisher passed away June 18, 2012 at his home. And three months earlier, Joy had passed away on March 14, 2012.

Courtesy of Mary Skelton
The Madison Square Garden Jumping Team
First Left Front Kneeling

CLEM CURTIS
1910-2012

At this writing, Clem has just surpassed his 102nd birthday
May 2012, with his wife Anne not far behind.

Clem Curtis and his wife Anne Courtemanche were both from Lebanon, NH, where they married on Anne's birthday, September 25, 1944. Clem was then on a one week furlough from in the U.S. Army's 10th Mountain Division troops where he first tested snowshoes and ran snow tractors on a glacier near Lake Louise in British Columbia. Then he was sent to Camp Hale in Colorado where he taught skiing and rock climbing. He returned to a new posting to a training base in Texas, but was honorably discharged before the rest of his division was sent to active duty in Italy. He and Anne then moved to Stowe in September 1945 where he had previously worked as a ski instructor and took a position as an assistant manager at the Mountain Company

On Feb. 22, 2010, correspondence began with Mary Curtis Skelton, the daughter of Clem and Anne Curtis when she contributed notes written by her father about his early skiing experiences, his various responsibilities at the Mount Mansfield Co., for which he worked for 12 years until 1956, and Clem's partnership with Melvin Bedell to found Curtis and Bedell, a successful building construction company.

Mary writes by email, "The first installment is from a notebook, handwritten by Dad. Not dated, but had to be around 1995, judging by his handwriting and notes in the margin,

'It was sixty years ago that I was invited to do some exhibition ski jumping in Boston Garden, Madison Square Garden, and other places. I couldn't believe I was skiing in the Gardens until I was there. The main arena was used for demonstrating ski jumping, a bit of slalom, and downhill. There was a ribbon of snow about 8' wide around the perimeter of the arena for cross country demonstrations and snowshoe racing. Macy's department store had a double runner sleigh drawn by two beautiful white horses. There were maybe six or eight girls on the sleigh, all dressed up in snowsuits, throwing snowballs made of cotton into the crowd.

'Boston Garden was nice, but quite plain. The start of the ski jump was about 3 ½ feet from the ceiling, so we were waiting all stooped over for the announcer to call our names

'Much of the floor was ice for the Ice Capades who stayed with us in the show for five years. Besides figure skating, speed skating and barrel jumping, by Alex Hurd, there was a comedian skater, Alf Trinkler, doing all kinds of antics. I was pleased to be skiing with Strand Mikkelson, National Champion of 1929, and Anton Tekang, National champion of 1932, and many great skiers from Norway, Sweden, Austria, Switzerland and Germany.

'1935 was about the beginning of safety bindings and many people came to us to try theirs. Some of them looked like real bear traps.

'In 1940, I joined the Sepp Ruschp Ski School. After three years in the service (10th Division Mountain Troops, where I taught skiing,)

I was assistant manager to Sepp for 10 years. I left the Mountain Company in 1956 and that was the end of my skiing career.'"

Mary speaking, "Dad also managed the Summit House, owned by the Mountain Company, from 1948-1956. This 100 year old hotel was at the top of the mountain, under the Nose. We had a little cottage near the hotel. Many of the same guests came back year after year, from Boston, New York, Albany, and beyond. Some time back I wrote a piece called 'Memoirs of a Mountain' about the time I remember up there, until I was 8. It's packed in storage now. At the Summit House, Dad was on call 24/7. He was also the postmaster –there was a rubber stamp that he would let me use to hand cancel the postcards and letters that guests sent. There was also a group of regular guests that would meet for cocktails at our cottage; they called themselves 'the six o'clock club.'"

The second installment from Mary came about two weeks later, "I was THRILLED to find these notes while cleaning out a desk."

Clem Curtis: "Around 1938-1940, Sepp Ruschp spoke with Ford Sayer, who was the manager of the Hanover Inn at the time, about hiring certified ski instructors. Ford told Sepp about me, and Sepp asked me to come interview. So I did. Sepp offered me a job; the pay was to be $5.00 a week, plus room and board. I accepted, and Sepp said he'd send me a letter of confirmation. But the letter never came. Finally, Sepp called me and said, 'are you coming to Stowe?' And I told him I never received the letter. Sepp said, "Well, come right now and I'll double the pay!" So I went. When I got there, an Austrian ski instructor showed me the letter- it was still in his pocket!

"I had been certified in North Conway, NH. I had to take a class held or sponsored by Johannes Schneider, a famous Austrian ski school founder. The actual instructor, I think his name was Benna Robisca, didn't want to take me, but Johannes told him he had to. So I took the class, then took the test, which was to demonstrate my teaching abilities, and passed the test.

"In Stowe, a group lesson was $2.00, (Hence my favorite expression: "Bend zee knees, two dollars, please..." A private lesson was $5.00, and the instructor got to keep $2.00 of that. I liked to teach beginners, best. One student, a good-sized lady, didn't want me for an instructor. But I said "I'll guarantee you a Christie." Sepp didn't think I could do it. But the woman finally agreed. I got her doing a snowplow, then taught her to side slip. Over and over, and when you do it fast enough, a snowplow and a side slip is a Christie! She was pretty pleased.

"I had one serious, could have been very serious, accident. Three of us were skiing to the clubhouse on one pair of skis. I told the fellow who was strapped onto the skis, 'If we wobble, drop your poles." But when we started to wobble, he threw the poles down. One of the handles bounced off the hard snow and the tip of the pole caught me just to the left of my eye. Pretty big scar still there!

"Lowell Thomas was a popular newscaster. He took lessons from Sepp, but sat for photos with the whole ski school. I still have that photo in our kitchen in Stowe.

"I helped Sepp lay out a couple of trails, as well as a lift on Spruce Peak, when it was still covered with trees. We found the spot on the bottom of the hill where the lift should end. I climbed a tree and tied my shirt to the top of the tree as a marker. Then we climbed to the top of Spruce, and marked the line for the lift.

"We lived in the Toll House, over what was the cafeteria. One night, Anne got scared – there were intermittent scraping noises coming from the floor below. We discovered rats moving cellophane wrapped crackers across the floor from the storeroom to their own hiding place!

"In the summers, until about 1947, I had an ice business in Lebanon. Had a truck and delivered 100 pound blocks of ice on my back. I had a rubber apron to protect my back from getting wet, but it did nothing to protect my back from getting cold. So my mother-in –law sewed padding into it for me.

"In the summer around 1948, I was asked to manage the Summit House, on the top of Mount Mansfield, and be the postmaster. We had a little cottage in the back, and Mary was just a few months old when we moved up for the first summer. Worst job I ever had. Chris was born on July 4, while we were living up there. They were treated like royalty by all the guests.

"I left the Mountain Company in 1956, and was given a lovely party, and a Lifetime Pass for all the uphill lifts, including the gondola. The pass expires this May, on my 100th birthday."

Clem was the innkeeper at the Summit House, until 1958 when the Mountain Co. began to plan for the controlled burning of the old hotel to demolish it. This was the same year that he joined the Stowe Rotary Club. When Clem was presented with the prestigious Rotary Paul Harris Fellowship award on September 2, 2010 many club members gave their testimony, some serious, many humorous. John Van Blarcom gave some final remarks after congratulating Clem on his honor and then recalled a story that Clem had told him, "As many know, Clem was a ski jumper for many years and ended up performing jumps at Madison Square Garden. There was not enough room there at the top, however, for the skiers to start in that complex, so jumpers had to go outside and come in though a window." "Well, Clem pulled if off," John said, and then added that "Clem is one of the greatest people he has known."

Clem has left other legacies in Stowe, among which was being instrumental in having the March of Dimes memorial brought down from the mountain and relocated to the Mayo farm area near the Weeks Hill Rd. where it would be seen by more visitors. Curtis and Bedell Construction Company built the first motel in Stowe, the Stowe Motel on the Mountain and Luce Hill Roads, as well as Topnotch, and Stowehof.

[Post script: One of the few remaining pioneers, Clem Curtis passed away Friday evening, Sept. 7, 2012 at age 102, while his wife Anne, died less than 48 hours later at age100 early Monday morning, Sept. 10 at their home]

LEADING SKI JUMPERS

Anton Lekang, Clarence Oleson, Clem Curtis and Strand Mikkelsen, who will compete in the ski tournament to be held in conjunction with the Fourth Annual National Winter Sports Exposition at Boston Garden.

Courtesy of Mary Skelton
Clem Is Third from Left

Vermont Ski and Snowboard Museum Collection

GORDON LOWE
1920-

Gordon was another member of the highly specialized U.S. Army's 87th Regiment, the 10th Mountain Division during World War II, as were David Burt, Clem Curtis, and Kerr Sparks. At the December 2, 2010, dedication of the bronze statue of the 10th Mountain soldier in the plaza between the new Stowe Mountain Resort and Spruce Camp, the president of the Resort read the names of the fifteen 10th Mountain men who had, over the years, been with the ski school, the ski patrol, and management at the Stowe Mountain Resort. Among these men was Albert "Midge" Tozloski of Stowe. Tozloski said he had lied about his age at the time in order to join the 10th Mountain.

Lowe comments that many World War II veterans from the 10th went on to apply their considerable skiing knowledge to a burgeoning stateside ski industry. In 1947, the 10th ski troops skied at Dutch Hill where Lowe headed up the Dutch Hill Ski School in Heartwellville, VT. The Dutch Hill Ski Area (1944-1985) was a popular, mid-sized ski area now listed in New England's lost ski areas. Lowe was then a US Eastern Amateur Ski Association instructor who spoke to local schools encouraging them to include skiing in their athletic programs.

In 1952, he moved to Stowe to take a position as a ski instructor, a job offered by Kerr Sparks. In September of that same year, William F. Mitchell designed the layout for the new 18-hole golf course in Stowe. Gordon Lowe of the Mountain Co. managed construction of the course in exchange for equity. The course opened in spring of 1963. The five top men in the new Club were Lowe, Henry Simoneau, Sepp Ruschp, Mitchell, and Chuck Savage, with Lowe as the course superintendent.

Gordon had many assorted duties at the Mountain Co.: he helped to build the Big Spruce chair lift, managed the State Ski Shelter, the ski shop at the Mountain, and the T-Bar and later he managed snowmaking, all transportation, and plowing. Eventually, he became vice-president of the Mountain Co. During C.V. Starr's reign, Gordon remarked that he once flew in Starr's plane to New York City and stayed at Starr's apartment, "Very plush."

The Trapp family and Gordon became great friends and he even skied with Maria on occasion.

Gordon retired from the Mountain Co. in 1975 and moved to North Hero, Vt., where he raised Scotch Highland cattle. He now resides in Shelburne, Vt.

On hand for the occasion was a group of former Mt. Mansfield employees as pictured above. Left to right are Clem Curtis, Ann Curtis, Helen (Maxie) Ruschp, Priscilla Hess, Henry Simoneau and Kerr Sparks.

may 28, 1992

PRISCILLA HESS
1921-2005

Priscilla (Pippy to her family) was born in Melrose, Mass and graduated from Melrose High School and Simmons College in Boston. One of the last survivors of the early Mt. Mansfield Co. group, she passed away on 4 September 2005 in Medford, MA.

Her dear friend Jane Weaver relates that Priscilla arrived in Stowe in 1948 and worked at The Lodge at Smugglers Notch under George Morrell, and then Nick Mara. Jane confirms that they were roommates back then. "Yes, Priscilla and I shared an apartment at the Harlow Hill House, owned by the Mountain Company, for 10 years – this is where the Austrian ski Instructors stayed every winter. This building is located next to the Mountain Co. warehouse – across from the Cross Country Touring Center. We spent holidays together with Jean and Gordon Lowe all those years. In the '80's I was included in holiday events with Priscilla and her family in Massachusetts and New Hampshire – and I still am!"

Sometime in the early '50's Priscilla moved to the accounting office of the Mountain Co. and later became the assistant treasurer under Milton Teffner. "She was a valuable employee – knew every facet of the business of the Mt. Mansfield Company. I once mentioned to Sepp that the company would have to close down if Priscilla left, and he agreed with me," comments Jane. "She was an enthusiastic skier and supporter of the Mt. Mansfield Ski Club." Jane writes that she started work for the Mt. Mansfield Co. as Office/Reservations Manager at The Lodge under Ivor Petrak, manager, on October 3, 1963 until spring of 1974, 10 ½ years. The three vice-presidents at that time were Gordon Lowe, Kerr Sparks, and Henry Simoneau. "It was like a family and I was part of it!"

Dickinson Collection

HELEN "MAXIE" (MURRAY) RUSCHP
1911-2009

She loved people, humor, and forthrightness.
Pat Haslam

Helen Murray Ruschp, better known as Maxie, was born in Utica, NY, 7 August 1911. Christi Ruschp Dickinson writes that "Maxie first came to Stowe with Helen Dougherty to ski and take lessons in 1936. Then, during World War II, she started coming to Stowe and working at the Toll House part-time. With the onset of gas rationing she no longer commuted and started to work permanently at the newly-formed Mount Mansfield Co.

"I think by 1943, when my brother Peter was born, she assisted my mother [Hermine] with the Toll House doing administrative duties, reservations, billing, etc. She later became the secretary and administrative assistant to Sepp Ruschp until her retirement in 1978. She is said to have had her finger in every pie! She married Mr. Ruschp in October 1985 as his second wife. Everyone knew her as "Maxie." And Maxie knew everyone!

"Julie Egenberg was asked about how her mother, Helen (Hennie) Batcheler Dougherty connected with Maxie. She said they were grade school classmates at the Halstead School in Yonkers, NY! In 1936, Maxie and Hennie visited another friend from Burlington, and they came up to ski at Stowe. The Dougherty's lived in Ohio then. Jack Dougherty traveled a great deal as a salesman, so the friends took time to travel.

"They spent the first year, 1936, staying at the Toll House, which was Sepp's first year as a ski instructor for the Mt. Mansfield Ski Club. They returned the following season and lived at Fred M. and Nan Pike's house on Pike St. (now 49 Pike St.) where Sepp and Hermine later lived. In 1937, Sepp brought Hermine over to our house and the three girls became great friends, and they skied all over. Mother (Hennie) had an old station wagon which was used to haul broken legs to the old Copley Hospital. During the war years, I believe Maxie was in Stowe almost full time. We saw her during summers after we had moved to Cazenovia, N.Y. and continued to spend a lot of time at the Toll House where Maxie was living and working for the Mountain Company. The Dougherty's and Maxie remained the closest of friends."

Polly (Rollins) Straub worked at the Mt. Company from 1969 to 1988. In April 2010, Polly wrote about her fond memories about Maxie and has some delightful stories, "Okay, lets get to Maxie… one of my very favorite people! My first day of work at the Mt. Mansfield Company was in November of 1969. I had been hired to fill a secretarial position in what was then called the News Bureau. Bill Riley was to be my boss. He hired me in the kitchen of my home during a cocktail party we were hosting. At work he had been dealing with three women splitting the seven day week. The two (Ann Van Gilder and Martha Walker) who had been handling Monday through Friday were leaving and I told him I was interested. When he heard I was willing to work five days a week, I had the job on the spot!

"On my first day on the job, I parked my car at the Toll House parking lot and proceeded to walk to the front door of the Office. Before I had taken very many steps, Maxie opened a window on the second floor and hollered out "Well, you beat your boss to work. That's a good sign." That was my introduction to Maxie. I had certainly heard about her, but I had never met her. I found her a bit intimidating to say the least. But she soon became a wonderful friend.

"Because Maxie had an eagle eye for misspelled words, we used to ask her to proof read material we produced. She was very good at it. The only problem was she often wanted to change the grammar and/or the context as well. She would have been good at that too, if we were writing a book, an article, etc. We were producing sell pieces, brochures, flyers, which do not often contain paragraphs or even complete sentences. She had trouble with that!

"For Maxie's 75th birthday, Patty Clark and I held a tea party inviting her numerous friends. We wanted it to be a surprise, but no way was that going to work! Maxie actually picked up the mail for a friend who lived near her at Stoneybrook and I guess she flipped through the envelopes. When she saw one addressed to her friend with my return address on it, the surprise was over. She called me, asked if I was planning something (it's a wonder to me she didn't just open her friend's mail!) and when and where was it going to be. We tried it again for her 80th and arranged for Bill Riley to bring her. He took her out to lunch and was going to tell her he had to stop at my house to pick something up. He miscalculated the amount of time needed for lunch and while they were spending an unusual amount of time driving around until it was time to bring her to my house, she figured it out. Not an easy person to surprise!

"Another thing I remember about Maxie was her promptness. When she said she would be back at 3 o'clock, she was back at 3 o'clock exactly. Not five minutes of or five minutes after. Not even one minute before or after. Exactly at 3 o'clock. And this was true whether she went down into the Village or was returning from a trip to New Jersey. No matter how long her trip, she knew when she was going to return. We used to accuse her of parking her car out on Route 108 until one minute before she was due to return and then driving in at the exact time.

Dickinson Collection
Maxie Having Fun in the Snow 1941

"Speaking of good things to eat, Maxie had lived in one of the Mt. Mansfield Townhouses for a couple of years when she came to me one day and asked me how to turn on the oven in her kitchen. I thought she was kidding at first. But it soon became evident that she had not yet used the oven in her condominium. She used to eat dinner with Sepp and Hermine every night and that meal was brought to the Ruschp house from The Lodge.

"Maxie was a unique person and I cherish my friendship with her. I feel very fortunate to have been able to be her friend."

****

[A note by the author: At Sepp's retirement party, I was visiting with Maxie about his years at the Mountain, hoping the Stowe Historical Society would someday acquire some of his reminiscences. She vowed she would take some notes during their winter at Long Boat Key, Florida, while they were on the beach. The result is his memoir to 1949 which is Part II of this work, as gathered by Maxie, then typed by Linda Adams and proofread by Bill Riley. PLH.]

Bill at his News Bureau Desk at the Mountain Company

BILL RILEY
1930-2010

Bill was employed by the Mountain Company for 30 years, the stories of which he continued to tell until his passing. Celebration of the Life, Bill Riley Program

Always smiling, affable, and full of stories about people and events, past and present, at the Mountain Company, that was Bill. He was the "voice" of the Mountain on radio for many of his 25 years there as head of the News Bureau, the position he took over from Bob Bourdon. "And even following his retirement from the Mountain Company, he maintained his contacts and there was little that happened at the Mountain that Bill couldn't tell you about, while, of course, offering his opinion," writes Peter Beck.

 Bill first came to Stowe in 1954 to ski after his discharge from the U.S. Air Force. "We have known Bill since he became a Ski Instructor. He lived at Harlow Hill, a place the Mountain Co. provided for the Austrian Ski Instructors who worked for the company. I also lived there and got to become friends with Bill..." writes Ruby Beeman. As a ski bum, he worked at the Round Hearth Lodge for room and board, tips, and most importantly, a ski pass. He quickly became an instructor with the renowned Sepp Ruschp Ski School on the Mountain, working up to the Mountain Company's News Bureau and later Marketing Director over a nearly 25-year period. One of his duties was to broadcast the ski conditions daily from the mountain by radio.

Very shortly before Bill's death in 2010, Peter Beck was able to chat with Bill after Easter dinner with Peter's family. Bill was asked about these jobs at the Mountain, and Bill replied that although he, Henry Simoneau, Kerr Sparks, and Gordon Lowe held various titles, they were all essentially Sepp Ruschp's assistants. As a job came up that needed attention, such as dealing with the Company's real estate, Sepp would assign it to one of them, regardless of their "title." Bill also commented about his departure in the 1960's, when Verne Johnson was president. After an incident about snow-making by upper management, Bill decided it was time to move on because management and methods of doing business had changed. At that time, Sepp was chairman of the board and suggested Bill get his real estate license, and so Bill did.

As Marketing Director, Bill came up with some novel ideas, such as overseeing promotional films "There is Always Snow in Stowe," and "Color it White and Call it Stowe." Kurt Zimmer, in a biographical sketch about Bill in the Stowe Reporter of July 22, 2004 issue commented, "One of Riley's greatest marketing tools were the movies that he directed, shot and distributed to ski clubs. Trailers for these movies were sent to movie theaters all over the country, and for many people it was their first exposure to the sport."

Bill was married to Betsy Snite in 1964. Betsy was the 1960 Olympic Silver Medalist at Squaw Valley, a native of Norwich, Vermont. After their marriage she retired from amateur Alpine racing. Betsy then worked at the Mountain Company's Ski Shops and in 1977, they opened Betsy Snite Sports, an upscale clothing shop on the Mountain Road.

After his retirement at the Mountain Co. Bill became associated with Brian Harwood, and Ken Squire to form the then-new Stowe radio station, WRFB, which later became WCVT, the classic Vermont station. He is believed to be the first in Stowe to sell cell phones when these were a new invention coming into general use. Many remember his marketing-tool license plate,"CELFONE." Everyone knew where he was.

The Stowe Historical Society Archives

Bill was a member of Stowe Rotary Club, Mount Mansfield Ski Club, the Stowe Planning Commission, Vermont Ski Museum, Stowe Land Trust, and other community and ski organizations. He helped to form the New England Ski Areas Association.

At Bill's memorial service in June 2010, outside the Vermont Ski Museum, Phil Camp, Sr. praised Bill as a confidant, partner in the creation of the New England Ski Areas Council, advisor, and with whom he generally spent a lot of time in these efforts. Phil remarked, "When I was named press chief for Alpine events at the 1980 Lake Placid Olympics, I was urged to find someone to be my chief of staff- someone to help balance the emotions and demands of the press- especially foreign media. Naturally I called Bill. He said, yes. He made a terrific partner. He helped make ME look good. But that was Bill. He played the marketing game superbly."

Courtesy of Mike Leach, MMSC Newsletter Archive
Charles Blauvelt, Henry Simoneau and Sepp Ruschp

HENRY SIMONEAU
1915—1995

*"I remember a run I took in 1949 on Mansfield
following instructor Henry Simoneau down Lord Trail
from the top, I turned when he turned. He didn't turn
often. It was wild."* Robert Rock, Oswego, NY.

Henry was born in Richmond Vermont in 1915, and graduated from Stowe High School in 1933. He was already a talented ski racer in high school. Henry, "a native lad," had set the record for the famous "Nose Dive" descent when Henry was less than 16 years old! In a Mt. Mansfield Ski Club newsletter, then named MMSC Skiing, is an item whereby, "Several prominent Club members are raising a fund with which to send Harry Simoneau, the Stowe Cannonball, to Sun Valley to train for the U.S. Ski Team." That was in December 1940. During World War II he served in the U.S. Army in the Far East Theater in India and Burma.

On the first official ride on the new double chair lift at Spruce (1960), Sepp Ruschp's son Peter and Heidi Simoneau, daughter of

263

Henry Simoneau, age 10, were the honored riders. In that same newsletter is listed the instructors at the Sepp Ruschp Ski School: Otto Hollaus, Kerr Sparks, Lionel Hayes, and Howard Moody. New instructors that year included Clem Curtis of Lebanon, NH, a certified teacher.

Simoneau was a champion ski racer and by December 1946 a ski instructor at the Sepp Ruschp Ski School at the Mountain. That was the 11th season of the ski school. Kerr Sparks and Curtis are on the roster of instructors as well as Gerald (Gary) Fisher, and Frances Harrison., and 6 others. He went on to become involved in the development of the Mountain as well as managing the Spruce Peak area and later manager of the Mt. Mansfield portion. In fact, his co-workers called Spruce Peak "Henry's Hill" which was "groomed to a fare-thee-well" under his guidance: "Henry claims that his hand-raked slopes will be skiable on a heavy frost!" He oversaw much of the construction of the original gondola.

Henry was the chairman of the Race Committee sponsored by the Mt. Mansfield Ski Club for many years. In the MMSC he writes annually about the races to be held for each season. He also planned for the annual women's downhill championships, the Stowe Derby, and the Sugar Slalom events each spring. Chuck Savage helped to handle many of the competitions as well.

In the 1970's, Henry Simoneau donated the now-famous "Smuggler's Bowl and that was the start of the Ski Bum Race Series. Even Charlie Lord and his team of Senior Citizens raced, it was reported, but the exact date is lost. After serving as a director and vice-president of the Mt. Mansfield Co., Henry retired in 1981.

A closed employee meeting at the Mt. Co. was held in mid-May 1990 to honor company founders with plaques honoring their accomplishments in building the "Ski Capital of the East," the honorees being Sepp Ruschp, Charlie Lord, Kerr Sparks, and Henry Simoneau. Simoneau died in February 1995.

Stowe Historical Society Archives

KERR SPARKS, JR.
1918-1993
&
FRANCES (HARRISON) SPARKS
1920-2012

*"Perhaps Kerr's most memorable contributions
stems from his gentle and creative character."*
Obituary. April 22, 1993, *Stowe Reporter.*

Born in Andover, Massachusetts in 1918, Kerr Sparks was athletic
and had a wide variety of interests. He was a football star in high
school and after graduation went on to become a ski instructor. In
1939, he became the eighth certified ski instructor in the US and
joined the Sepp Ruschp Ski School in Stowe, a very early staff

265

member. He directed the ski school for 43 years after Sepp Ruschp needed a replacement. Later, he was also property manager and a vice president of the Mount Mansfield Co. Sparks was instrumental in founding the Eastern Professional Ski Instructors Association and served as its first president. By March 1950, he had already served for three years as manager of the Sepp Ruschp Ski School.

In his obituary in the newsletter of the MMSC newsletter of November 1993, he is commended for his strength and bravery demonstrated during his service in the 10th Mountain Division. He won a battlefield commission and was awarded a Bronze Star and Purple Heart for his service in the Aleutian Islands and the Italian Campaign.

Kerr was originally a landscape designer and expert horticulturist, during the off-season. And, pursuing yet more creativity became adept at basket weaving, fly fishing, dowsing, and golf. According to Hesterly Buckley, most of the attractive plantings at the Toll House, then managed by Gub and Doris Langdon, were planted by Kerr.

The Sepp Ruschp Ski School report in the Mt. Mansfield Ski Club Newsletter of Jan. 1, 1940, states that, "This winter Sepp will be assisted by two fine ski teachers, Otto Hollaus, an Austrian State Qualified Instructor, and Kerr Sparks, certified by the USEASA. The school provides for a two-hour lesson period every morning, commencing at 10 a.m., and a two-hour period every afternoon at 2 PM rates are $1.50 for half day and $2.00 for a whole day."

It is interesting to note that the 1946 season roster of ski instructors at the Sepp Ruschp Ski School are listed the names of Bob Bourdon, Mary Mather, Kerr Sparks, Joan Stent, and Frances Harrison, among very few others. Kerr Sparks married first, Joan Stent in 1944, and second Frances (Frankie) Harrison, and Bob Bourdon married Mary Mather in 1946. The Ski School was a Mecca for marriages!

Frankie Sparks was born on October 18, 1920, in Rosemont, Pa. She grew up loving nature and animals and became an accomplished horsewoman, states her obituary. She was a Motor Corp Volunteer with the Red Cross during World War II. In 1945, she moved to Stowe with her best friend Mary Mather Bourdon and became a certified ski instructor. This is where she met her husband. They were married in 1948. Frankie was a very active member of St. John's in the Mountains church in Stowe. She passed away February 23, 2012, in Shelburne, Vt.

267

Courtesy of Elizabeth J. Teffner

MILTON TEFFNER
1908-1968

Born in Batavia, New York, Milton Teffner attended Bryant-Stratton Business College in Buffalo and then worked in western New York for various businesses including the Army Corps of Engineers. He and his wife, Susie, moved to Stowe in 1936 when they purchased and operated the Three Green Doors, as a guest house. They moved back to Tonawanda, New York, in 1940. They farmed until 1952, when they returned to Stowe and operated Teffner's Lodge until 1958. Subsequently, that lodge became the Golden Kitz, and is now named the Riverside Inn.

Also, in 1952, at the invitation of Sepp Ruschp, Teffner joined the Mt Mansfield Company as treasurer of the Mountain Co. His tenure as Treasurer and valued employee of the fledging Mountain Company spanned 16 years. One of the early employees of the Company was Priscilla Hess, who was first his secretary, and later assistant treasurer.

About 1959, Milton was sent to Spokane, Washington to negotiate the purchase of a double chair lift with The Riblet Tramway

Co. The new lift was installed in 1960. Betty Teffner, widow of Milton's son, Ted, relates that the Teffners drove across the country to Washington, making Milton's business trip a family affair.

Milton served as treasurer of the Stowe Area Association and the Stowe Country Club.

Stowe Historical Society Archives
Bob Skiing and Reading his New Book, 1934

BOB BOURDON
1916-1995

"A Man for All Seasons,"
Exhibit title, Vermont Ski Museum, July 2004.

Bob's earliest claim to fame began when he was the first person in the United States to ride the first-ever ski tow at Woodstock, Vermont, on Gilbert Hill. He was a native of Woodstock where skiing was developing as a sport. That was in 1934 at age 18. In 1936, he won the first sanctioned race, the Vermont Ski Championship on the Nose Dive Trail at Stowe to set a record.

Bob obtained his professional instructor's certificate in 1938; and by 1941, Sepp Ruschp had induced him to come to Stowe where he joined the staff of the Ski School.

He suffered a serious accident in 1943 whereby the ski injuries registered him as 4F so that he could not serve in the U.S. Army during World War II. But in 1945-46, he was part of the U.S. Army Ski and Jumping Teams including a championship in Cortina, Italy. His wife Betsy has a shot of him in Cortina coming off the jump with the American flag streaming behind him. When Betsy was asked why Bob was classified 4F during the war, and yet served later, she said that he was 4F until the war was almost over at which time he said, "They were taking everyone up to and including the walking wounded." So he was drafted and sent to Italy where he heard about a "racer chaser" of a general. On his 11th attempt to see the general, Bob finally met him and talked him into putting him on the ski team. The rest is history. Bob won several other championships, but then turned to teaching skiing. Back in the States, he was an instructor in Woodstock, Sun Valley, Jackson Hole, and later at Stowe.

Bob's wife Betsy described his ski accident on Nose Dive in 1943 in more detail, "He refused to get in the [rescue] basket to be taken down the Mountain so he skied down. He met someone on the trail during one of the many stops, who said there had been an accident 'up there'. Robert said, 'Well, you're looking at him.' No one realized how seriously he was hurt. However, Janet Savage offered to drive him to the hospital. When a nurse finally saw the x-rays of his ribs she said, 'Oh dear! You better go upstairs.' He did. One month later he was allowed to go home. Second day out, he skied the mountain HARD."

There is an interesting tidbit about Bob's ski accident in the "Sally Joy News." published in Stowe at the Sally Joy Farm, 30 March 1943. It is an item about Bob's stay in the hospital following his injury: "One of Stowe's best liked ski instructors and one of the nicest guys you'd ever want to know is now confined to the Morrisville Hospital where he's been on the Danger List since Thursday, March 18. He was coming down the Nose Dive during rather icy conditions he hit a tree, smashed his right side-breaking ribs in 13-16 places. Internal bleeding, the fear of a punctured lung found him a week later on March 25, still with only a 50-50 chance. Ski instructors can't get accident insurance. I don't know whether he has Hospitalization. I do know that his recovery will be costly... and (possibly) some of Bob's good skiing friends may care to chip in..."Maxie" [Helen Murray] is acting as Treasurer of the ''Bob Bourdon Fund for Courageous Skiers.' And I mean courageous, for Doc Phil Goddard told me that if it were not for Bob's fighting spirit this past ten days, he'd not be here."

By 1947, Bob had moved to Stowe and became something of a skiing legend. By then he was an instructor at the Sepp Ruschp Ski School as well as winning races. As an accomplished professional photographer all year-around, he was hired to manage the Mount Mansfield Company's News Bureau, year unknown. His photos were published in Vermont Life, Life, and other magazines. One of his photos appeared on the cover of Life Espanol when he covered the opening of Portilla, Chile, where Othmar Schneider directed his ski school.

The C.V. Starr Memorial Trophy. The hand forged trophy was created by blacksmith Robert Bourdon of Stowe. The figure was split and hammered from one piece of iron from an action photo of Stowe's Olympic Silver Medal Winner, Billy Kidd.

Stowe Historical Society Archives
C.V. Starr Memorial Trophy

Bob was multi-talented, authoring two books on skiing technique in 1954 and 1964. He created trophies for the C V Starr and Stowe

Derby races for the Mount Mansfield Ski Club which were highlighted in the exhibit in his honor in 2004 at the Vermont Ski Museum. Simple, functional sculptures became well known to both the skiing and local communities. He took up blacksmithing, being mostly self-taught, and gunsmithing. That career lasted for 30 years. But music was a large part of his life. He played the trumpet, his first love, in many jazz bands. His own group was "The Bob Bourdon Quartet." He and his brother were charter members of the Vermont Symphony Orchestra.

One of Bob's photos for the Mt. Mansfield News Bureau is included on the website for the New York Folklore journal, Voices, in the Fall-Winter issue 2003. The image depicts Helen Hartness Flanders "collecting songs" from innkeeper Olive (Ollie) May in front of the fireplace at The Fountain in Stowe, in the 1940's.

Stowe Historical Society Archives

MARY (MATHER) BOURDON
1923-2003

Mary (Mather) Bourdon was born in horse country at Ardmore, Pa., as was Nose Dive Annie Bonfoey, and is said to have left there at age 21. In the early 1940's, when skiing was just developing, she went with friends to ski in Stowe. There she met Bob Bourdon already a well-known ski racer and instructor, musician, and photographer.

Bob was classified as 4F and, at first, could not serve in the Army during World War II because of a serious ski injury. Towards the end of the war, he was able to enlist as the Army loosened its requirements when more men were needed to serve.

While Bob was away, Mary worked at Los Alamos, N.M. and trained as a pilot to ferry bombers to distant locations. She spent winters teaching skiing and had already become a professional ski instructor by the time Bob returned to Stowe after World War II. They were married January 27, 1945, at Stowe. Bob's occupation on the marriage certificate reads: ski instructor.

There were few women ski instructors on the staff of the Sepp Ruschp Ski School, and Mary Mather was one of the earliest women in the ski school who are listed on the roster of the winter of 1944-45 along with Bob Bourdon, Bob DeForest, and Joan Stent at the Toll House.

Her obituary claims she spent most of her 25 years in Stowe teaching skiing and working with Bob in the Mt. Mansfield News Bureau writing marketing material for the Mt. Mansfield Co. By 1971, she left Bob to become a rancher in Sheridan, Wyo. Mary passed away 24 Nov 2003 in Wyoming.

ERWIN S. LINDNER
1915-1980

by Brian Lindner

Many decades before the Stowe Mountain Rescue team was formed, there was one key phone number to call for rescues in the vicinity of Mt. Mansfield. No documentation remains to show how many times "Alpine 4014" was called to notify Erwin "Lindy" Lindner of a lost or injured hiker, rock climber, or skier, but it was in the dozens. Lindner was the ranger at the Smuggler's Notch State Campground from 1943 to 1962. Employed by the Vermont Department of Forests and Parks, his duties consisted of running the campground (Where Spruce Camp is today) and the picnic area in the Notch plus the tourist station at the top of the Notch. In winters, he was in charge of the state-operated Nose Dive parking lot at the base of the Mansfield lifts. Because the State Shelter at the base of the lifts was owned by the state of Vermont, he and his family were provided with the apartment at the north end of the building. It was tight quarters for a family of five and one never knew when the front door would pop open with a skier thinking he/she was coming into the restaurant. Privacy in winter months was always at a premium as skiers could easily see everything going on in the living room.   Born 26 May 1915 in Underhill, he migrated around to the Stowe side of the mountain where he remained until his untimely passing on February 22, 1980 at age 65. The son of a German mother and Austrian father, he grew up on the family farm with seven sisters and three brothers. In 1940, along with his oldest brother he enlisted in the Vermont National Guard, Company F, 172nd Infantry. The Lindner brothers ended up in the armory in Northfield, which was a long drive around Mt. Mansfield in a time of primarily dirt roads. In February 1941 the Vermont National Guard was federalized and the Lindner brothers suddenly found themselves shipped off to the southern states as members of the 43rd Division. The heat, humidity, and especially the presence of snakes didn't suit either brother very well. When they heard that an entirely new division was being formed to fight in mountains and cold weather, they immediately sought to make the transfer. The 87th Regiment of the famous 10th Mountain Division (ski troops) was being formed but it wasn't easy to get transferred. The 10th required formal applications plus at least two letters of recommendation from prominent citizens. The records are long gone about who recommended either brother but they soon found themselves on a train to Fort Lewis, Washington to be ski troopers. When the 10th opened its special training facility at Camp Hale in Colorado they were among the first to arrive and began to learn the skills of mountain warfare. They learned rock climbing, survival skills and skiing. The 10th trained in the worst possible mountain conditions which made each soldier an individual survivalist with a multitude of back country skills.

There are two versions of what happened next which caused Lindy to be medically discharged. One version has it that he wanted a pair of aviator sunglasses to help prevent snow blindness but upon making the request he suddenly found himself with the optometrist who quickly discovered he was blind in one eye. Up to this point he had memorized the Army eye charts and faked his way through each test. The second version is based on a supposition from Army records: Lindner retained his shooting records which proved him to be well above the standard. In one day's entry at Camp Hale he was shooting with his normal precision then the book called to switch partners and cover one eye.

The records end at that point. Either way, to his life-long disappointment, he was medically discharged and given money to return home to Vermont. Unemployed, he sought work as a civilian and was hired that fall as the Ski Patrol Director of the Mt. Mansfield Ski Patrol. Clearly, the skiing, first aid and rescue skills he had learned in the ski troops had placed him well ahead of any other applicants. Thus began his service for the next three seasons as Stowe's second paid ski patrolman. The top station on the patrol was in the Octagon and he soon met one of the workers named Florence Adams, daughter of Claude and Margaret, and they became engaged. On May 6, 1946, they were married in Burlington. Even Claude Adams was involved in working for the Mountain Company.

After his retirement from farming, he collected a quarter for every car that parked at the ski area from the 1940's to 1960. Dressed in his red and black wool shirt, old grey fedora hat, and giant bushy moustache, he was probably one of Stowe's most photographed individuals. He was Lindner's father-in-law.

Some of the ski patrol log books from the 1940's survive and are filled with Lindner's handwriting. Clearly, during his time on the patrol it was all about ankles in the old leather boots and "bear trap" bindings. Entry after entry showed him and others responding to broken ankles on the Nose Dive, Skimeister, and Toll Road trails. In 1947, Lindner became a full-time employee of the Department of Forests and Parks probably because of the connections he made as a member of the ski patrol. Men such as Bill Mason, Charlie Lord, Ab Coleman had all become life-long friends and most knew Perry Merrill, the commissioner of the department. This brings us back full circle to his rescues. Just as today, hikers, skiers, and tourists venture into back country situations where they are prepared for any emergency. From 1943 until 1962 Lindner was the person to call for every one of these emergencies which drew upon his woodsman, first aid, and survival skills learned in the ski troops and on the ski patrol. Until his passing some of the rescued parties send Christmas cards every year over the decades to express their ongoing gratitude.

The one surviving document about a rescue was written in 1959 by Vermont State Trooper Walter J. Lamere. In his memo Trooper Lamere speaks about a hiker stranded in Smuggler's Notch several hundred feet above Route 108. Trooper Lamere remarked on Lindner's "immediate response [and whose] help and knowledge of this type of situation led to a safe and quick rescue."

Lindner passed away of natural causes and is buried in Riverbank Cemetery in Stowe.

ERLING STROM
1897-1986

"Bend your knees, trust in God, and let your nose run." Motto of Erling Strom to his pupils.

In 1900, at about the age of 2 or 3 years, Erling Strom was put on skis. In Norway, everyone strapped on skis at an early age, so it became natural for everyone to travel in this manner in winter. He was a schoolboy jumper growing up and competed at Stockholm in the Nordic Winter Games that lead to the founding of the international Olympic Games. By the time he entered the Norwegian Army in 1918, he was an expert skier. After his discharge, he sailed to the United States to build a career in winter sports.

The passenger list of 19 March 1919 records the arrival in New York of Erling Strom departing from Christiania (Oslo), Norway at age 21. He went first to Arizona and worked as a cow hand, but soon went to Colorado to find work. He worked in the oil fields at Ft. Collins, and then went to the Estes Park, Boulder area. Over the years Strom made many trips by ship back to his homeland. In 1922, he worked his way back to the US by ship when his position in the crew was "extraman." In 1926, at age 29, his US destination was to "return to Estes Park, Colorado." His return from Oslo back to Estes Park in 1929 lists his occupation as "sports director," and he is still single. Between 1929 and mid-1930, Strom moved east to Lake Placid where he was the sports director at the Lake Placid Club, as listed in the 1930 census at North Elba, NY. His wife Sigrid and daughter Siri came from Norway in 1934, and joined him at Lake Placid until they moved to Stowe in 1940 to establish a ski lodge for guests.

In 1940, the Stroms bought the Mark Poor farm, the brick house on the Mountain Rd. that now houses Cactus Cafe and Darkside Snowboards. They renovated the house to accommodate

Wendy Snow Parrish Collection
The Strom Lodge in the 1940's

20 ski guests. He enticed his Norwegian friend, Johan Bull, to move to Stowe. Bull, well-known for his cartoons and illustrations in The New Yorker magazine and other periodicals, painted the dining room wall with a mural about Norse mythology. Strom installed a tow rope in his back yard to serve his own and nearby lodge guests. Lessons were given on request. "My own daughter Siri became a good skier on that hill, and our nearest neighbor, Lena Gale, ended

up as a Vermont Champion in Eastern GS final in 1952 and was sent to Europe to train by C. V. Starr."

Strom once related details about a group of New York businessmen coming to Stowe in 1940, who created the first big chair lift on Mt. Mansfield, and [there was] Sepp Ruschp's excellent ski school, and how, "when Cornelius Vander Starr entered the picture things really did begin to happen...and of considerable importance was that he also could pay for it all."

"Mt Mansfield Skiing," Mt. Mansfield Ski Club newsletter, Dec. 16, 1946: "An effort will be made this winter by the Club to promote the enjoyment of ski touring and mountaineering in the Mt. Mansfield region. This activity is under the leadership of Erling Strom, Rolf Holtvedt, and David Burt. Mr. Strom made the first ski ascent of Mt. McKinley, the highest peak in North America. Guided trips off the beaten path are being planned..."

In 1949, he was described as a 52 year old ski mountaineer and one of the pioneer ski instructors in the United States. He pioneered cross-country skiing in the United States and in Canada, operating in the Mt. Assiniboine Camp, British Columbia, from 1928 until the 1970's.

The Stroms ran their lodge for 30 years when in the fall of 1970 the lodge was sold to the Holmbergs, "the nicest people in the world," writes Strom. The Holmbergs kept the old murals as that was the real reason they bought the place, the Holmbergs said. The murals have since been painted over.

Lowell Thomas wrote a detailed reminiscence about Erling Strom in the Stowe Reporter of April 3, 1986, shortly after the death of Strom on March 17, 1986. Thomas described the purchase of the Stowe lodge, Strom's frequent travels to Mt. Assiniboine, and his regular trips to Norway. Thomas wrote, "Strom had been teaching for 20 years by 1940, which was when folks had skied before mountains were slashed of timber and opened to sweeping slopes. Then tows and lifts were added to serve them. Today there are speedsters who can't wait long enough to be transported to a mountain summit or the top of a trail so they can rush down in the fastest time possible."

Strom once related to Thomas, "We never took our skis off after we finished a run. We just went back up the mountain, packing out the trails and conditioning ourselves at the same time."

He was inducted into the U.S. National Ski and Snowboard Hall of Fame and Museum in 1972. His book, Pioneers on Skis, was published in 1977. Then, in 1977, he returned to Norway having retired. He passed away in Oslo in March 1986.

Vermont Ski and Snowboard Museum Collection

MARVIN MORIARTY
1937-
&
BILLY KIDD
1943-

Vermont Ski and Snowboard Museum Collection

In 1954, young Marvin Moriarty won the Eastern Junior Slalom and Combined races. That year Billy Kidd and he went west to the competition in the Junior Nationals with Billy Woods. Billy won second in the Combined, Skip Bryan was 4th in the Slalom, but Marvin was injured.

Two years later at age 17, he was the youngest skier to be picked for the 1956 Olympic Team, but disaster happened: two weeks prior to the Olympics he broke his ankle in the Hannenkahm downhill races in Kitzbuhel, Austria.

Kim Brown writes in the Stowe Reporter in January 2011 that he recalls Marvin as perhaps the most famous pacesetter for the old Stowe Standard races on the Mountain in those days. "These were races contested on the Standard trail long before grooming existed. There were lots of moguls"

In 1956, Annabel Moriarty decided to knit a hat for her skier son to keep his ears warm. The first hat, a pentagonal shaped white one, was done as she learned on her new-to-her second-hand knitting machine. When other skiers saw this hat others wanted them, too. Many of the first hats were knitted by hand. This became a part-time business and soon the family realized they would need to hire help to keep up with the burgeoning orders. When a distributing firm asked to handle the hat, Annabel agreed to purchasing small looms for workers to use in their homes and a cottage industry was created for 55 home knitters. Her business boomed for more than 40 years. After about 2006, the sales of the hats declined.

Marvin now lives in retirement in Vero Beach, Florida.

Stowe Historical Society Archives

ANN "NOSE DIVE ANNIE" (COOKE) TAYLOR 1910-2007

She was nick-named "Nose Dive Annie" by Roland Palmedo, because she "practically lived" on that precipitous trail for advanced skiers. She hiked up and skied down daily regardless of weather conditions. Hagerman, Mansfield, Stowe's Loftiest Mountain.

[While interviewing friends and descendants of the pioneers for this book, almost everyone asked me about whether the colorful and famous "Nose Dive Annie" would be represented. PLH]

Ann was born in Ardmore, Pennsylvania [as was Mary Mather Bourdon], and brought up in Quincy, Illinois. At the age of 6, Ann's father, Lawrence P. Bonfoey, introduced her to flying when he often took her aloft in an open two-seater bi-plane. At 12, she began taking flying lessons, becoming one of only 25 women to earn a flying license in the United States in the early 1940's. She loved tennis and competed at Wimbledon. She married J. Negley Cooke, known

286

as "Cookie," in 1928 after which they moved to Vermont by the mid-1930's.

Charlie Lord chronicles the preliminary location of the Nose Dive trail, to be the first racing trail at Mt. Mansfield, in the summer of 1933. By winter of 1935-1936 seasons, the trail was skiable. Ann earned a reputation for her daring and rapid ski ascents after climbing up with skins on her skis, and her expert technique on the descents of the brand-new Nose Dive. She became known as "Nose Dive Annie," her name synonymous with the Nose Dive. Thus began her ski racing debut in Stowe, and in 1939 she was elected as an alternate on the U.S. Women's Olympic Ski Team. The first official rider on the new single chair lift when it opened December 1940 was Ann B. Cooke, the wife of the then vice-president of the Mt. Mansfield Lift Co. However with the outbreak of World War II, she instead served her country as a flight instructor for both U.S. Navy and Army pilots.

By 1941, her marriage had ended, and she began to design her own ski clothing which became very popular. She often skied in uniforms from the Civil War as well as her own creations, such as a matador cape and hat. Her clothing appeared on covers and articles of Vogue, Harper's Bazaar, and in the windows of Lord & Taylor on Fifth Ave., and other stores in New York City. Then in 1947, she married Vernon "Moose" Taylor, Jr. and by 1954, they had moved to Vail, Colorado where they raised their family. As one of the founders of the Vail ski area, the Taylors built one of the first ski chalets in the new town. By then, Ann had set her clothing design business aside to be a full-time wife and mother.

Nose Dive Annie passed on October 28, 2007, at her Denver home at the age of 97. In 2009, after her death, the Colorado Ski and Snowboard Hall of Fame honored Ann Bonfoey (Cooke) Taylor as a Pioneer.

Stevens

Teacher and pupils at the Burlington airport

Stowe Historical Society Archives

Ann with a group of pilots she was training during World War II

Dottie, Tom and Rita Buchanan take a break from their work to peer through connecting window from kitchen to dining room. Ted McKay was out doing errands when photo was taken.

Stowe Historical Society Archives

RITA BUCHANAN
(1928-

They Came to Stowe to Ski but Stayed to Build a Lodge.
Headline, *Burlington Free Press*, Dec. 27, 1956.

Before Rita and Tom Buchanan moved to Stowe, Rita worked in Connecticut. She would meet up with Werner Beckerhoff in Springfield, VT on Fridays after work and they would drive up to Stowe together, relates Helen Beckerhoff.

Ted McKay and Tom Buchanan purchased the land on which Winterhaus was built in 1955. Rita and Tom Buchanan, and Dottie and Ted McKay came from Connecticut to ski and stayed to build a lodge. Dottie told the Burlington Free Press correspondent that they were eager to get here. "We had very little money, some talent, but a lot of energy," said Dottie. They started in July 1955 and gave themselves a year, which turned out to be not enough. Their first booking was for 50 officials coming from the United Nations in New York to ski during the Christmas holiday.

The delegation representative was told that The Lodge was not completed, but still habitable to which the representative said they did not mind. That was in 1956. In the December 27, 1956 issue of the Burlington Free Press is the detailed article describing the opening of the lodge. There was so much to get ready in such a short time, that a distress signal was sent out and a group from Stowe village formed a building bee and came to help out. They painted, did small carpentry jobs, scrubbed, and even did some wiring. Food supplies began to arrive. Bunks were delivered just in time. The signature snowflake "Winterhaus" sign was put up outside.

Daughter, Dede Buchanan LaRow, provided further details. "My parents purchased a second parcel of land known as "The Robinson Farm." It is the same Robinson family upon whose land is the development "Robinson Springs." The farmer that owned this land, on which I now live, deeded his springs to the Town of Stowe, and that is where the town water comes from for the upper part of the Mountain Road. The springs are located on Edson Hill. 'Good Time Charlie's' night spot was in the barn and was started up by my father—which is how Mom came to work there. His intention was to have an alcohol-free nightclub for teens, etc., with live bands, but it became too popular.

"I guess it got pretty wild and there was a lot of partying in the parking lot, so they closed it down. Throughout my life I have come across people in a wide variety of situations—work, college, social gatherings, etc.—that have told me they used to go to 'Good Time Charlie's' and how much fun it was. Jim Shepard's ski shop was in the barn afterward [its first location until it moved across the Mountain Road], and then it was used as office space for Black Magic Chimney Sweeps which was run by Don Post and Chris Curtis."

Rita told this writer about the time that a very nice lady bus driver came to Winterhaus with a busload of kids which she said "would tear up the place." With this advance warning steps were taken that averted disaster, and chaos did not happen.

Courtesy of Dede LaRow, Daughter
Photograph by Michael R. Sorkin
Rita's Sepp Ruschp Ski School Instructor Badge

Rita was one of the few women ski instructors in the 1950's. Helen Wilhelm Wright confirms that there were very few women ski instructors in the 1950's and they only taught children. "Sepp was not big on women instructors." Dede Buchanan LaRow interviewed her mother, Rita, in January 2011. Rita "seconded" Helen's report that Sepp Ruschp did not like female instructors. So Dede asked her how she got in to the "Club," and Rita said, "It was because they needed us. They were so busy and so shorthanded. They had fifteen people lined up for lessons and they had no instructors, so I asked if I could help out, and that's how I started. It also seemed like they needed me on the days when the wind chill was minus 40 degrees. The men seemed to work less on those days."

Sally Curran Smith adds that she and Rita both took their ski instruction certification tests in New York, along with two men in 1958. The two women passed the tests and were certified, but the men weren't!

THE GALE SHAW, SR. FAMILY
Ann, Marilyn, Theresa, Barbara, and Gale Shaw, Jr.

Everyone in the Gale Shaw, Sr. family participated in some way to the developing ski industry in Stowe. Mr. Shaw was a prominent businessman who was active in the community. He served as one of the grand jurors, a Lamoille County Savings Bank director, as postmaster for Mt. Mansfield from 1936-1945, and was a general insurance agent. After his father, Howard E. Shaw passed away in 1924, Gale took over the family business and became president and treasurer of Stow are, Inc., and H.E. Shaw General Store. He also became a director of the Mt. Mansfield Co., while his wife, Theresa, was chairwoman of the Social Committee for a time. Sally McMahon, granddaughter of Gale, Sr., supplied entries from his business ledgers from the 1940's:

Friday, Feb. 22, 1946—Saw Cornelius V. Starr.

Friday, May 3, 1946—Flew to NYC.

Saw Mr. Starr. He offered $250,000 to help a development.

April 19, 1947—Went to Mt. Mansfield Lift meeting regarding Gordon Bull made   manager; cost of road to chair lift, building a tower about tree tops for people to look off, money for trails. Says, [J. Negley] Cooke thinks the state will help them an awful lot on trails, etc. . . ." The family owned major land holdings saw mills, etc., in town. Daughter Ann said her father loved to fish, but never skied. "He was the private, quiet one."

All of Gale and Theresa Shaw's four children were racers! They got their start when the children were taught to ski by their mother, and later Sepp Ruschp took over their training. They skinned up the Toll Road to ski down. And not to be forgotten, Theresa Shaw was chosen Vermont's Snow Queen in 1935.

The oldest child, Marilyn (1924-1989) was already making a name for herself when in 1938 at the national championships at Nose Dive in Stowe; Elizabeth Woolsey saw Marilyn ski and recognized her as "comer,". She had then placed 7th on that contest at 13 years old, and with only three years of skiing experience, Woolsey invited Marilyn to train. She continued to win various contests at Mt. Tremblant, the New Hampshire Slalom at Plymouth, and other areas around the country. The American Ski Annual of1940 writes: "Marilyn Shaw skied extremely well to win the National Combined Championship at Sun Valley at age 16." Woolsey states, "From her record it appears that she is a slalom specialist and a very steady runner. She should be an example to every young skier in her steadiness and in the lack of recklessness in her downhill running." The same year she was "Girl of the Month" in Youth Magazine. Another comment after the 1940 win on her 16th birthday, states her win is more remarkable due to Miss Shaw's age. Sun Valley will not soon forget this little Vermont school girl who carried off the honors."

At age 16, she was the youngest woman in history on the US Ski Team, an original member of the Mt. Mansfield Ski Club, spirited Vermonter, and a 1940 Olympian. An unknown admirer of hers is quoted as saying, "Those that haven't climbed on the Marilyn Shaw band wagon had better start climbing. In the meantime don't forget to give some credit to Sepp Ruschp who taught her a great deal of what she knows."

By 1942, Marilyn had entered Wellesley College and continued to compete. She was a stand-in, skiing for Sonja Henie in "Sun Valley Serenade" in April 1941. In 1944, she married Edward McMahon of Morrisville, VT, in Sacramento, CA. The U.S. Ski Hall of Fame inducted Marilyn onto their roster in 1986.

Sister Ann Savela said about her second sister, "Barbara shadowed Marilyn on her journeys to competitions and caught the competition bug," which can be contagious. They had both skied successfully during their high school years and became member of the American Women's Ski Team. Barbara attended the University of Vermont and Middlebury College, but graduated from Katherine Gibbs Secretarial School in June 1946. About a month later she married Hilton Wick, and worked in the Boston area until they moved to Burlington, VT in February 1948.

In November of 1955, Barbara became the owner of The Ski Shop on the Shelburne Rd. in Burlington as one of the earliest women's business operators. She was skilled at marketing, a discriminating buyer of merchandise, and an adept saleswoman. For a few short years Barbara owned and operated H.E. Shaw General Store in Stowe village, established by her grandfather. She later sold the business to her sister, Ann and her husband Ken Savela. .Barbara loved people and was very fond of her trademark corn cob pipe.

Third sibling, Gale, Jr. learned to ski jump off a wooden ski jump that had been built across from the Stowe Center on Birch Hill. When he was about 11 years old, Sears Raymond took him to a ski race in Montpelier where he won in his age group...and thus he became hooked on the sport," declares his wife, M.J. Pepi Gabl, an Austrian who Sepp Ruschp brought to his ski school honed Gale's technique. Gale's father sent him to the Vermont Academy for his high school years where he skied for events at the school in cross country, downhill, jumping, and slalom. Being the star of his team, he was elected captain during his senior year in 1949. At Middlebury College, he raced and won often, becoming captain of the team during his senior year in 1953. And not to be forgotten, M.J. Shaw was executive director of the Mt. Mansfield Ski Club for several years.

After graduation, Gale enlisted in the U.S. Army and was stationed at Verdun, France. While there he was approached by his superior officer and was told to report to Franconia, NH to try out for the US Olympic Ski Team. He arrived back in the States just in time to put on his skis and race a downhill course at Franconia Notch. The fog was so thick that day that Gale wasn't sure he was still on the course. When he did find the finish, he decided right then that the French girls were more interesting than ski racing, and headed back to Europe where his superior officer banished him to the army ski patrol at Berchtesgaden where he happily skied out the remainder of his enlistment. Back in the states, he was president of the Mt. Mansfield Ski Club in 1958-1959 and helped Sepp organize international ski races here in Stowe,

Gale, Jr. and M.J. had three children, all skiers: Gale III (Tiger), Andrew, and Dani. Tiger, former Olympian, was inducted into the Vermont Alpine Racing Association in October 2009; Andy (Beach), the 1986 NCAA GS champion, was inducted to the University of Vermont Hall of Fame in 2005; and Dani was an All-American skier at Middlebury.

Last in line of the siblings was Ann. Beginning at the age of 5, she skied continually, and progressed through high school in Stowe when she began to enter racing competitions. Ann comments that when she entered the University of Vermont in 1949, she started the program to establish a ski team. In that first year, she earned a slot on the U.S. Ski Team competing against Canada. She captained the team in 1950. In her sophomore year, she received a tryout for the 1952 Olympics at Sun Valley, and as a junior, she earned fifth place in the slalom at the nationals which were held in Stowe that year. Ann represented UVM at Middlebury Winter Carnivals, and in 1953 she won the New York State Slalom Championships. She raced in the New England's, the Easterns, the Trans-National, and the National Seniors during here career.

Courtesy of Ann Shaw Savela
First University Ski Team, 1949
Toni Peloquin, Judy Aronson, Ann Shaw and Lena Gale

An interesting story from Ann about her grade point average while at UVM and spending so much time practicing for, and racing in competitions, she told of going to a well-known professor and artist Francis Colburn and explained, "I race and I am gone a lot. Can I take your course to get by?" And he said, "Sure!" Her graduation took place in 1953.

As a versatile athlete, she played basketball in high school, and excelled at golf, winning several championships in the 1970's. Ann and her husband Ken Savela owned the H.E. Shaw General Store in the village until their recent retirement, when their daughter Anne-Marie and her husband Sal Vespa took over. She was inducted into the University of Vermont Athletic Hall of Fame in 1984.

Courtesy of Lena Gale Allen

LENA GALE ALLEN
1928-

In on the ground floor of early ski competitions in town were Lena and Emma-Lou Gale. Although twelve years apart, they both got their start at very young ages, Lena was five years old when she first put on homemade skis crafted by her grandfather and her father. The skis were long, slender pieces of wood with a slot in the middle. "Grandpa made toe straps to go through the slot, and then we took Mason jar rubbers and put them over our toe, and around the back of our heels, to keep the skis on," relates Lena. Their brother Don also participated, as everyone in the family were outdoor people. These were the children of Charles and Ruth Gale of the Gale Farm on the Mountain Road.

The Charlie and Ruth Gale family did not take in ski guests, but the girls grandmother, Jennie Sanborn Gale (1891-1983) did take in guests at nearby Rocky River Lodge (the former West Branch Meeting House) on the Mountain Rd. Later, this Lodge was operated by Susie Sanborn Irish, Jennie Gale's niece. While Susie Sanborn was dating her future husband, Lee Irish, they would take Lena skiing. They had found some maple skis for her which she really liked. The skis had bindings which were fastened down for downhill and loosened for cross-country. She and her brother Don would "hike" on skis across the fields to Strom's Hill (now Mountainside at Cottage Club Road and the Mountain Road). The brick house (now Cactus Cafe) was then Strom's Lodge. "Being shy, we would stand aside and listen to Strom's lessons to his guests. After Mr. Strom went home, we would practice what we had heard." And then ski back to the farm again.

Later Susie and Lee took her to the Toll House where Lena would learn the proper way to hold onto the rope tow after many previous failings. "The Toll House slope was our first use of a real ride uphill to ski downhill!"

Lena skied in high school along with sisters Marilyn, Barbara, and Ann Shaw. She relates that she started ski racing while in high school and continued to race while attending Green Mountain Junior College, and at the University of Vermont on the college ski team. She became obsessed with skiing and every weekend that she could manage it, she would hitch a ride back to Mt. Mansfield to practice downhill or slalom. A football player and great skier [name unknown] would set up slalom courses on the Nose Dive corridor and make her practice until she was exhausted. "Up and down, climbing all the time, as they used just the short steep pitch in the middle of the trail for practice..." No helmets back then. After graduation from UVM, she worked at a ski shop in the Stowe Center. She continued practicing every day before going to work until 9 PM, and then practice again after that. That was a daunting daily routine! Luckily her boss would give her time off to race on weekends.

The winter of 1951-2, she won just about every race in the East. She was Vermont State Champion, placed first in the Eastern's Downhill, Slalom, and Combined as well as first in the Canadian Championships and other races in the US and Internationals. Once she was second behind Andrea Mead Lawrence in the Combined. She was sponsored by the Mt. Mansfield Co. to go to either South

America or Europe for a winter of skiing. She chose Europe. In December of that year, she and ten other young people went to New York City as protégés of C.V. Starr who was their sponsor. Beginning in winter 1951, she raced at Mt. Greylock, MA in the US Eastern Giant Slalom, Ste. Marguerite, Quebec, and at Pico, in Rutland, Vermont. The next year, the US Nationals and Internationals were held in Stowe in which she participated, and in 1953, she raced in Seefeld and Kittsbuehl, Austria, Garmisch, Germany, and St. Moritz, Switzerland.

Courtesy of Lena Gale Allen
Lena Racing Downhill

Emma-Lou echoes much of what Lena described about growing up on the farm, learning the ropes at Strom's, and then merging into the ski competition world. She remembers that the only other girl skiing when they were in junior high was Susie Adams, who did not continue in high school. Most of the time, Emma Lou skied with Shamus Daly, Paul Percy, Ellsworth Nichols, and Billy Kidd. "I was skiing on 210 downhills and 205 slaloms and could sometimes beat the boys down Big Spruce on my downhills. The Mountain Co. was very generous and saw that all of us got to ski free on Tuesday and Thursday afternoons, and our racing crew on Friday afternoons as well. Those of us who were racing at that time got to ski behind Chickie Igaya, Bob Bourdon, or any of the ski instructors who gave up their afternoons to let us follow them down the National and Lift Line trails, many times non-stop. Fun for kids! We skied in races all over New England with Charlie and Peg Daly being chaperones on several trips."

Em continues, "Sometimes we would bum rides up to the mountain at 7 a.m. with whomever we could catch on their way to work and could then start our day with the 'milk run.'" They would ski all day and ride home with some one they knew. But sometimes when they were doing their last run down the Toll Road they would miss everyone so skied home, only six miles to the farm. "Many days we would go to Spruce Peak in the mornings and set slalom courses, Marvin Moriarty and Billy Kidd set the best ones, and we would hike up and ski down, memorizing them, and a treat would be to ski to the bottom and ride up the lift. When there were lines on weekends we couldn't ski free so hiked up and down and our reward was to go over and run downhill on the 'big mountain' in the afternoons."

Both sisters say that when skiing at the mountain all the instructors sort of kept an eye on them, and this was a perfect way to grow up.

The Foster Place

ANNE (MORGAN) (SIMONEAU) AUGUST 1922-

Anne remembers many stories from the early days skiing at Stowe. She said that Craig Burt, Sr. took them on cross country picnics on the lumber trails which were later developed to become ski trails. Early visitors to Ranch Camp either skied in or went by sleds with their baggage. That was about 1945. Races were held on the Toll Road, Nose Dive, Bruce, and S-53 trails which they used to cross over to Lift Line and Starr trails.

She met Henry Simoneau in 1946 on the slopes. She ran the Foster Place beginning in 1949, succeeding Woody Woodhouse, and ran it until 1957, when she married Henry. During the time she managed the Foster Place, she heard stories about her across-the-road neighbors, Dr. Marguerite Lichtenthaeler and Mrs. Helen Montanari, who took in boarders and raised English sheep dogs. The sheep dogs drew sleds for the guests. And the ladies are said to have chaperoned their guests very closely!

Anne described in a telephone interview that "post Foster Place managership" she ran a Tea Room in the Eggleston's house across from the stable on the Mountain Rd. She was drawing in skiers by the dozens because of her serving of mouth-watering cinnamon toast, the fragrance of which wafted out to the main road. Her familiar nick-name developed in her family because when she was young, she was shaped like a polly-wog, hence her nick-name, "Wogs."

Alex Nimick met Ruthie Porter in the 1940's at the Foster Place at Stowe Forks, one of the earliest ski lodges, once owned by the Burts. She was another one of several managers of this famous hostel and served for three seasons.

Other snippets of her many stories: "There were some broadcasts by Lowell Thomas from The Lodge as well as from the Green Mountain Inn, and that George Morrell, the owner of the Lodge, would not permit blue jeans to be worn by women."

Anne now lives at Wake Robin in Shelburne, VT where other ski pioneers from Stowe now reside, Gordon Lowe, Dee and David Partridge, and Frankie Harrison Sparks.

Boston & Maine Railroad

On board a ski train bound north from Boston

Stowe Historical Society Archives
Interior Shot of a Coach on the Ski Train from Boston

GEORGE R., JR. AND VERA FEARING

As told by daughter, Hesterly (Fearing) (Black) Buckley

Hesterly (Fearing) (Black) Buckley sent these delightful remembrances from her parent's day, as well as her own, virtually a portrait of Stowe in the 1940's and 1950's, a broad range of people and places.

"In 1933-34, my parents were involved in a club called the Hochgebirge Ski Club from Boston. My parents were George R. Fearing and wife Vera. They, and others, would take the train from Boston and be met at Waterbury and then stay at "The Lodge" then owned by George Morrell. Mr. Morrell's daughter, Dinny, was in Stowe as late as the mid-1970's and was a good friend of Darby Chambers. They walked up the Toll Road and ski down the Nose Dive, according to my mother, and would make three or four runs a day! I still have the skins they used for climbing somewhere as there was no lift then. Imagine being in such good shape! It makes me tired just to think about it Sepp arrived [shortly before] the lift did

303

[1940] and Cornelius V. Starr bought the Lodge and invested in the Mountain and that was the beginning of Stowe as we know it.

"Arthur Dana was a friend back then, and he settled on West Hill. V. Z. Reed, Verner's father, had his house, Edson Hill Manor, and his own ski lift, but I don't think he had any connection to Mr. Starr.

"In the '40's, Anne (Morgan) (Simoneau) August and her friend Wa Wa Lannen carried on as innkeepers at Foster Place, near Dr. Lichtenthaeler's where the Hockey School is now, and where Stowe Prep used to be. Helen Murray, better known as Maxie, and her best friend Helen (Hennie) Doherty lived near the Toll House, next to Claire Lintilhac's. To make a long story short, they all fell in love with Stowe and Maxie stayed on as Sepp's private secretary. Priscilla Hess came on the scene about the same time, as a book keeper. Hennie and her husband John Dougherty, came up skiing and to see Maxie, and eventually built their house near the Toll House where they retired.

"Kerr Sparks was originally a landscape architect from the Boston area (Swampscott), and became a ski instructor. During the war he was a member of the 10th Mountain Division with Sepp and Henry Simoneau. Kerr and his (then) wife Matilda/Tildy settled in Stowe. They soon divorced and she married Vernor Reed, Jr. and Kerr married Frankie [Harrison]. .. Most of the attractive plantings at the Toll House, then run by Gub and Doris Langdon were planted by Kerr about the same time, just after the war, "Parker Perry bought the Green Mountain Inn and married Dottie Whipple, hence the name "The Whip" for the bar. Stowe was dry in those days and you brought your own. Also, about the same time, my brother Dick Fearing started the first Top Notch where the Olde England Inn is today. He later sold to Dick Hood, Don Schole and Peter Parker, and started Tyrola Lodge where Foxfire is today. None of the motels on the Mountain Road existed. The Partridge Inn was owned by the Hannes Lipponers and was the Mountain Chalet. Warner Brothers was across from the Episcopal Church, which was then a district school, and Darby Almy was the cook. Ten Acres was run by Charlie and Blanche Blauvelt before they built Roundhearth.

"Back to Kerr, he became head of the Ski School, and then as the area grew and Spruce was built, Sears Raymond came on the scene. Rob Salvas was one of the builders of the hut at the top of Spruce. Alice and Gerry Hartigan worked at the Lodge, Alice as a waitress and Gerry as sommelier.

"If you go up and down the Mountain Road, most of the Austrian and German names came from their days as ski instructors who all stayed at Harlow House. Many others worked at the Lodge as chefs, or as in the case of Ivor Petrac, as managers.

"Incidentally, Annabelle Moriarty started out as a cleaning lady and then she became a caterer before she made her famous hats for her racer son, Marvin."

****

As later participants in the 1950's, we remember Gerry and Alice Hartigan at the Lodge; Bill and Connie Bull who, with Freddie and Betsey Killingbeck, built and operated the Old Shoe ski dorm in the village; George Barton, sommelier at The Lodge; Roman Wickart (1924-1993) who came to Stowe from Switzerland in 1955 to teach skiing for the Mt. Mansfield Co.; and many others. Developing these personalities and others will be left to future historians.

Stowe Historical Society Archives

NORMA (MAGNUS)
(WALKER) BARTOL
1929-

Norma Magnus Walker Bartol's connection to the early ski days in Stowe was discovered within her March 1, 2013 column published in the Greenwich Time, Greenwich, CT. She became a ski bum in Stowe for two years back in 1949 and 1950, when her cousins Charles "Shot" and Willie Warner bought a farmhouse, converted it to become a ski lodge, and asked her to join them. They spent much of their free time at Topnotch, (later Sans Souci, and today, Ye Olde England Inn). Topnotch at that time was owned by Dick Fearing, sister of Hesterly Fearing Buckley. Dick came to Stowe in 1946 or 1947 and renovated an old house, across from the Lipponers' Mountain Chalet, to become the lodge. Hesterly, in her mid-teens, remembers washing dishes and chamber-maiding for her brother. The Warner/Magnus cousins also spent time at the popular gathering spot, the Foster Place. Back in that day, Darby (Almy) later Chambers, worked for the Warner brothers at their farmhouse which was located at the corner of the Mountain

Road and Luce Hill Road, which they purchased from the Kittles in 1945. Today this is the Riverside Inn.

The Mt. Mansfield Ski Club newsletter contains columns by Norma, from the New York City perspective, and by Pansy Prince from the Boston point of view, beginning December 1, 1951, and ran occasionally through the 1950's. She still writes columns for the Greenwich Time today. In her March 1, 2013 article, Norma recalls several names of Greenwich and New York City people and organizations who contributed to the development of skiing in Stowe: Minnie Dole, C. V. Starr, the Amateur Ski Club of New York, Roland Palmedo, the founding of the National Ski Patrol system, and Franklin Edson, of Greenwich.

One fascinating detail, relayed by telephone on April 29, concerns the "chalet car," a private railroad car owned by the railroad but rented by a group from the New York City area, which traveled from New York City and stopped in Waterbury. Alexander Mc Ilvaine was the leader. She also describes an unofficial and infamous New Year's Day "Hangover Handicap" race between the Warner brothers, the Foster Place, and Topnotch teams, when they would each hang onto the other, then snowplow down the mountain. First team down was the winner. "The best fun," she said.

Stowe Historical Society Archives
Two Skiers Waiting for a Ride to the Mountain

Acknowledgements

Many, many people have contributed their knowledge, photos, and stories about the early years of the development of the Stowe ski industry and the participants who made it all happen. It is all very much appreciated. These include first and foremost, Barbara Harris Sorkin without whose generous offer of help to edit and produce this book, a special thank-you. We had no previous knowledge of this being one of her talents.

Special thanks go out to Christi Ruschp Dickinson for the permission to publish her father's memoir, and providing photos and memorabilia from her personal collection. Also thank you Tom Amidon, executor of Sepp Ruschp's estate, for providing permission to us to publish both Sepp's memoir, and the photos of Bill Riley.

And my deepest appreciation to Biddle Duke for giving us permission to reprint the Charlie Lord ski articles in the book and to John P. Lord of Groton VT, son of Charlie Lord, who loaned to us Charlie's photo albums.

The following Stowe Historical Society members Chuck Dudley, Barbara Baraw, Wendy Snow Parrish, Connie Bull, and Lois Kiefer, who have been especially helpful over the last couple of years of putting this book together.

Mike Leach, who describes himself as "the defacto historian of the MMSC" scanned all the MMSC Newsletters onto the Club's website, which made access easy and an invaluable source for this book. And thank Mike for the many suggestions to other sources that have helped me in the research.

Many thanks to my readers, husband Peter Haslam, Sr., Johanna Darrow, and descendants or friends of the pioneers who have encouraged me each step of the way and a special thanks to Kate Haslam Paine for the great job she did on our regional publicity campaign.

And though I will inevitably omit many who should be mentioned, I would like to express special gratitude to Jane Weaver, Polly Rollins

Straub, Marc Sherman (beautiful cover photograph) Denise Burt Cushwa (family papers of her grandfather, Craig Burt, Sr.), John P. Lord (of Groton, VT for loan of his father's photo albums and reading), Dr. John Gale and daughter Judith Gale (for information regarding George W. Gale), Karin Gottlieb, Michael Sorkin (tech support, photography and lots of patience), Marion Kellogg, Wanda Morton, Meredith Scott (director, Vermont Ski Museum), Lee Darrow (for tracking information on Cooke and Simoneau houses being razed in 2003 to make way for the new Stowe Mountain Resort), Jeannette Pearson, Greg Morrill (Stowe Reporter, his retro columns), Norwich University Archives librarians (Northfield, VT: Suzanne Desch, Gail Wiese, and Jennifer Payne), Helen Wilhelm Wright, Christine and Bruce LaRow, Mary Curtis Skelton, Gretchen Besser (National Ski Patrol Historian) David and Dee Partridge, Rick Moulton (Huntington, VT), Marcia Smith and Molly Pease (Stowe Free Library).

Sources

Part I: The Physical Development of the Mountain

Davis, Thomas C. "Ski Pioneers—The Early Days on Mt. Mansfield."
  Vermont Life Magazine, Winter 1989. 5–8.

Earle, Elinor. "Charlie Lord, One of the World's Seven Wonders."
  Stowe the Magazine, Winter 1992–1993. 35–41.

Geggis, Anne. "Vt. Ski Pioneer Dies at 95." *Burlington Free Press*,
  December 1997.

Hartt, Pete. "Charlie Lord Dead at 95." Obituaries. *Stowe Reporter*,
  December 25, 1997.

Lord, John P. Loan of Charlie's photo albums.

Marsh, Erline V. "The Coming of Charlie Lord." *Stowe Heritage*,
  n.d. 20–26.

Marsh, Erline V. "Trailmaster of Mount Mansfield: Charlie Lord."
  Country Courier, May 22, 1992.

Moulron, Rick. *Legends of American Skiing*. DVD. Huntington,
  VT: Keystone Productions, 1982. http://www.rickmoulton.com/
  merchandise/legends.shtml.

Mt. Mansfield Ski Club. Newsletters/Bulletins. http://www.
  teammmsc.org/newsletter. 1930–1960.

Schwartz, Nan B. "Ranch Valley Days: Charlie Lord Remembers."
  Stowe Country, Winter 1988.

Part II: The Sepp Ruschp Memoir

"A Celebration of the Life of Sepp Ruschp." Memorial service
  program, July 14, 1990.

Ancestry.com. *New York, Passenger Lists, 1820–1957*. Online
  database. Provo, UT: Ancestry.com Operations, Inc., 2010.

Ancestry.com. *Passenger Ships and Images: S.S. Deutschland*.
  Online database. Provo, UT: Ancestry.com Operations Inc, 2007.

Burt, Craig O. *We Lived in Stowe: A Memoir*. Middlebury, VT: Ranch Camp Publishers, 2003.

Dickinson, Christina Ruschp. Personal and e-mail interviews and family papers, 2011, 2012.

Fillion, Don. "The King of the Mountain." *Vermonter Magazine*, February 13, 1977. 4.

"Hundreds Celebrate the Life of Sepp Ruschp." *Mt. Mansfield Ski Club Newsletter*, November 1990. 1, 8.

Mt. Mansfield Ski and Snowboard Club. http://www.teammmsc.org.

Mt. Mansfield Ski Patrol. http://www.mtmansfieldskipatrol.org.

National Ski Areas Association. https://www.nsaa.org.

Navarro, Mirey A. "Sepp Ruschp, 81; Skier Who Brought Sport to US is Dead." Obituaries. *New York Times*, June 10, 1990. http://www.nytimes.com/1990/06/10/obituaries/sepp-ruschp-81-skier-who-brought-sport-to-us-is-dead.html.

Oliver, Peter. *Stowe: Classic New England*. Boulder, CO: Mountain Sports Press, 2002.

"Sepp Ruschp Elected President of the National Ski Association." *Mt. Mansfield Skiing* 26, no. 4 (July 1960): 2. http://www.teammmsc.org/newsletter_1960s.html.

Stowe Historical Society. Archives.

Stowe Reporter, various issues. [Indexed to 1996 at Stowe Free Library, Vermont Room.]

Vermont Ski and Snowboard Museum. Archives. http://www.vtssm.com/collections/library-a-archives.

US Ski and Snowboard Hall of Fame and Museum. http://skihall.com.

Part III: People Remembering People

Craig Burt Sr.

Bigelow, W. J. *History of Stowe, Vermont: from 1763 to 1934*. 2nd ed. Stowe, VT: Stowe Historical Society, 1988.

Burt, Craig O. *We Lived in Stowe: A Memoir*. Middlebury, VT: Ranch Camp Publishers, 2003.

Cushwa, Denise Burt. Personal interview and review of her family papers, September 2011.

Duffy, John J., Samuel B. Hand, and Ralph H. Orth, eds. *The Vermont Encyclopedia*. Lebanon, NH: University Press of New England, 2003.

Mt. Mansfield Ski Club. Newsletters/Bulletins. http://www.teammmsc.org/history.html.

Obituary. *Burlington Free Press*, April 16, 1965.

Oliver, Peter. *Stowe: Classic New England*. Boulder, CO: Mountain Sports Press, 2002.

Stowe Historical Society. Archives.

Vermont Ski and Snowboard Museum. http://www.vtssm.com.

Roland Palmedo

Boe, Gene. "King Roland from Mad River." *Vermont Skiing*, Winter 1966. 27, 29.

Duffy, John J., Samuel B. Hand, and Ralph H. Orth, eds. *The Vermont Encyclopedia*. Lebanon, NH: University Press of New England, 2003.

Luray, Martin. "The Remarkable Mr. Palmedo: A Ski Profile." *Ski Magazine*, December 1959.

Mt. Mansfield Ski Club. Newsletters/Bulletins. http://www.teammmsc.org/history.html.

Obituary. *Skiing Magazine*, September 1977. 21.

Obituary. *Ski Life*, September 1977. 40.

Palmedo, Lt. Commander Roland, USNR. "A Tropical Tour." *Williams College Ski Team American Ski Annual*. 95–97.

Roland Palmedo Collection. New England Ski Museum. December 2008.

Ronald Palmedo Library. US Ski and Snowboard Hall of Fame and Museum, Ishpeming, MI.

Vermont Ski and Snowboard Museum. Archives.

Frank Griffin

Ancestry.com. *1930 Federal Census.* Online database. Provo, UT: Ancestry.com Operations Inc.

Burt, Craig O. "Frank E Griffin: Ski Pioneer." *Vermont Sunday News,* June 18, 1961.

Leab, Richard C. Senior Assistant, Pittsfield (MA) Public Library. E-mail correspondence, Jan. 2012.

Tyler, Linda M. City Clerk, City of Pittsfield. E-mail Correspondence, Jan. 2012

George W. Gale

Burt, Craig O. *We Lived in Stowe: A Memoir.* Middlebury, VT: Ranch Camp Publishers, 2003.

Gale, Judith A. (daughter of John Sumner Gale, MD). Personal interview and manuscript—Chapter 4, "Skiing," concerning George W. Gale, father of John S. Gale, draft as of June 9, 2010, with permission to quote.

"George Warren Gale." Obituaries. *Burlington Free Press.* August 31, 1964.

Hagerman, Robert L. *Mansfield: The Story of Vermont's Loftiest Mountain.* 2nd ed. Canaan, NH: Phoenix Publishing Company, 1975.

Haslam, P. L. *Stowe, Vermont History and Genealogy: The Susan W. Downer Collection.* Stowe, VT: Stowe Historical Society: 2001. 52.

Abner Coleman

Davis, Thomas C. "Ski Pioneers—The Early Days on Mt. Mansfield." *Vermont Life Magazine,* Winter 1989. 5–8.

Harrison, Blake. "The Technological Turn: Skiing and Landscape Change in Vermont 1930–1970." *Vermont History* 71, no 3 and no 4, Summer–Fall 2003: 211.

Coleman, A. W., ed. *Mt. Mansfield Skiing.* Newsletter, Mt. Mansfield Ski Club. Various issues. December 8, 1951, p. 3; November 1993, p. 9.

Obituary. *Times-Argus,* Barre, VT, June 3, 2000.

Oliver, Peter. *Stowe: Classic New England.* Boulder, CO: Mountain Sports Press, 2002. 53, 59, 148, 170.

Stowe the Magazine, Winter 1992–1993. 38, 39.

Albert W. Gottlieb

"Al Gottlieb Resigns." *Stowe Reporter,* August 26, 1971.

"Ex-Forestry Official Albert Gottlieb Dies." *Burlington Free Press,* January 3, 1978.

Gottlieb, Elizabeth R. E-mail correspondence.

"Gottlieb to Retire." *Burlington Free Press,* October 29, 1970.

Obituary. *Stowe Reporter,* January 3, 1978.

Rae, Karin Gottlieb. E-mail correspondence.

Stowe Historical Society. Archives.

"Vermonter Remembers Win Over Flying Finn." *Burlington Free Press,* October 5, 1973.

Perry H. Merrill

Davis, Jeremy. "The History of Vermont Skiing: One Hundred Years of Growth." April 20, 1998. http://www.nelsap.org/vt/history.html.

Davis, Thomas C. "Ski Pioneers—The Early Days on Mt. Mansfield." *Vermont Life Magazine,* Winter 1989.

Duffy, John J., Samuel B. Hand, and Ralph H. Orth, eds. *The Vermont Encyclopedia.* Lebanon, NH: University Press of New England, 2003.

Mt. Mansfield Ski Club. Newsletters/Bulletins. http://www.teammmsc.org/history.html.

"Perry H. Merrill, 99; Created Vermont Parks." Obituaries. *New York Times*, December 25, 1993. http://www.nytimes.com/1993/12/25/obituaries/perry-h-merrill-99-created-vermont-parks.html.

"Resorts Weather the Storm." *Burlington Free Press*, July 22, 1991.

Vermont Ski and Snowboard Museum. http://www.vtssm.com.

Cornelius Vander Starr

Ancestry.com. *WWI and WWII Draft Registration Cards.*

"Cornelius Vander Starr 1892–1968," Memorial, in-house publication. New York: C. V. Starr & Co., 1970.

"Neil V. Starr." Obituaries. *Mendocino Beacon*, December 27, 1968.

Obituary. *Burlington Free Press*, n.d.

Oliver, Peter. *Stowe: Classic New England*. Boulder, CO: Mountain Sports Press, 2002.

Vermont History, Summer–Fall 2003. 211.

Viuhkola, Carylon. Mendocino County Historical Society, Ukiah, CA.

Webster, Barbara. Mendocino County Historical Society, Ukiah, CA.

Wei Chi Poon and Jainye He. Special Collection named for C. V. Starr, dedicated October 2007. East Asian Library, University of California, Berkeley.

Who's Who in America 34 (1966–1967). Chicago, IL: Marquis Co., 1967.

C. Minot "Minnie" Dole

Adler, Allen. *New England and Thereabouts: A Ski Tracing*. Nelco Press, 1985. ISBN 10:0961776307.

Adler, Allen. "Recognizing the Tenth's Vermonters." *Vermont Ski Museum Newsletter* 10, no. 1 (Winter 2010): 8.

Besser, Gretchen R. *Alpenglow Ski Mountaineering History Project*. The National Ski Patrol, 1983. http://www.alpenglow.org/ski-history/.

Besser, Gretchen R. *The National Ski Patrol: Samaritans of the Snow*. Woodstock, VT: The Countryman Press, 1983.

Brooks, Thomas. "Division Founder Dole Faced Opposition from the Start." *Blizzard: Published By and For the Soldiers of the 10th Mountain Division* 9, no. 1 (2010). http://10thmtndivassoc. org/2010_Issue_1_Blizzard.pdf.

Burt, Craig O. *We Lived in Stowe: A Memoir.* Middlebury, VT: Ranch Camp Publishers, 2003.

Colorado Ski and Snowboard Museum Hall of Fame. http://www. skimuseum.net.

Dole, C. Minot. "A History of Mt. Mansfield Skiing." The Historical Committee of the Mt. Mansfield Ski Club, n.d.

Dole, Minot. *Adventures in Skiing.* The Adventure Library. New York: Franklin Watts, 1965.

Dole, Minot (C. M.) Jr. Personal interview, June 10, 2011.

Obituary. *Greenwich Time*, March 16, 1976: A7.

St. John's in the Wilderness Episcopal Cemetery, Brighton, NY. Gravestone inscription and memorial marker, images. http:// freepages.genealogy.rootsweb.ancestry.com/~frgen/franklin/ brighton/wilderness.htm.

J. Negley "Cookie" Cooke

Adler, Allen. *New England and Thereabouts: A Ski Tracing.* Nelco Press, 1985.

Colorado Ski and Snowboard Museum Hall of Fame. http://www. skimuseum.net.

"J. Negley Cooke." *Honored Members.* US Ski and Snowboard Hall of Fame and Museum. http://skihall.com/index. php?_a=document&doc_id=11&id=73.

New England Ski Museum. http://newenglandskimuseum.org.

Obituary. *Stowe Reporter*, August 1978.

Vermont Ski and Snowboard Museum. http://www.vtssm.com.

Jacques Charmoz

Charmoz, Frederique (daughter of Jacques Charmoz). E-mail correspondence beginning January 2012.

Jacques Charmoz: The Website. http://www.jacquescharmoz.com.

Mt. Mansfield Ski Club. Newsletters/Bulletins, December 12, 1938–January 30, 1939. http://www.teammmsc.org/history.html.

Gary Fisher

Buckly, Hesterly (Black). E-mail correspondence.

Haslam, Peter, Jr. E-mail correspondence.

Mt. Mansfield Ski Club. Newsletters/Bulletins. http://www.teammmsc.org/history.html.

Obituary. *Stowe Reporter*, June 28, 2012.

Wright, Helen (Wilhelm). E-mail correspondence.

Clem Curtis

Gear Box: Weekly Newsletter of the Stowe Rotary Club, September 9, 2010.

McCormack, Lisa. "Love Story: After 60 Years of Marriage, They Still Hold Hands." Stowe Scene. *Stowe Reporter*, September 9, 2004. 1, 15.

Scrapbooks of clippings and photos of Clem Curtis, 10th Mountain Division training, loaned by the Curtis family, 2011.

Sharp, Margery. "Clem Curtis: Ski Pioneer and Builder." *The Transcript*, Morrisville, VT, November 11, 2010.

Skelton, Mary Curis (daughter of Clem Curtis). E-mail interview, with notes by her father.

Gordon Lowe

Altadonna, Lynn P. *Stowe Country Club History: 1948 to 2006.* Stowe Country Club Blog. http://thestowecountryclub.blogspot.com/p/stowe-country-club-history.html.

Dutch Hill Ski Area. Heartwellville, VT http://www.nelsap.org/vt/dutch1.html.

Stead, Nancy. "10th Mountain Soldier Honorable at New Home." *Stowe Reporter*, December 2, 2010. Scene p. 16.

Lowe, Gordon. Interview at Shelburne, VT, July 2010.

"The Lincoln Detachment: 10th Mountain Division Training in New Hampshire." New England Ski Museum. http://newenglandskimuseum.org/the-lincoln-detachment-10th-mountain-division-training-in-new-hampshire/.

Priscilla Hess

Bull, Connie. E-mail interview, 2010.

Obituary. *Stowe Reporter*, September 8, 2005.

Weaver, Jane. E-mail interview.

Helen "Maxie" (Murray) Ruschp

Dickinson, Christi Ruschp. Personal interviews, 2011, 2012.

Egenberg, Julie Dougherty. Handwritten correspondence, November 2011.

Straub, Polly Rollins. E-mail interview, October 2011.

Bill Riley

Beck, Peter. E-mail correspondence and interview, 2010.

"Bill Riley." Obituaries. *Stowe Reporter*, April 10, 2010.

Camp, Phil. Eulogy, April 2010.

Mt. Mansfield Ski and Snowboard Club. http://www.teammmsc.org.

Zimmer, Kurt. *Stowe Reporter*, July 22, 2004. 23.

Henry Simoneau

Elkins, Frank. "New Ski Lift Is Dedicated at Stowe." *Burlington Free Press*, December 1954.

Gilcrist, Gil. "Chit Chat." *Mt. Mansfield Skiing* 16, no. 2 (December 1, 1950): 5, 7. http://www.teammmsc.org/Newsletters/MtMansfield Skiing/1950s/December%201950.pdf.

"Mt. Mansfield Co. Honors Founders." *Stowe Reporter*, May 24, 1990.

Obituary. *Stowe Reporter*, February 16, 1995.

Reed, Tildy. "Old Times at the Toll House Slopes." *Stowe Reporter*, April 15, 1982.

Simoneau, Henry. "Mt. Mansfield Ski Club Races—1951." *Mt. Mansfield Skiing* 17, no. 1 (December 1, 1950): 7. http://www.teammmsc.org/Newsletters/MtMansfieldSkiing/1950s/December%201950.pdf.

Williams, Robert B. "Patrol Interests." *Mt. Mansfield Skiing* 23, no. 2 (January 1957): 6. http://www.teammmsc.org/Newsletters/MtMansfieldSkiing/1950s/January%201957.pdf.

Kerr Sparks Jr. and Frankie (Harrison) Sparks

Death certificate. Vermont Vital Records, Vermont State Archives.

"Frances Harrison Sparks." Obituaries. *Burlington Free Press*, February 23, 2012.

Mt. Mansfield Ski Club News. 60th anniversary edition, November 1993.

Mt. Mansfield Ski Club. Newsletters/Bulletins. http://www.teammmsc.org/history.html.

Obituary of Kerr Sparks.

Obituary. *Stowe Reporter*, April 22, 1993.

Photo of Kerr Sparks and Nancy Graham. *Burlington Free Press*, December 7, 1957. Stowe Historical Society Archives.

"Sports News." *Eagle*, Lawrence, MA, March 24, 1950. Stowe Historical Society Archives.

Milton Teffner

Mt. Mansfield Skiing 22, no. 1 (December 1955).

Obituary. *Stowe Reporter*, May 24, 1968.

Ruschp, Sepp. "In Memoriam." *Stowe Reporter*, May 24, 1968.

"Sixth District Gazette." *CCC Weekly*. Camp Charles M. Smith, Waterbury, VT. December 26, 1936. 8.

Teffner, Betty. Personal interview, family papers, and album.

Bob Bourdon

"A Man For All Seasons: Bob Bourdon." Exhibit. Vermont Ski Museum, Stowe, VT, July 22, 2004.

Bourdon, Betsy. E-mail interview, January 13, 2010.

Coleman, A. W. "Cameraman on Skis: a Young Vermonter." *Vermont Life Magazine*, n.d. Photography by Robert Bourdon. 41–47.

Laughlin, James. *Skiing in America*, December 6, 1954.

Mt. Mansfield Ski Club. Newsletters/Bulletins. http://www.teammmsc.org/news.html.

Obituary. *Stowe Reporter*, January 1996.

Oliver, Peter. *Stowe: Classic New England*. Boulder, CO: Mountain Sports Press, 2002.

"Sally Joy News." *Stowe* 43, no. 1 (March 30, 1943). Parker Perry papers, Stowe Historical Society.

Mary (Mather) Bourdon

Obituary. *Stowe Reporter*, undated clipping, about December 2003.

Mt. Mansfield Ski Club. Newsletters/Bulletins. http://www.teammmsc.org/history.html.

Mt. Mansfield Ski Club. Newsletters with rosters. http://www.teammmsc.org/history.html.

Vermont Life. Undated clipping, photos by Bob Bourdon.

Erwin Lindner

Lindner, Brian. Short biography of his father.

Erling Strom

Ancestry.com. *Norway Burial Index, DIS-Norge, 1700–2010.* http://search.ancestry.com/search/db.aspx?dbid=70487.

Bull, Henrik. E-mail interviews, Fall 2010.

Elkins, Frank. "Ski Slopes and Trails." *New York Times*, December 12, 1949.

"Erling Strom: Reminiscences of a Ski Pioneer." *Stowe Reporter*, April 3, 1986.

Scott, Chic. *Powder Pioneers: Ski Stories from the Canadian Rockies and Columbian Mountains.* Surry, British Columbia: Rocky Mountain Books, 2005. 58.

Stowe Guide and Magazine, Winter 2010–2011. Re: Johan Bull and Erling Strom.

"Stroms at Mansfield" and "Stowe." Stowe Historical Society Archives: "Inns and Lodges." Unsourced, undated clippings (c. 1954).

"Stroms No More." *Stowe Reporter*, December 24, 1970. Stowe Historical Society Archives.

Marvin Moriarty and Billy Kidd

Brown, Kim. "Ski Bum Spirit Is Alive and Well Here in Stowe." *Stowe Reporter*, January 6, 2011.

Colorado Ski and Snowboard Museum Hall of Fame. Accessed June 10, 2012. http://www.skimuseum.net.

"Moriarty and His Mother's Hat," *International Skiing Heritage Journal*, September 1999.

"Mother's Knitting Machine Puts Eclat in Skiers' Hats." *Christian Science Monitor*, December 19, 1972.

Mt. Mansfield Ski Club. Newsletters/Bulletins, 1954, 1956. http://www.teammmsc.org/history.html.

Mt. Mansfield Ski Club News. 60th anniversary edition, November 1993.

Mt. Mansfield Skiing 18, no. 1 (December 8, 1951): 3.

Nohl, Dixie. "A View from the Top." Undated clipping from unknown newspaper, after the 10th Olympic Games.

Sports Illustrated, January 24, 1966.

"30 Years of Sepp and Stowe." *Vermont Skiing*, undated clipping (1966?). Stowe Historical Society Archives.

Vermont Ski Hall of Fame inductee, October 28, 2006.

Nose Dive Annie (Bonfoey) (Cooke) Taylor

Bull, Henrik. E-mail correspondence, February 2010.

Colorado Ski and Snowboard Museum Hall of Fame. http://www.skimuseum.net.

Hagerman, R. L. *Mansfield: Stowe's Loftiest Mountain.* 2nd ed. 1975.

New England Ski Museum. http://newenglandskimuseum.org.

Obituary. *Denver Post*, November 2, 2007.

Oliver, Peter. *Stowe: Classic New England.* Boulder, CO: Mountain Sports Press, 2002.

Rita Buchanan

Buchanan, Rita. Personal interview, June 2010.

LaRow, Dede Buchanan. Interviews of her mother, Rita Buchanan, December 2010 to February 2011.

Smith, Sally C. E-mail comments, 2012.

"They Came to Stowe to Ski But Stayed to Build a Lodge." *Burlington Free Press*, December 27, 1956.

"Tom Buchanan." Obituaries. *Stowe Reporter*, February 2, 2012.

The Gale Shaw Sr. Family: Ann, Marilyn, Barbara, and Gale Shaw Jr.

Adler, Allen. *New England and Thereabouts: A Ski Tracing.* Nelco Press, 1985. 58.

"Barbara Shaw Wick." Obituaries. *Burlington Free Press*, November 17, 2001.

"Gale H. Shaw Sr." Obituaries. *Burlington Free Press*, August 31, 1964.

Harty, Pat. "Stem Turns." *Boston Globe*, December 12, 1949.

McMahon, Sally. Entries from Gale Shaw Sr. business ledgers to Dr. Ned Lang, president. Stowe Historical Society Archives, March 1996.

Mt. Mansfield Skiing 6, no. 5 (April 25, 1940). http://www.teammmsc. org/Newsletters/MtMansfieldSkiing/1940s/April%201940.pdf.

Mt. Mansfield Skiing 8, no. 3 (January 15, 1942). http://www. teammmsc.org/Newsletters/MtMansfieldSkiing/1940s/ January%201942.pdf.

Savela, Ann Shaw. Personal interviews, February 2012 and May 2012.

Shaw, M. Janet. E-mail interview about Gale Shaw Jr., February 2012.

University of Vermont. Archives, February 2012

University of Vermont Athletic Hall of Fame, February 2012. http:// www.uvmathletics.com/hof.aspx.

Vermont Ski and Snowboard Museum Archives. http://www.vtssm. com.

Lena (Gale) Allen

Allen, Lena Gale. E-mail interviews, February 2012.

Allen, Lena Gale. *Hip Boots in the Spring.* Autobiography, privately printed, 2000.

Craig, Emma-Lou Gale. E-mail correspondence, February and October 2012.

Masterton, C. Robert. *The Mt. Mansfield Story*, 1951. Photos by Bob Bourdon.

Mt. Mansfield Ski Club. Newsletters/Bulletins. http://www. teammmsc.org/history.html.

"Stowe Skier to Train Abroad This Winter." *Mt. Mansfield Skiing* 19, no.1 (December 1952).

Anne (Morgan) (Simoneau) August

August, Anne. Personal interview, June 2010, and by phone July 2012.

Earle, Elinor. "The Foster Place." *Stowe Guide*, Winter–Spring 2005.

George R. and Vera Fearing

Buckley, Hesterly. Personal and e-mail interviews, 2011, 2012.

Norma (Magnus) (Walker) Bartol

Bartol, Norma. E-mail and phone interviews, May 2013.

Bartol, Norma. "New York to Stowe." *Mt. Mansfield Skiing* 18, no.1 (Dec. 8 1951): p. 2. http://www.teammmsc.org/newsletter_1950s. html.

Index

Duffy (the cook) | 11, 12, 17, 28, 304, 313, 315
Duke, Biddle | xi, 3, 309
Durrance, Dick | 17, 32, 58
Durrance, Jack | 61
Dutch Hill | 251, 319
Dutch Hill Ski Area | 251, 319

E

Eagleton, Harold | 35
Eastern Professional Ski Instructors Association | 266
Edson, Frank | 213, 235
Edson, Franklin | 307
Edson Hill | 3, 7, 52, 171, 290, 304
Edson Hill Manor | 304
Egenberg, Julie | 256, 319
Elliman, Trowbridge | 238
Engl, Sig | 176
Ericksen, Stein | 232
Estes Park, CO | 280, 281

F

Far East Theater | 263
Fearing, Dick | 304, 306
Fearing, George R., Jr | 303
Fearing, Vera | 303, 325
Federation Internationale de Ski (FIS) | 87, 240
Fette Hill | 13, 24
First Battalion, 87th Regiment | 237, 251, 277
First World War | 99, 316
FIS Championships | 240
Fisher, Gary | 243, 244, 318
Fisher, Gerald | 68
Fisher Ski Co. | 108
Flanders, Helen Hartness | 273
Flickinger, Ruth | 225
Forest Service | 14, 33, 35, 39, 63, 78, 225, 227

Foster, Gilman | 208
Foster Place | 208, 209, 301, 302, 304, 306, 307, 325
Fountain, The | 31, 59, 208, 213, 234, 273
Foxfire | 304
Frahner, Karl | 72
Frenchy | 17
Ft. Bragg, CA | 230
Ft. Collins, CO | 280
Fuller, Edi | 33, 62

G

Gabl, Pepi | 294
Gale, Charles and Ruth | 297
Gale, Emma-Lou | 297, 324
Gale, George | 32
Gale, George W. | 218, 220, 310, 314
Gale, Jennie | 13, 31, 297
Gale, John S. | 218, 314
Gale, Judith | 218, 310, 314
Gale, Lena | 281, 296, 297, 299, 324
Gale, Nina | 219
Gale, Richard | 15
Gale, Robert G. | 218
Garrity, Bill | 71
Garrity, Fred | 70, 71
Ghost Trail | 235
Gibbs, Orlo | 11, 15, 54
Gilbert Hill | 270
Gilchrist, Dick | 51
Gillette, Ned | 176
Goddard, Dr. Phil | 272
Gondola Base | 39, 78
Gondola lift | 95
Goodrich, Art | 4, 26
Goodrich, Arthur | 221
Goodrich, George | 41
Goodrich, Nathaniel | 40, 52
Good Time Charlie's | 290
Gosnay, Stan | 68
Gottlieb, Karin | 310, 315

J

Japan | 110, 112, 231
Jenkins, Ab | 48
Jenney, Orlo | 54
Jerome, Harry | 4
John J. Clair Memorial Award | 240
Johnson, Mr. | 154, 187
Johnson, Sven | 73
Johnson, Verne | 260
Jones, Casie | 68
Judge, Chet | 4
Junior Program | 35, 70

K

Karl (Zwack) | 117, 118
Keeler, Everett | 41
Kidd, Billy | 178, 284, 299, 300, 322
Killingbeck, Freddie and Betsey | 305
Koblenzer, Freddie | 29, 34, 64
Kramer, Fritz | 29, 35, 65

L

Lake Lamoille | 41
Lake Louise | 245
Lake Mansfield | 16, 61, 208, 209
Lake Mansfield Trout Club | 208, 209
Lake Mansfield Valley | 16
Lake Placid Club | 281
Lake Placid, NY | 162, 216, 261, 281
Lake Placid Olympics | 261
Lamere, Walter J. | 279
Lamoille County Savings Bank | 292
Lance, Joe | 38, 77
Langdon, Gub and Doris | 266, 304
Langlais, Monique | 73
Langley, Roger | 235, 236
Lang, Otto | 156
Lannen, Wa Wa | 304
LaRow, Dede Buchanan | 290, 291, 323
Lawrence, Andrea Mead | 298

Leach, Mike | xiii, 241, 263, 309
Lewis, Joe | 118
Lichtenthaeler, Dr. Marguerite | 301, 304
Lift Line trail | 300
Lindner, Brian | ix, x, 225, 276, 321
Lindner, Erwin (Lindy) | 4, 35, 70, 276, 277, 321
Lindner, Lindy | 4
Lintilhac, Claire | 304
Linz, Austria | 83, 85, 91, 93, 174, 176
Little Spruce | 36, 37, 71, 72, 74, 75, 76, 168
Lodge, The | 31, 32, 33, 34, 36, 38, 51, 60, 61, 62, 63, 65, 71, 77, 86, 122, 141, 153, 161, 162, 164, 171, 172, 181, 184, 232, 242, 253, 254, 258, 282, 289, 290, 302, 303, 304, 305, 306
Longfellow, Livvy | 150
Lord, Charlie | ix, xi, 1, 2, 3, 5, 13, 17, 26, 28, 30, 40, 43, 49, 52, 84, 129, 152, 170, 208, 213, 218, 221, 225, 228, 264, 278, 287, 309, 311
Lord, John P | 311
Lord trail | 3, 33, 64, 263
Lovejoy, Mark | 50
Lowe, Gordon | 72, 86, 251, 252, 253, 254, 260, 302, 318, 319
Luce Hill | 10, 16, 58, 63, 249, 307
Lullaby Lane | 36, 68, 72, 75
Lumber camps | 12, 13, 14
Lyons, Chelsea | 130

M

Madison Square Garden | 245, 246, 249
Mad River | 5, 212, 214, 239, 240, 313
Mad River Glen | 212, 214, 240
Magoon, Quincy | 54
Main Street Restaurant | 39, 78
Malcolm, Mary H. | 231

Vivian, (a cook) | 23, 60, 129
Voice of America | 150
Voices, NY Folklore journal | 27, 273
Volkswagen | 104
Vt. Headmasters Club | 61

W

Wade Pasture | 63
Wagner, Dr. Ernest | 60
Walker, Martha | 256
Ware, Clyde | 230
Warner Brothers | 304, 306, 307
Warner, Warren | 4
Warner, Willie | 306
Waterbury Ski LIft | 126
WCVT | 261
Weaver, Jane | 319
Weinstein, Martin | 26
Wells,-- | 19, 26, 40, 53
Wells, Bob | 53
Wells, Mahlon | 26
Wells, Robert | 40
Wesson, George | 4, 70, 71
West Branch Meeting House | 297
West Hill | 7, 52, 244, 304
Whipple, Dottie | 304
White, Freddie | 11, 15
Wickart, Roman | 305
Wick, Hilton | 294
Wilson, Boone | 152
Wiltshire, Dwight | 11, 15, 44
Winter Carnivals | 10, 56, 206, 295
Winterhaus | 289, 290
Winter Olympics | 240
Wogs | 209, 302
Women's Golf World Amateur Team
    Championship | 176
Woods, Billy | 73, 284
Woodstock, VT | 128, 147, 182, 270,
    271, 316
Woolsey, Elizabeth | 293

World War 1 | 316
World War 11 | 316
WRFB radio | 180
Wright, Helen Wilhelm | 244, 291, 310
Wright, Loren | 29, 35
Wright, M/M Loren | 29, 35

Y

Ye Olde England Inn | 306
Yoerg, Adi | 73
Yong, Joe | 28
Yosemite Park ski school | 148
Youth Magazine | 293

Z

Ziegenbein, Capt. | 118
Zimmer, Kurt | 260, 319
Zwack, Karl | 117, 118